Modern Hebrew

An Essential Grammar

Third Edition

This new edition of *Modern Hebrew: An Essential Grammar* is an up-to-date and practical reference guide to the most important aspects of modern Hebrew as used by contemporary native speakers of the language.

It presents an accessible description of the language, focusing on the real patterns of use today. The Grammar aims to serve as a reference source for the learner and user of Hebrew irrespective of level, by setting out the complexities of the language in short, readable sections that are clear and free from jargon.

It is ideal either for independent study or for students in schools, colleges, universities and adult classes of all types.

Features of this new edition include:

- Expanded coverage of nouns, verbs and adjectives
- A glossary of grammatical terms
- A full exercise key
- More examples throughout

Lewis Glinert is Professor of Hebrew Studies at Dartmouth College, New Hampshire, USA.

Routledge Essential Grammars

Essential Grammars are available for the following languages:

Chinese
Danish
Dutch
English
Finnish
Modern Greek
Modern Hebrew
Hungarian
Norwegian
Polish
Portuguese
Spanish
Swedish
Thai
Urdu

Other titles of related interest published by Routledge:

Colloquial Hebrew
By Zippi Lyttleton and Tamar Wang

Modern Hebrew

An Essential Grammar

Third Edition

 Lewis Glinert

 Routledge
Taylor & Francis Group

NEW YORK AND LONDON

To the memory of Sarah Katz
A teacher of inspiration

First published 1991
by the School of Oriental and African Studies (University of London)
as *Chik-Chak! A Gateway to Modern Hebrew Grammar*

Second edition published 1994 in the USA and Canada
by Routledge
270 Madison Avenue, New York, NY 10016

Simultaneously published in the UK
by Routledge
2 Park Square, Milton Park, Abingdon, Oxon, OX14 4RN

Reprinted 1996, 1999, 2000, 2002, 2003

Third edition published 2005 by Routledge

Routledge is an imprint of the Taylor & Francis Group

© 1991, 1994, 2005 Lewis Glinert

Typeset in Gill, Sabon and Hebrew Frank Ruehl by E. Sinason
Printed and bound in Great Britain by MPG Books Ltd, Bodmin

Library of Congress Cataloging in Publication Data
Glinert, Lewis.
Modern Hebrew: an essential grammar – third edition
p. cm. – (Routledge essential grammars) Includes index
1. Hebrew language – Grammar – Textbooks.
1. Title. II. Series: Essential Grammar.
PJ4567.3.G58 2004
492.4 ' 8421 – dc22   2004000795

British Library Cataloguing in Publication Data
A catalogue record for this book is available from the British Library
ISBN 0–415–70081–7 (hbk)
ISBN 0–415–70082–5 (pbk)

Contents

Contents

LEVEL TWO

Contents

Contents

xii

Preface

Modern Hebrew: An Essential Grammar is intended as a grammar and workbook for the first two years of modern Hebrew at high school or university.

The book covers the features of syntax and morphology – colloquial and more formal – that are most useful to the average student. Many other features of modern Hebrew might arguably have been included – but we wished to keep things short and sweet. For a much fuller picture of the language, teachers and advancing students are referred to our *The Grammar of Modern Hebrew* (Cambridge University Press, 1989).

Modern Hebrew is *not* a graded, step-by-step coursebook. Of those there are many. It supplies what they generally lack: a simple, up-to-date outline of Hebrew structure.

The grammar and exercises are arranged by topic, with several sections on the noun, several on the adverb, and so on. Using the contents or index, students will be able to home in on the points of grammar that they wish to learn, in whichever order suits them best. The exercises should provide an entertaining challenge, but a carefully managed one: the exercises for Level One require no knowledge of Level Two (and in fact little knowledge of *any* subsequent sections in Level One), and all vocabulary is listed in the custom-built word list.

If some of this vocabulary is rather more colorful than the usual beginners' fare, so much the better. The old 'basic Hebrew' word lists upon which modern Hebrew courses have rested for forty years are starting to look distinctly dated.

Thus the exercises in this book are more than just an exercise-ground for the grammar: they also introduce a colorful spectrum of vocabulary, spanning the colloquial and the elegant, current affairs, kitchens and kibbutzim, and religious and secular culture.

To the teacher

The way we have divided the material between Levels One and Two may cause surprise. Some of the things traditionally fed to beginners do not appear until Level Two – and not by accident. Hebrew education has had an unhealthy tradition of fussing over inflections while ignoring syntax, and the written word, even to this day, gets more attention than the colloquial language. We have endeavored to redress the balance.

At the same time, in leaving *all* defective verb inflections until Level Two, we have taken advantage of the fact that language teachers today no longer deal with each grammatical structure fully as soon as it crops up. Instead, a word with לָלֶכֶת or יוֹדַעַת may be learned simply as a vocabulary item, or even just as part of an expression, until the time is ripe for the grammatical facts of the verb הָלַךְ or the guttural verb to be confronted *in toto*. The signal we have tried to convey in leaving all defective verbs till Level Two is that there are many more important – and above all, simpler – things to be learned systematically before these.

A word on colloquial language, 'slang', and 'grammatical errors': some teachers may be surprised to see that we have given primacy to the norms of the average educated Israeli speaker rather than the traditional norms of school grammar books. For example, forms of the type כָּנַסְתֶּם appear throughout the verb tables, rather than the 'classical' form כְּנַסְתֶּם. Similarly, our *nikkud* seeks to echo colloquial pronunciation rather than Biblical norms. The reason is simple: the main purpose of modern Hebrew teaching, as of modern French or Spanish teaching, is to teach students to understand and simulate an average educated speaker – not to sound like a newsreader or funeral orator.

Thanks are due to the Research and Publications Committee of the School of Oriental and African Studies for sponsoring the first, experimental edition of this book, to Simon Bell of Routledge for bringing it to full fruition, to Professor Reuven Tzur of Tel Aviv University for his wizardry with the Hebrew Mac and to my students at the universities of London and Chicago, perforce anonymous, for being such magnificent guinea-pigs in the evolution of an idea.

יבואו כולם על שכרם

London 1993/5753

About the third edition

This third edition is a response to the comments and suggestions of the many teachers and students who have used this book over the past ten years. Mindful in particular of the needs of intermediate students, I have introduced several new points of syntax and expanded the coverage of noun, verb, and adjective morphology and their semantics, as well as the exercises to match. Thanks are due to the reviewers for their valuable advice and criticisms, and above all to Routledge for their unstinting commitment to the teaching of the Hebrew language around the globe. **Yishar kocham.**

Lewis Glinert
Dartmouth College, USA
2003/5764

Glossary

Action nouns indicate an action: *destruction, dancing, development.*

Actives are the forms of the verbs that indicate 'doing an action': he *grabbed.*

Adjectives are words that describe: a *bad* boy, the eggs are *bad.*

Adverbials are any word, phrase or clause that tells us how, when, where, or why: he stopped *suddenly,* he stopped *after the lights,* he stopped *to scratch his nose.*

Adverbs are any one-word adverbial: he sings *loudly,* he *always* knows.

Agreement shows that a word hangs together with a particular noun – the word may agree in number and gender (sometimes even in person) with that noun: times *are* changing (not: *is* changing).

Bases are the basic uninflected forms, before the addition of inflectional prefixes and endings. Thus the bases of *kibbutzim* and *madricha* are *kibbutz* and *madrich.*

Binyan: a verb pattern. There are seven *binyanim,* allowing one to build a variety of verbs from a single root.

Clauses are sentences nested inside the larger sentence: he thinks *you're crazy.*

Comparatives denote *more, most, as* (e.g. *easy as*) and the like.

Construct phrases are two Hebrew words side by side (usually two nouns and usually a set phrase), much like English *soccer game, apple tree.* The first noun in the Hebrew is called 'the construct noun' and often displays a special construct ending.

Definite article: the word 'the'.

Degree words are a special sort of adverb, indicating degree: *very* cold, *somewhat* strange, *more* slowly, I *quite* agree.

Demonstratives single out: *this* tape, *that* disk, *such* ideas (demonstrative determiners), give me *this,* what's *that* (demonstrative pronouns).

Determiners are words added to a noun to indicate its identity: *which* guy, *any* time, *this* tape, the *same* guy.

Feminine. *See* **masculine.**

Gender. *See* **masculine.**

Generic plural: refers to 'x in general': I hate *exams*, *dentists* chew gum.

Gerunds are a verb form that does the job of a noun: on *arriving* in Israel . . ., before *meeting* his fiancée . . . .

Imperative: a verb form expressing a request: *kiss* me! *stop*!

Infinitive: a special verb form that is unchanged for gender or plural, and has an abstract meaning. In English: *to go, to be, to squeeze.*

Inflections are the variations in number, gender, tense, etc. that can be created in a word by adding prefixes, suffixes, etc.: *take, takes, took, taken . . . long, longer, longest.*

Masculine and feminine: all Hebrew nouns have a certain 'gender', either masculine or feminine. This has nothing essentially to do with male or female.

Mishkal: a noun or adjective pattern, with a distinctive set of vowels, prefixes or suffixes.

Nouns indicate a person or thing – concrete or abstract: *mat, mate, materialism.*

Object: the object of a verb is the person or thing undergoing the action: I got *jelly*.

Object marker: the small word (**preposition**) that often introduces objects in Hebrew and English: I looked *at* Joel, he thought *of* jelly.

Ordinals indicate order by number: *first, third, twenty-fourth.*

Partitives indicate 'part of': *some of, all of, three of, most.*

Passives: forms of verbs indicating 'undergoing an action': he *was grabbed, I am asked* by many people. (Compare **actives.**) Hebrew has special *binyanim* for the passive.

Person: depending on whether the subject of the verb is *I* or *we* ('first person'), *you* ('second person') or *he, she, they*, or any noun ('third person'), the form of the verb may vary, even in English: *I am, you are, Jane is.*

Personal pronouns denote *I, you, he, she, it, we, they.*

Plural indicates 'more than one': *dogs* vs. dog.

Possessive indicates to whom or what something belongs or relates: *Jane's* husband, *my* surprise, the end *of* the world.

Prefixes are bits prefixed to words – future tense prefixes, noun prefixes, etc.

Prepositions are short words commonly indicating an object or when, where, how, etc.: *to* Sara, *for* me, *with* Daniel, *under*, *by*, *through*, *after*.

Pronouns stand in for a specific noun: *they*, *them*, *this*, *someone*, *who*, *what*.

Quantity words indicate quantity: *a lot of*, *some*, *several*, *most*, *half*, *seven*.

Reflexive verbs involve doing something to oneself: *he shot himself*.

Relative clauses add information about some noun: the car *that I bought* does 30 to the gallon.

Roots are 'skeletons' of consonants from which the typical Hebrew word is built.

Singular indicates 'one': *dog* vs. dogs.

Subjects of sentences are the nouns doing the action (more strictly speaking: nouns with which the verbs agree): *films with subtitles* annoy me.

Suffixes are bits attached as word endings – dog*s*, confess*ed*, scient*ific*.

Tenses are the various verb forms expressing past, present and future time.

Verbs indicate actions (occasionally states): *fry, enjoy, adore*.

Hebrew grammatical terminology

Commonly used Hebrew equivalents for our grammatical terms:

action noun	שם פעולה
active	פעיל
adjective	שם־תואר
adverb	תואר־הפועל
adverbial	תיאור
agreement	התאם
base	בסיס
clause	פסוקית, משפט
comparative	מלת השוואה
conjunction	מלת קשר
construct noun	נסמך
construct phrase	צירוף סמיכות
definite article	תווית יידוע
degree word	מלת דרגה, דרג
demonstrative	מלה רומזת
determiner	תווית
direct object	מושא ישיר
embedded	משועבד, נטוע
feminine	נקבה
gender	מין
generic plural	ריבוי סתמי
gerund	שם־הפועל
imperative	ציווי
indirect object	מושא עקיף

infinitive	ל + שם־הפועל
inflection	נטייה
interrogative	שאלה
masculine	זכר
negative	שלילי
negator	מלת שלילה
noun	שם־עצם
object	מושא
object marker	סמן מושא
ordinal	מספר סידורי
particle of being	אוגד
partitive	פרטיטיווי
passive	סביל
person	גוף
personal pronoun	כינוי גוף
phrase	צירוף
plural	ריבוי
possessive	קניין
prefix	קידומת, תחילית
preposition	מלת־יחס
pronoun	כינוי
quantity word	מלת כמות, כמת
reflexive verb	פועל חוזר
relative clause	משפט זיקה
root	שורש
singular	יחיד
stress	הטעמה
subject	נושא
subordinate	משועבד
suffix	סיומת, סופית
tense	זמן הפועל
verb	פועל

Level One

1 The simple sentence: basic word order

In the basic modern Hebrew sentence, the subject comes before its predicate, e.g.

Subject + verb

Subject + adjective

Subject + adverb

Examples:

יוֹרָם צָף	Yoram floats
יוֹרָם עַצְבָּנִי	Yoram's uptight
יוֹרָם שָׁם	Yoram's there

Note: We will also encounter the reverse order – verb + subject etc.

2 The simplest sentences: 'Me Tarzan, you Jane'

a The pattern יוֹרָם עָיֵיף 'Yoram is tired'

For sentences of the type 'Yoram is tired, the falafel is cold', i.e. *noun* + 'be' + *adjective*, Hebrew commonly omits the verb:

הַפַלַפֶל קַר	The falafel [is] cold
הַפַלַפְּלִים הָאֵלֶה קָרִים	These falafels [are] cold

Alternatively – especially after a longish subject like כָּל הַפַלַפְּלִים הָאֵלֶה 'all these falafels' – Hebrew often inserts the 'particles of being' הוּא, הִיא, הֵם, הֵן. Which one is chosen depends on whether the subject is masculine or feminine, singular or plural:

Masc. sing.	יוֹרָם שֶׁלָנוּ הוּא עָיֵיף	Our Yoram is tired
Masc. pl.	הַפַלַפְּלִים הָאֵלֶה הֵם קָרִים	These falafels are cold

3

Fem. sing.	שָׂרָה שֶׁלָּנוּ הִיא עֲיֵיפָה	Our Sara is tired
Fem. pl.	הַפִּיצוֹת הָאֵלֶּה הֵן קָרוֹת	These pizzas are cold

Note: These particles are identical with the pronouns for 'he, she, they', which will be dealt with in 3.

b The pattern יוֹרָם בְּתֵל-אָבִיב 'Yoram's in Tel Aviv'

The same is true for sentences like 'the cats are in the closet, Shmulik is over there, the letter's from Grandma' (i.e. sentences with an adverbial as their predicate). Either there is no word for 'be':

הַחֲתוּלִים בָּאָרוֹן	The cats [are] in the closet
שְׁמוּאֵלִיק שָׁמָּה	Shmulik [is] over there
הַמִּכְתָּב מִסַּבְתָּא	The letter['s] from Grandma

or one uses one of the particles of being הוּא, הִיא, הֵם, הֵן.

הַחֲבִילוֹת הֵן בִּשְׁבִיל הָרַבָּנִית
The packages are for the rabbi's wife

הַמִּכְתָּב הוּא מִסַּבְתָּא
The letter's from Grandma

c The pattern 'Yoram is a . . .'

So far, we have seen sentences of the type 'someone is *adjective*' or 'someone is *adverbial*'. But for 'someone is *noun*', i.e. a noun sentence, Hebrew generally must insert the particles of being הוּא, הִיא, הֵם, הֵן:

יוֹרָם הוּא רַב	Yoram is a rabbi
הַבּוּלִים הֵם מַתָּנָה	The stamps are a gift
הָאַחִים שֶׁלָּה הֵם טַיָּיסִים	Her brothers are pilots

The main exception, shown in (d), is where the subject is a pronoun:

אֲנִי תַּיָּיר   I am a tourist

זֶה סְקַנְדָּל   This is a scandal

Another exception is where one is *identifying* someone or *defining* something. Then one normally uses זֶה for 'is':

מִי זֶה יוֹרָם ? יוֹרָם זֶה הַשּׁוֹעֵר
Who is Yoram? Yoram's the janitor

אִמָּא, מַה זֶה קַלֶטֶת? – קַלֶטֶת זֶה קַסֶטָה, מוֹתֶק
Mommy, what's a kaletet? – A kaletet is a cassette, darling

---

d *The pattern 'I am ..., he is ...'*

Hebrew does not generally use a word for 'am, is, are' after a *personal pronoun*:

אֲנִי רַב   I am a rabbi

אַתְּ מְשׁוּגַּעַת   You're nuts

הוּא הַבֶּן־אָח שֶׁלִּי   He's my nephew

הֵם מִמִּינְסק   They're from Minsk

---

3   The personal pronouns

The personal pronouns are:

Plural		Singular	
אֲנַחְנוּ	we	אֲנִי	I
אַתֶּם	you	אַתָּה	you (masc.)
אַתֶּן	you (fem.)	אַתְּ	you (fem.)
הֵם	they	הוּא	he
הֵן	they (fem.)	הִיא	she

5

The feminine plural pronouns, אַתֶּן and הֵן, are rather formal and typical of newscasters, newspapers, books and so on. In casual usage, their masculine counterparts אַתֶּם and הֵם are used instead, thus:

הַבָּנוֹת? נוּ, הֵם בְּצַהַ"ל   The girls? Well, they're in the Army

For 'it' and other pronouns, see 16.

These personal pronouns are used either as the subject of a sentence or as its predicate:

As subject: אֲנַחְנוּ עִם שָׂרָה, בְּסֵדֶר?   We're with Sara, OK?

As predicate: בְּסֵדֶר, בְּסֵדֶר, זֶה אֲנַחְנוּ!   OK, OK, it's us!

But as objects, e.g. as in 'congratulate *us*', or after a preposition, e.g. as in 'with *us*', 'for *us*', different pronouns are used (e.g. אוֹתָנוּ) – see 35.

4 The definite article ה

'The' is usually ה, pronounced *ha*. It is always prefixed to the noun, e.g. הָאוֹר 'the light'. (So, too, are all other one-letter words, such as בְּ 'in' and כְּ 'as'.)

Note: Newsreaders and teachers may pronounce it as הֶ with certain words, but coming from an ordinary person this will sound pedantic.

When combining בְּ and לְ with ה 'the', one has to *run them together* to make בַּ and לַ, thus

בַּבּוֹקֶר   in the morning   (not בְּהַבּוֹקֶר)

לַסּוֹף   to the end   (not לְהַסּוֹף)

On adding ה to an accompanying adjective (הַיֶּלֶד הַטּוֹב), see 12 on agreement of הַ. On the use of אֶת with הַ, see 34(a).

5 The Hebrew for 'a', 'some'

Hebrew generally has no word for 'a', nor for 'some' (the plural equivalent of 'a'):

קַח עוּגָה	Take a cake
קַח עוּגוֹת	Take some cakes
יֵשׁ פֹּה שְׁגִיאוֹת	There are some mistakes here

6–8 MASCULINE AND FEMININE, SINGULAR AND PLURAL

6 Masculine and feminine nouns (gender)

Every Hebrew noun is either masculine or feminine. Such gender does not have very much to do with maleness or femaleness: although most nouns denoting a male or a female are indeed masculine or feminine, respectively, nouns denoting *objects* are masculine or feminine without any apparent rhyme or reason.

Gender shows up in two ways: (a) it commonly affects the form of the noun, and (b) it invariably affects the form of any verb or adjective relating to it:

Rule (a) The vast majority of feminine nouns end in either הָ or ת. Most masculine nouns, by contrast, have no such ending. Examples:

Feminine nouns:	פִּיצָה pizza	תְּמוּנָה picture
	טַלִּית prayer-shawl	מִרְפֶּסֶת balcony
	עֲדִיפוּת preference	
Masculine nouns:	בָּצֵק dough	צִיּוּר painting
	כּוֹבַע cap	

7

There are some exceptions: a fair number of feminine nouns have no ending, particularly names of limbs, e.g. יָד 'hand, arm', אוֹזֶן 'ear', כָּתֵף 'shoulder'. Some common segolate nouns (nouns like יֶלֶד, פַּחַד with stress on the first syllable) are feminine, e.g. אֶרֶץ 'country', דֶרֶךְ 'route', פַּעַם 'time', and several others, e.g. רוּחַ 'wind', עִיר 'town', צִיפּוֹר 'bird'. Countries and towns are feminine singular (just like the words אֶרֶץ, עִיר) e.g.

אַרְצוֹת הַבְּרִית מִתְנַגֶדֶת	The US is opposed
תֵל אָבִיב יְקָרָה	Tel-Aviv is expensive

and a handful of masculine nouns end in ה or ת, e.g. שֵׁירוּת 'service'.

Rule (b) A combination of masculine and feminine nouns is counted as masculine:

שִׁפְרָה וּמָרְדְכַי קוֹפְצִים אַחַר־כָּךְ
Shifra and Mordechai are stopping by later

הַנְיָיר־דֶבֶק וְהַמַעֲטָפוֹת נִמְצָאִים אֶצְלְךָ?
Are the scotch tape and envelopes with you?

Rule (c) Any adjective or verb relating to the noun must take on masculine or feminine form, in agreement with that noun (on agreement, see further 13):

Masculine:	הַבָּצֵק קָשֶׁה	The dough is hard
Feminine:	הַפִּיצָה קָשָׁה	The pizza is hard

7 The feminine and plural of nouns

a The endings יִם and וֹת – for the simplest noun type

Nouns mark their plural by the endings יִם and וֹת. Nearly all masculines take יִם and nearly all feminines וֹת.

Before adding יִם, the masculine noun first drops any הָ or יִ ending it has. And before adding וֹת, the feminine noun first drops the singular feminine ending הָ or ת. Thus:

Masc.				
מֵיכָל	tank	מֵיכָלִים	tanks
תִּיק	bag	תִּיקִים	bags
מוֹרֶה	teacher	מוֹרִים	teachers
מַעֲשֶׂה	deed	מַעֲשִׂים	deeds
יְהוּדִי	Jew	יְהוּדִים	Jews
עִתּוֹנַאי	journalist	עִתּוֹנָאִים	journalists

Fem.				
מְגֵירָה	drawer	מְגֵירוֹת	drawers
טִירָה	castle	טִירוֹת	castles
יָדִית	handle	יָדִיוֹת	handles
מַפִּית	napkin	מַפִּיוֹת	napkins

There are some exceptions, e.g. the masculine noun שׁוּלְחָן 'table' has the plural שׁוּלְחָנוֹת. Conversely, feminine שָׁנָה 'year' has the plural שָׁנִים. For more about these exceptions, see 60(d).

The form that a noun happens to take in the plural has no effect on its intrinsic gender. Thus שׁוּלְחָנוֹת 'tables' is as masculine as שׁוּלְחָן 'table', and hence the agreement שׁוּלְחָנוֹת מַקְסִימִים 'gorgeous tables'.

b | The plural of nouns of the type דָּבָר

To make the plural of a noun is often more than just a matter of adding an ending: the internal vowels may have to be changed, depending on the form of the word. Obviously, this generally affects pronunciation rather than spelling, as Hebrew is mostly written without vowels. We begin with the 'third-from-the-end rule':

When the vowel *a* becomes third vowel from the end (thanks to the presence of an ending), many nouns omit it. Thus:

דבר thing *(davar)*   Plural: דברים *dvarim* (not *davarim*)

שקד almond *(shaked)*   Plural: שקדים *shkedim* (not *shakedim*)

Further examples: בְּצָלִים~בָּצָל   onion

גְּמַלִּים~גָּמָל   camel

שְׁכֵנִים~שָׁכֵן   neighbor

However, many nouns do not observe this rule, e.g. חֲכָמִים~חָכָם 'sage', עֲנָנִים~עָנָן 'cloud', צַדִּיקִים~צַדִּיק 'righteous man', פַּסָּלִים~פַּסָּל 'sculptor', בַּמָּאִים~בַּמַּאי 'director'. There are two main reasons:

1 *Either* they begin with one of the four letters א, ה, ח, ע (so-called 'guttural' letters), which for ancient phonetic reasons require the acoustic 'support' of a full vowel;

2 *or* the *a* has the vowel point ַ rather than ְ (which again for historical reasons could not drop). Among these are the many nouns of the kind מַשְׁבְּרִים~מַשְׁבֵּר 'crisis', כַּפְתּוֹרִים~כַּפְתּוֹר 'button' – here, naturally, the *a* does not drop as this would create a hard-to-pronounce run of three consonants in a row (imagine *kftorim*).

To know if a noun has ְ or ַ is a matter of recognizing characteristic patterns – or consulting a dictionary.

| c | *The plural of nouns of the type* סֶרֶט *(segolate nouns)*

Most nouns are stressed on the *last* syllable, e.g. מָקוֹם 'place'. But many nouns, with ֶ (termed the 'segol' vowel) as their last vowel, are stressed on the *next-to-last* syllable. These are called segolate nouns. Here are some examples (we have marked the stress by ٭):

סֶרֶט film   סֵפֶר book   טוֹפֶס form

Note: Some segolates actually have -a- as their last vowel or as both vowels – owing to the presence of a so-called guttural letter: ה, ח, ע, e.g. פֶּרַח 'flower', רוֹחַב 'width', נַעַר 'lad', פַּחַד 'fear'. But they are still segolates in every other respect.

The plural of segolate nouns involves an internal change in their vowels:

1 The first vowel is usually dropped, forming a variant of the 'third-from-the-end rule' (recall the preceding section), as the stress has now been shifted onto the plural ending.

2 The second vowel becomes *a*:

סְרָטִים ←	סֶרֶט		רְמָזִים ←	רֶמֶז	
séret →	sratim		rémez →	r'mazim	
סְפָרִים	סֵפֶר		שְׁבָטִים	שֵׁבֶט	
séfer	sfarim		shévet	shvatim	
טְפָסִים	טוֹפֶס		גְרָנוֹת	גּוֹרֶן	
tófes	tfasim		góren	granot	
פְּרָחִים	פֶּרַח		צְלָעִים	צֶלַע	
pérach	prachim		tséla	tsla'im	

Further examples:

בֶּרֶז tap   שֶׁמֶן oil

תֶּדֶר frequency   יֵצֶר drive

שֵׂכֶל intelligence   צוֹמֶת junction

צוֹפֶן code   שֶׁקַע socket

שֶׁבַח praise

As with nouns like דָבָר in 7(b), segolates that begin with one of the four letters א, ה, ח, ע ('guttural' letters) do not allow the first vowel to be dropped. Instead it usually becomes *a*:

עֲרָבִים~עֶרֶב	evening	חֲלָקִים~חֵלֶק	part
חֲבָלִים~חֶבֶל	rope	אֲרָזִים~אֶרֶז	cedar

A small group of feminine nouns behaves rather like segolates, e.g.:

שְׁכָבוֹת - שִׁכְבָה	layer
דְּמָעוֹת - דִּמְעָה	tear
שְׂמָלוֹת - שִׂמְלָה	dress

d | The plural of nouns ending in וּת

We have just seen that the plural of feminine יָת nouns is formed by first dropping the ת and then adding וֹת, thus כַּפִּיּוֹת ← כַּפִּית.

Feminine וּת nouns, too, form their plural by dropping ת but then add יּוֹת. Thus:

חֲנוּיּוֹת ← חֲנוּת	store	סוֹכְנוּיּוֹת ← סוֹכְנוּת	agency

e | The feminine of nouns denoting people, e.g. מוֹרָה 'teacher'

Virtually all nouns denoting *people* have a masculine and a feminine form, e.g.

מוֹרָה~מוֹרֶה	male teacher ~ female teacher
כּוֹכֶבֶת~כּוֹכָב	male star ~ female star

The form of the feminine largely depends on the form of the masculine. As a rough rule:

1 Nouns of the מוֹרֶה or דָּבָר or סֶרֶט type (see 7(a–c)) take ָה:

מַרְצָה woman lecturer		שְׁכֵנָה woman neighbor	
יַלְדָּה little girl			

2   Nouns for inhabitants of most major European or Near Eastern countries take ◌ָה:

אַנְגְּלִיָּה Englishwoman   עֲרָבִיָּה Arab woman

יְהוּדִיָּה Jewish woman

3   Nouns of the פַּעָל type (66) take ◌ֶת:

חַיֶּלֶת girl soldier   גַּנֶּנֶת kindergarten teacher

4   Nouns of the פַּעְלָן type (66) take ◌ִית, as do inhabitants of most other countries:

פַּחְדָנִית~פַּחְדָן coward   מַדְעָנִית~מַדְעָן scientist

יַפָּנִית~יַפָּנִי Japanese

5   Foreignisms take ◌ִית:

סְטוּדֶנְטִית~ סְטוּדֶנְט student   פְּרַיְיאֶרִית~פְּרַיְיאֶר fool, mug

6   Nouns shaped like present tense verbs behave like these verbs. See 72.

Other notable words: תַּלְמִידָה~תַּלְמִיד 'student', שָׂרָה~שָׂר 'minister', עִיתוֹנָאִית~עִיתוֹנַאי 'journalist', רוֹפְאָה~רוֹפֵא 'doctor'

8   The feminine and plural of adjectives

Virtually all adjectives have four forms: masculine singular and plural, and feminine singular and plural. All but the first are marked by distinctive suffixes and often by internal vowel changes as well.

a   The simplest adjective type: טוֹב, דָתִי

1   The simplest adjectives add the following endings, with no other changes in spelling or pronunciation*:

Example: טוֹב 'good'

Fem. sing.	ָה	טוֹבָה
Masc. pl.	ִים	טוֹבִים
Fem. pl.	וֹת	טוֹבוֹת

* Changes in nikkud can be ignored, except where there is also a change in pronunciation.

2 There are a vast number of adjectives with the suffix ִי either created out of nouns by adding ִי or based on some international word (with ִי taking the place of *-ic*, *-ical*, etc.). These, too, simply add the following endings:

Examples: דָתִי 'religious', פִיזִי 'physical'

Fem. sing.	ת	דָתִית	פִיזִית
Masc. pl.	ִים	דָתִיִים	פִיזִיִים
Fem. pl.	וֹת	דָתִיוֹת	פִיזִיוֹת

Many adjectives with ־ִי are foreign loans; as if to show this fact, Hebrew keeps the stress on the base of the word rather than on the ending. Hence (marking stress by ˅):

פִּֽיזִי, פִּֽיזִית, פִּֽיזִיִים, פִּֽיזִיוֹת

Further examples:

Like טוֹב: נִפְלָא 'wonderful', נֶאֱמָן 'loyal', רַע 'bad', חָזָק 'strong', חַם 'warm', יַצִיב 'stable', רִאשׁוֹן 'first'

Like דָתִי: יַמִי 'marine', כַּלְכָּלִי 'economic', רִאשׁוֹנִי 'preliminary', בַּעֲיָיתִי 'problematic'

Foreignisms: קוֹמוּנִיסְטִי 'communist', כִימִי 'chemical', נוֹרְמָלִי 'normal'

b *Adjectives ending in* הֶ

Like nouns (7(a)), adjectives ending in הֶ drop this before adding הָ, ים, ות. (See 50 for similar behavior by ל׳ה verbs.)

Example: נָאֶה 'attractive'

Fem. sing.	הָ	נָאָה
Masc. pl.	ים	נָאִים
Fem. pl.	ות	נָאוֹת

Further examples:

יָפֶה beautiful   כֵּנֶה honest

כֵּהֶה dark   מְשׁוּנֶה strange

c *Adjectives of the type* גָּדוֹל *'large'*, קָטָן *'small'*

In many adjectives, the first vowel is *a* and many of these belong to the גָדוֹל־קָטָן type, i.e. (like nouns of the type דָבָר) they drop their *a* when adding endings (the 'third-from-the-end rule'):

When a vowel *a* becomes third vowel from the end (thanks to the presence of an ending), many adjectives omit it.

Thus:

Examples: גָּדוֹל 'large', קָטָן 'small'

Fem. sing.	הָ	גְדוֹלָה (gdola)	קְטַנָה (ktana)
Masc. pl.	ים	גְדוֹלִים (gdolim)	קְטַנִים (ktanim)
Fem. pl.	ות	גְדוֹלוֹת (gdolot)	קְטַנוֹת (ktanot)

15

Further examples:

נָכוֹן right | יָשָׁר straight

נָעִים pleasant | שָׁחוֹר black

סָגוּר closed | בָּרוּר obvious

However, just as with nouns, many adjectives are exceptions to this rule and belong under 8(a): חָזָק, חֲזָקָה, חֲזָקִים, חֲזָקוֹת. Examples:

אָדִיב polite | הָגוּן fair

חָזָק strong | חָכָם wise

עָצוּם huge | עַתִּיק ancient

Just as with nouns (7(b)), there are two main reasons for this:

1 *Either* they begin with one of the four letters א, ה, ח, ע ('guttural' letters) which for ancient phonetic reasons do not allow the vowel to be dropped;

2 *or* (very occasionally) the *a* has the vowel point ַ rather than ָ. These have to be learned as you go along or you should consult a dictionary.

9 Noun + adjective phrases, e.g. יֶלֶד קָטָן 'small boy'

For 'small boy', 'wet dog' and other phrases composed of *adjective + noun*, Hebrew put the noun first:

יֶלֶד קָטָן small boy | כֶּלֶב רָטוֹב a wet dog

To distinguish these from whole sentences ('dogs are wet'), Hebrew tends to insert the particle of being הוּא, הֵם etc.:

כְּלָבִים הֵם רְטוּבִים | Dogs are wet

10 Quantity phrases

Words for 'a lot of, a few, more, how many, twenty, all (ice-creams etc.)',
i.e. quantity words, usually precede their noun:

הַרְבֵּה גְּלִידוֹת	a lot of ice-creams
כַּמָּה גְּלִידוֹת?	how many ice-creams?
מְעַט סוּכָּר	a little sugar
עוֹד כּוֹסוֹת	more glasses
עֶשְׂרִים סְפָלִים	20 cups
כָּל הַמִּכְסִים	all the lids
רוֹב הַדִּי־גֵ׳יים	most of the DJs
נוֹרָא הַרְבֵּה תְּאוּנוֹת	a great many accidents
הַרְבֵּה מְא׳ד תְּאוּנוֹת	very many accidents

Generally, the same quantity word is used whether the noun is being
treated as something *countable* (as in 'lots of e-mails, how many letters')
or something *uncountable* (as in 'lots of e-mail, how much mail'):

הַרְבֵּה אִי־מֵיילִים lots of e-mails		הַרְבֵּה אִי מֵייל lots of e-mail	
כַּמָּה מִכְתָּבִים? how many letters?		כַּמָּה דּוֹאַר? how much mail?	
מְעַט מִכְתָּבִים a few letters		מְעַט דּוֹאַר a little mail	

However, כַּמָּה in the (non-interrogative) sense of 'a few, some' is used
only with *countable* nouns, i.e. it cannot be used for English 'a little':

כַּמָּה מִכְתָּבִים	a few letters, some letters

A few quantity words follow their noun, namely the numeral אֶחָד 'one' and a few 'adjectives of quantity': רַב 'much, many', אֲחָדִים 'a few', מְעַטִים 'a few':

סֵפֶל אֶחָד	one cup
סְפָלִים אֲחָדִים	a few cups
פַּחַד רַב	much fear
סְפָלִים מְעַטִים	a few cups

Notice that מְעַט can either precede the noun or follow it. Following it, it denotes 'a few', not 'a little'.

▌▌ Noun + determiner phrases ('this . . ., the same . . ., which . . .')

Determiners are words that indicate the identity of a noun, such as כָּזֶה 'such', זֶה 'this', אוֹתוֹ 'that, the same', אֵיזֶה 'what, which?', כָּל 'any'.

זֶה, כָּזֶה and הַהוּא 'that' follow the noun, whereas כָּל, אֵיזֶה, אוֹתוֹ and other determiners must precede it:

אִידְיוֹט כָּזֶה	such an idiot
רוֹשֶׁם זֶה	this impression
הַמִרְקָע הַהוּא	that screen
אוֹתוֹ אִידְיוֹט	the same idiot
אֵיזֶה רוֹשֶׁם !	what an impression!
כָּל מִרְקָע	any screen
אֵיזֶה כַּרְטִיס	some ticket
אַף כַּרְטִיס	not a single ticket
שׁוּם כַּרְטִיס	no ticket

12–13 AGREEMENT

12 Agreement of הַ

a *For noun + adjective:* הַכֶּלֶב הָרָטוֹב *'the wet dog'*

When noun + adjective phrases like those in 9 have a definite noun (i.e.
one with הַ, or a name), the adjective automatically takes a הַ prefix, too:

הַיֶּלֶד הַקָּטָן	the little child
גְּבֶרֶת קְוֶוטְש הַזְּקֵנָה	Old Mrs Kvetch

If the adjective does not show agreement for definiteness, we are dealing
with a whole sentence, not a phrase. Contrast these:

Phrase	הַיֶּלֶד הַקָּטָן	the little child
Sentence	הַיֶּלֶד קָטָן	the child is little

b *For noun +* זֶה: הַכֶּלֶב הַזֶּה *'this dog'*

זֶה 'this' following a noun with הַ becomes הַזֶּה, but in fact כֶּלֶב זֶה and
הַכֶּלֶב הַזֶּה mean the same: 'this dog'. The difference is stylistic: כֶּלֶב זֶה
sounds formal or official; everyday speech prefers הַכֶּלֶב הַזֶּה.

13 Agreement for gender and number

a *Adjective agreement*

Any adjective relating to a noun must adopt either *masculine* or *feminine*
form in agreement with that noun. Similarly, it must agree in number
(singular or plural). Thus:

מֵיכָל רֵיק	an empty tank
מְגֵירָה רֵיקָה	an empty drawer
מֵיכָלִים רֵיקִים	empty tanks
מְגֵירוֹת רֵיקוֹת	empty drawers
הַמֵּיכָל רֵיק	the tank is empty
הַמֵּיכָלִים רֵיקִים	the tanks are empty
הַמְגֵירָה רֵיקָה	the drawer is empty
הַמְגֵירוֹת רֵיקוֹת	the drawers are empty

Even if a singular noun denotes a *group*, such as מִשְׁפָּחָה 'family', צֶוֶת 'team', וַעַד 'committee', it is treated as singular for purposes of agreement:

הַוַעַד הֶחְלִיט לְתַקֵן אֶת הַשֶׁלֶט
The committee has decided to mend the sign

Pronouns require similar agreement:

אֲנִי עֵר   I (masc.) am awake   אֲנִי עֵרָה   I (fem.) am awake

Most adjectives take the following agreement endings:

fem .sing. ה or ת   masc. pl. ים   fem .pl. ות

For details of these, see 8.

b Agreement of verbs

Verbs agree with their subject, and not only in gender and number but also in person, as and when the verb makes such distinctions available.

Present tense verbs distinguish masculine from feminine, and singular from plural:

| רוּסִים בָּאִים | Russians are coming |

| רוּסִיּוֹת בָּאוֹת | Russian women are coming |

Past and future tense verbs additionally distinguish 1st, 2nd, and 3rd person, e.g.:

| אֲנִי אֶמְשׁוֹךְ | I'll pull |

| אַתָּה תִּמְשׁוֹךְ | You'll pull |

| הוּא יִמְשׁוֹךְ | He'll pull |

For full details see 18 onwards.

c Agreement of 'particles of being'

The particles expressing 'is' and 'are' (described in 2(a)) agree for gender and number with their subject noun:

masc. sing. הוּא	fem. sing. הִיא	masc. pl. הֵם	fem. pl. הֵן

Thus:

| Masc. sing. | יוֹרָם שֶׁלָּנוּ הוּא עָיֵיף | Our Yoram is tired |
| Masc. pl. | הַפָלָפֶלִים הָאֵלֶה הֵם קָרִים | These falafels are cold |

d Agreement of determiners: זֹאת, כָּזֹאת, etc.

Determiners that point to someone or something, i.e. words denoting 'this, that, the same, such, a kind of' (demonstratives), agree for gender and number with their noun. Most other determiners (e.g. כָּל 'any, every', שׁוּם 'no') do not agree. Taking each determiner in turn:

21

	Masc. sing.	Fem. sing.	Masc. pl.	Fem. pl.
this	זֶה	זוֹ or זוּ, זֹאת	אֵלּוּ or אֵלֶּה	
that	הַהוּא	הַהִיא	הָהֵם	הָהֵן
that, the same	אוֹתוֹ	אוֹתָהּ	אוֹתָם	אוֹתָן
such, a kind of	כָּזֶה	כָּזוֹ or כָּזֹאת, כָּזוּ	כָּאֵלּוּ or כָּאֵלֶּה	

Examples:

הַמַּחְשֵׁב הַזֶּה	this computer	הַמַּחְשְׁבִים הָאֵלֶּה	these computers
הַדַּוְושָׁה הַזֹּאת	this pedal	הַדַּוְושׁוֹת הָאֵלֶּה	these pedals
וִירוּס כָּזֶה	a virus of sorts, such a virus	וִירוּסִים כָּאֵלּוּ	viruses of sorts, such viruses
בְּחִינָה כָּזֹאת	a test of sorts, such a test	בְּחִינוֹת כָּאֵלֶּה	tests of sorts, such tests

The determiner אֵיזֶה (in its various meanings) has a feminine form אֵיזוֹ and a plural form אֵילוּ in formal usage. Colloquially, however, one generally meets אֵיזֶה:

אֵיזֶה אַכְזָבָה !	what a disappointment!
בְּאֵיזֶה תַּאֲרִיכִים ?	on which dates?

Note: Instead of זוֹ and כָּזוֹ, one most often hears זוּ and כָּזוּ in colloquial speech.

---

e *Agreement of quantity words*

Most quantity words generally do *not* agree with their noun. Thus:

22

הָמוֹן נִסָיוֹן	lots of experience
הָמוֹן נִיסוּיִים	lots of experiments
כַּמָה אוֹטוֹבּוּסִים	a few buses
כַּמָה מוֹנִיוֹת	a few cabs

But those that are really adjectives do agree:

מִשְׂרָדִים רַבִּים many offices   מַדְפָּסוֹת רַבּוֹת   many printers

Some numerals agree, too. See 14.

14 Numerals

a The numerals 1 to 10

The numerals for 1 to 10 agree for gender with their noun. But unlike adjectives, the *feminine* is the basic form of the numeral, whereas the *masculine* adds הָ (for 3 to 10) together with various other adjustments:

Feminine numerals 1–10			
שֵׁשׁ בַּנָנוֹת	6 bananas	בַּנָנָה אַחַת	1 banana
שֶׁבַע בַּנָנוֹת	7 bananas	שְׁתֵּי בַּנָנוֹת	2 bananas
שְׁמוֹנֶה בַּנָנוֹת	8 bananas	שָׁלוֹשׁ בַּנָנוֹת	3 bananas
תֵּשַׁע בַּנָנוֹת	9 bananas	אַרְבַּע בַּנָנוֹת	4 bananas
עֶשֶׂר בַּנָנוֹת	10 bananas	חָמֵשׁ בַּנָנוֹת	5 bananas

Masculine numerals 1–10			
שִׁשָּׁה סֶנְדְוויצ׳ים	6 sandwiches	סֶנְדְוויץ׳ אֶחָד	1 sandwich
שִׁבְעָה סֶנְדְוויצ׳ים	7 sandwiches	שְׁנֵי סֶנְדְוויצ׳ים	2 sandwiches
שְׁמוֹנָה סֶנְדְוויצ׳ים	8 sandwiches	שְׁלוֹשָׁה סֶנְדְוויצ׳ים	3 sandwiches
תִּשְׁעָה סֶנְדְוויצ׳ים	9 sandwiches	אַרְבָּעָה סֶנְדְוויצ׳ים	4 sandwiches
עֲשָׂרָה סֶנְדְוויצ׳ים	10 sandwiches	חֲמִשָּׁה סֶנְדְוויצ׳ים	5 sandwiches

The feminine form (the basic form) is also used for performing a count, and here the word for 'two' will be שְׁתַּיִם (the so-called 'free-standing form') rather than שְׁתֵּי:

אַחַת, שְׁתַּיִם, שָׁלוֹשׁ . . .

b *The numerals 11 to 19*

The numerals 11 to 19 also have masculine and feminine forms, but, colloquially, the feminine does the job for both (and, as always, is also used for counting):

	Fem.	Masc.		Fem.	Masc.
16	שֵׁשׁ-עֶשְׂרֵה	שִׁשָּׁה-עָשָׂר	11	אַחַת-עֶשְׂרֵה	אַחַד-עָשָׂר
17	שְׁבַע-עֶשְׂרֵה	שִׁבְעָה-עָשָׂר	12	שְׁתֵּים-עֶשְׂרֵה	שְׁנֵים-עָשָׂר
18	שְׁמוֹנָה-עֶשְׂרֵה	שְׁמוֹנָה-עָשָׂר	13	שְׁלוֹשׁ-עֶשְׂרֵה	שְׁלוֹשָׁה-עָשָׂר
19	תְּשַׁע-עֶשְׂרֵה	תִּשְׁעָה-עָשָׂר	14	אַרְבַּע-עֶשְׂרֵה	אַרְבָּעָה-עָשָׂר
			15	חֲמֵשׁ-עֶשְׂרֵה	חֲמִשָּׁה-עָשָׂר

Examples:

שְׁלוֹשׁ־עֶשְׂרֵה פָּרוֹת   vs.   שְׁלוֹשָׁה־עָשָׂר שְׁוָרִים
13 cows   13 bulls
(but colloquially: שְׁלוֹשׁ־עֶשְׂרֵה שְׁוָרִים)

אַחַד־עָשָׂר כַּדּוּרִים   vs.   אַחַת־עֶשְׂרֵה גוּלוֹת
11 balls   11 marbles
(colloquially: אַחַת־עֶשְׂרֵה כַּדּוּרִים)

These forms are a peculiar combination of the regular masculine or feminine 1–9 form (with a few adjustments) with a special word for '10': עָשָׂר for masculine, עֶשְׂרֵה for feminine. Notice that the ה ending appears on only one bit of each numeral.

| c | *The numerals 20 to 99* |

The numerals for the 'tens' (20–90) do not have separate masculine and feminine forms. They make use of the same base as the *masculine* numerals just listed – thus '30' is '3' with ים added. The exception is '20', which is based on עָשָׂר '10' and not on '2':

60	שִׁשִּׁים		20	עֶשְׂרִים
70	שִׁבְעִים		30	שְׁלוֹשִׁים
80	שְׁמוֹנִים		40	אַרְבָּעִים
90	תִּשְׁעִים		50	חֲמִשִּׁים

For 21, 34, 77, etc. the order is *ten* + וְ + *unit*. As with numerals like '1, 4, 7', the unit agrees with its noun:

עֶשְׂרִים וְשֵׁשׁ קוּפְסוֹת   26 boxes   עֶשְׂרִים וְשִׁשָּׁה קַרְטוֹנִים   26 cartons

Two details must be pointed out:

1 For '21, 31', etc. אֶחָד or אַחַת do not this time follow the noun: עֶשְׂרִים וְאַחַת קוּפְסוֹת '21 boxes'.

2 For '22, 32', etc. one always uses the 'free-standing' form שְׁנַיִם or שְׁתַּיִם rather than שְׁנֵי, שְׁתֵּי: עֶשְׂרִים וּשְׁתַּיִם קוּפְסוֹת '22 boxes'.

For the hundreds and thousands, see 81 in Level Two.

15 Partitives: 'many of the . . ., all the . . .'

To express 'of' ('many *of* the . . ., some *of* the . . ., three *of* the . . .'), use מִ:

הַרְבֵּה מֵהַשּׁוֹטְרִים	many of the cops
חֵלֶק מֵהַסֶּרֶט	part of the film
שֵׁשׁ מֵהַמוֹרוֹת	six of the teachers
כַּמָה מֵהֶם ?	how many of them?

There are a few exceptions: כָּל 'all', רוֹב 'most of', שְׁאָר 'the rest of' and a few others require the construct (see 17(c), (d)) instead of מִ:

כָּל הָעוֹלָם	all the world
כָּל הַתִּיקִים	all the files
רוֹב הַמוֹדָעוֹת	most of the notices
שְׁאָר הַגְלוּלוֹת	the rest of the pills

16 Pronouns and words standing in for nouns

a Definite pronouns

The personal pronouns have already been listed in 3. Note that when referring back to a particular noun just mentioned, where English might use 'it', Hebrew commonly uses הוּא (for a masculine noun) or הִיא (for a feminine):

הַסְוֶוֹדֶר הַזֶּה? אֲבָל הוּא לֹא נָקִי!

This sweater? But it isn't clean!

אֵיפֹה הַמְּנוֹרָה? הִיא בְּתִיקוּן

Where is the lamp? It's being fixed

יֵשׁ לְךָ גִיטָרָה? נוּ, אֵיפֹה הִיא?

You have a guitar? So where is it then?

And similarly, one uses אוֹתוֹ, אוֹתָהּ (see 35(b)):

יֵשׁ לְךָ חֶבֶל? אָז תֵּן לִי אוֹתוֹ!

Do you have string? Then let me have it!

For a vaguer, less specific 'it', Hebrew uses זֶה:

מַה, אֵין תְּשׁוּבָה? זֶה אָיוֹם וְנוֹרָא!

What, no answer? It's awful!

דַּי! זֶה סְקַנְדָּל!

Stop! It's a scandal!

כָּל הַבַּלַגַן שֶׁלְּךָ? זֶה בָּאוֹטוֹ מֵאֲחוֹרָה

All your mess? It's in the back of the car

Note: זֶה can also mean 'this' (plural: אֵלֶּה 'these'). See 11.

b *Indefinite pronouns: 'someone, something . . .'*

'Someone' and 'something' are expressed by taking question words (i.e. interrogatives, see 39(b)) and adding שֶׁהוּ. Note the spelling and the stress on the first part of the word: מַשֶּׁהוּ 'something', מִישֶׁהוּ 'someone' and, if one knows that the 'someone' refers to a woman: מִישֶׁהִי.

'Somewhere' is usually בְּאֵיזֶשֶׁהוּ מָקוֹם (i.e. 'in some place'), and 'some time, once' is פַּעַם:

זֶה בֶּטַח בְּאֵיזֶשֶׁהוּ מָקוֹם	It's definitely somewhere
תֵּן צִלְצוּל פַּעַם	Give a call some time

27

c Adjectives without their noun: הַיָּרוֹק 'the green one'

Where English might use the pronoun 'one, ones' in phrases like 'green ones, the green one, this one, which one?', Hebrew lets the adjective or other word stand by itself with whatever agreement is needed:

בֵּיצִים רַכּוֹת זֶה גוֹעַל-נֶפֶשׁ, אֲנִי רַק אוֹהֶבֶת קָשׁוֹת
Soft eggs are gross, I only like hard ones

אֵיזֶה סִיכָּה אַתְּ רוֹצָה, הַיְרוּקָה?
Which clip do you want, the green one?

הַשִׂמְלָה הַזֹּאת לֹא בְּסֵדֶר? נוּ, אָז קְחִי אֶת זֹאת
That dress is no good? Then take this one

For 'the one that . . ., the ones that . . .', Hebrew uses זֶה שֶׁ and אֵלֶּה שֶׁ:

אֵיפֹה אֵלֶּה שֶׁעוֹשִׂים בִּיפּ?   Where are the ones that go 'beep'?

d Numerals without their noun

Numerals, like adjectives, can be used without mentioning the noun each time. They will still agree. For '2', the free-standing form שְׁתַּיִם, שְׁנַיִם must be used rather than שְׁתֵּי, שְׁנֵי:

לָמָה קִיבַּלְתִּי שְׁלוֹשָׁה תְּמָרִים וְהוּא קִיבֵּל אַרְבָּעָה?
Why did I get three dates and he got four?

אֲנִי מִתְלַבֵּט אִם לְהַכְנִיס אַרְבַּע בַּטֶרִיוֹת אוֹ שְׁתַּיִם
I'm in two minds whether to put in four batteries or two

e Quantity words without their noun

Other quantity words, too, can be used without a noun:

יֵשׁ לְךָ הָמוֹן, תֵּן לִי עוֹד קְצָת   You have loads, give me a bit more

17 Possessives and constructs

a *Possessive 'of':* הָאָח שֶׁל יוֹרָם *'Yoram's brother'*

Possessive 'of' (or 's) is commonly שֶׁל:

הַבֵּן שֶׁל הַנָּשִׂיא	the son of the President (the President's son)
הַסֶּלוּלָרִי שֶׁל מַייק	Mike's cell-phone

Notice that the word order is as with English 'of': the thing possessed comes first.

שֶׁל מִי denotes 'whose?'. For example:

שֶׁל מִי הַכִּיפָּה שָׁם ?
Whose is the yarmulka over there?
  (Of whom is the yarmulka over there?)

הַבֵּן שֶׁל מִי מִתְחַתֵּן עִם הַבַּת שֶׁל הָרַב?
Whose son is marrying the rabbi's daughter?
  (The son of whom is marrying the rabbi's daughter?)

b *Possessive 'my, your', etc.:* הָאָח שֶׁלִי *'my brother'*

'My' is commonly שֶׁלִי:

הַכֶּלֶב שֶׁלִי   my dog (*lit.* 'the dog of me')

שֶׁלִי is made up of שֶׁל 'of' + an ending representing the pronoun אֲנִי 'I': in other words, 'of me'.

1 These possessives follow the noun, just like שֶׁל הַנָּשִׂיא 'of the President' in 17(a).

2 ה 'the' is added to the first noun, because 'my dog' means *'the* dog of mine'.

29

The full list is as follows:

our	שֶׁלָּנוּ	my	שֶׁלִּי
your (masc. pl.)	שֶׁלָּכֶם	your (masc. sing.)	שֶׁלְּךָ
your (fem. pl., formal)	שֶׁלָּכֶן	your (fem. sing.)	שֶׁלָּךְ
their (masc. pl.)	שֶׁלָּהֶם	his	שֶׁלּוֹ
their (fem. pl., formal)	שֶׁלָּהֶן	her	שֶׁלָּהּ

For the possessive *suffixes*, commonly used in formal Hebrew, e.g. כַּלְבְּךָ, see 73.

c *The construct: set phrases*

To make two nouns into a set phrase of the type 'soccer game', Hebrew places them side by side, but in the opposite order to English: the noun that *does the qualifying* comes last, just as an adjective follows its noun. The whole thing is called a construct phrase or smichut, and the first noun is called the construct noun:

מִשְׂחַק כַּדּוּרֶגֶל   soccer game
(*lit.* game soccer. Compare מִשְׂחָק טוֹב good game)

To remember the order, just imagine that there is a שֶׁל 'of' between the nouns:

מִשְׂחָק שֶׁל כַּדּוּרֶגֶל   game of soccer

Further examples: סוֹף שָׁבוּעַ 'week end', עֵץ תַּפּוּחַ 'apple tree', אֶרֶץ יִשְׂרָאֵל 'Land of Israel'.

With particularly fixed set phrases, a hyphen is sometimes used:

בֶּגֶד־יָם   swimsuit

As with English set phrases and 'of', Hebrew construct phrases and שֶׁל
cover a wide range of semantic relationships, particularly the following:

1 made of, composed of, a measure of:

שִׁינֵי זָהָב gold teeth   טִיפַּת גֶּשֶׁם rain drop

צֶוֶת רוֹפְאִים team of doctors   כַּף מֶלַח a tablespoon of salt

2 function:

שִׂמְלַת חֲתוּנָה wedding dress   כַּרְטִיס אַשְׁרַאי credit card

מִשְׂרַד הַתַּחְבּוּרָה Ministry of Transport

3 naming and branding:

מְדִינַת אוֹרֶגוֹן the State of Oregon   קִיבּוּץ דְּגַנְיָה kibbutz Deganya

נַחַל הַיַּרְקוֹן the River Yarkon   יְמֵי־שִׁישִׁי Fridays

שְׁנַת 2004 the year 2004   מִפְלֶגֶת הַלִּיכּוּד the Likud party

עֲצֵי אוֹרֶן pine trees   מַצְלֵמַת קָנוֹן a Canon camera

4 using certain nouns as the equivalent of an adjective, e.g.:

עָנָק	דִּירַת עָנָק	a giant apartment
מִשְׁנֶה	וַעֲדַת מִשְׁנֶה	a subcommittee
חִינָם	שִׂיחַת חִינָם	a free call
בְּכוֹרָה	הוֹפָעַת בְּכוֹרָה	debut

---

d *Construct endings*

A construct phrase is often more than just a matter of putting two nouns
together. The first noun frequently requires a special 'construct ending'
and / or an internal change of vowel.

For words that already have an inflectional ending, there are two construct endings:

1 The feminine ending הָ always becomes תַ:

אֲרוּחָה meal ~ אֲרוּחַת־עֶרֶב evening meal (supper)

בְּרֵכָה pool ~ בְּרֵכַת־שְׂחִיָּה swimming pool

2 The plural ending ים always becomes יֵ. But the plural ending וֹת is unchanged:

סַלִּים baskets ~ סַלֵּי לֶחֶם bread baskets

קַוִּים lines ~ קַוֵּי טֶלֶפוֹן telephone lines

אֲרוּחוֹת meals ~ אֲרוּחוֹת־עֶרֶב evening meals (suppers)

For words without such an inflectional ending, e.g. יֶלֶד, מָטוֹס, קִיבּוּץ, there is no construct ending, but there may be an internal vowel-change (as indeed there may be for other words, too), e.g. *מְטוֹס נוֹסְעִים* 'passenger plane'. For details, see 73(a).

When one wishes to make a construct phrase plural, it is usually the first noun that becomes plural; the second noun remains unchanged (and usually singular): אֲרוּחוֹת־עֶרֶב 'evening meals (suppers)'.

e ה in construct phrases

To add 'the' to a construct phrase, formal Hebrew attaches the ה only to the second word:

אֲרוּחַת הָעֶרֶב the evening meal

But colloquial Hebrew often treats set phrases such as these like a single word, attaching ה to the *front*: for example, הָאֲרוּחַת־עֶרֶב 'the evening meal', הַחַיּוֹת־בַּיִת 'the household pets'. While common and quite acceptable in casual speech, this practice is frowned upon in written Hebrew.

18–23 THE INFLECTIONS OF THE VERB

18 Introduction

Most verbs have five major sets of inflections:

> Three tenses: past, present, future
> Imperative (i.e. request)
> Infinitive (i.e. 'to . . .')

For example (referring to the verb by its simplest form, the 'he' form of the past tense):

קִיצֵר:

The three tenses:

יְקַצֵּר	מְקַצֵּר	קִיצֵר
will shorten	shortens	shortened

Imperative: קַצֵּר!   shorten!

Infinitive: לְקַצֵּר   to shorten

Most verbs also have a related 'action noun', e.g. קִיצוּר 'abbreviation'. We have listed it together with the inflection tables, though in fact it is not quite as regular as the inflections proper (for example, the action noun for רָקַד 'dance' is not רְקִידָה as expected but רִיקוּד). For the use of the action noun, see 64.

Note: Verbs also have a gerund, related to the infinitive (e.g. קַצֵּר 'shortening'), but it is too uncommon to be listed here. See 97 for its use.

In addition, any given verb belongs to a particular grammatical pattern (known as a *binyan*). There are seven binyanim (see 25). Every verb also has a root, with certain types of root being peculiar in some way, leading to significant upsets in the verb's inflections. But whichever binyan or root-type they belong to, verbs form their tenses and other inflections in a fairly uniform way; in the next five sections, we list these shared features.

19 The past tense

a Form of the past tense

All verbs form their past tense by adding a *suffix*, as follows:

נוּ	(we)	תִּי	(I)
תֶּם	(you, masc. pl.)	תָּ	(you, masc. sing.)
תֶּן	(you, fem. pl.)	תְּ	(you, fem. sing.)
וּ	(they)	*no suffix*	(he)
		הָ	(she)

Note: The suffixes in the first three lines (the 1st and 2nd person suffixes) are not stressed. Those in the last two lines are sometimes stressed, depending on the type of verb.

Using the verb קָם 'get up' as a model:

אֲנַחְנוּ קַ֫מְנוּ	we got up	אֲנִי קַ֫מְתִּי	I got up
אַתֶּם קַ֫מְתֶּם	you (masc. pl.) got up	אַתָּה קַ֫מְתָּ	you (masc. sing.) got up
אַתֶּן קַ֫מְתֶּן	you (fem .pl.) got up	אַתְּ קַ֫מְתְּ	you (fem. sing.) got up
הֵם קַ֫מוּ	they got up	הוּא קָם	he got up
		הִיא קַ֫מָה	she got up

We have marked stress by ⁺ on the first syllable. It is a feature of this type of verb that stress never falls on the past tense endings.

The past tense inflects for *person* as well as for gender and number, but unlike the present tense (see 19(b), (c)) it cannot distinguish gender for 'I', 'we', and 'they'.

A point to ponder: some of these suffixes bear a resemblance to the personal pronouns themselves: י to אֲנִי, ת to אַתָּה, etc.

34

b *Syntax of the past tense*

The 1st and 2nd person forms in the past tense are often used without the
pronoun, particularly in formal style:

מָתַי קַמְתָּ?   When did you get up?   הֶחְלַטְתִּי   I have decided

The 3rd person forms normally require הוּא or הִיא or הֵם or a noun:

מָתַי הוּא קָם?   When did he get up?   הִיא קָמָה   She's got up

אֲחוֹתִי קָמָה   My sister got up   הַפָּרוֹת קָמוּ   The cows rose

הֵם קָמוּ כְּבָר   They've got up already

c *Meaning of the past tense*

The meaning of the Hebrew past tense essentially covers four English past
tenses: 'I got up, I have got up, I was getting up, I had got up.' An added
כְּבָר 'already' or בְּדִיוּק 'just' can increase precision:

אֶתְמוֹל קַמְתִּי מְאוּחָר   Yesterday I got up late

כְּבָר קַמְתִּי, בְּסֵדֶר?   I've already got up, OK?

כְּשֶׁאַתָּה בָּאתָ, אֲנִי בְּדִיוּק קַמְתִּי   When you came, I was just getting up

20 The present tense

a *Form of the present tense*

All verbs form their present tense with suffixes of the kind that are also
used for nouns and adjectives:

masc. sing. *no suffix*		fem. sing. ◌ָה or ◌ֶת	
masc. pl. ◌ִים		fem. pl. ◌וֹת	

And using the verb קָם 'get up' as a model:

אֲנִי . . . אַתָּה . . . הוּא קָם		I (masc.) . . . you (masc.) . . . he . . . get(s) up
אֲנִי . . . אַתְּ . . . הִיא קָמָה		I (fem.) . . . you (fem.) . . . she . . . get(s) up
אֲנַחְנוּ . . . אַתֶּם . . . הֵם קָמִים		We . . . you (pl.) . . . they . . . get up
אֲנַחְנוּ . . . אַתֶּן . . . הֵן קָמוֹת		We (fem.) . . . you (fem. pl.) . . . they (fem.) . . . get up

b *Use of the present tense*

The present tense verb ordinarily requires a personal pronoun (or a noun), as in the preceding table.

The meaning of the Hebrew present tense basically covers the two English tenses 'I get up' and 'I am getting up' (including the meaning 'I am due to get up'):

מָתַי אַתְּ קָמָה בְּשַׁבָּת?	When do you get up on Shabbat?
מָתַי אַתְּ קָמָה מָחָר?	When are you getting up tomorrow?

21 The future tense

a *Form of the future tense*

All verbs form their future tense by using the following *prefixes* plus *suffixes*. (The reason for giving these 'skeletal' prefixes without vowels is that the vowels vary according to the verb pattern.)

Plural			Singular		
נ . . .		we	א . . .		I
ת . . . וּ		you	ת . . .		you (masc.)
			ת . . . י		you (fem.)
י . . . וּ		they	י . . .		he
			ת . . .		she

Using the verb קָם as a model:

Plural			Singular		
אֲנַחְנוּ נָקוּם		we will get up	אֲנִי אָקוּם		I will get up
אַתֶּם/אַתֶּן תָּקוּמוּ		you (pl.) will get up	אַתָּה תָּקוּם		you (masc. sing.) will get up
			אַתְּ תָּקוּמִי		you (fem. sing.) will get up
הֵם/הֵן יָקוּמוּ		they will get up	הוּא יָקוּם		he will get up
			הִיא תָּקוּם		she will get up

1 Notice the similarities to the personal pronouns: א to אֲנִי, and so on for ת 'you' and נ 'we'; but not for ת 'she' or י 'he, they'.

2 Plural וּ is added to distinguish 'you' sing. from pl., and 'he' from 'they'. For this reason it is not found with נ.

Note: In elevated style, a special form may be used for the feminine 2nd and 3rd person plural (one form for both): ת . . . נה, e.g. תְּקוּמֶֽנָה 'they will arise'. We will disregard it here. It is listed in traditional grammars.

b *Use of the future tense*

Future tense has two main uses:

1 It can be a *prediction*, equivalent to the English future;

2 in the 2nd person it can be a *request*.

In practice, confusion between the two uses rarely arises.

Examples of a prediction:	אָקוּם	I'll get up
	תָּקוּם	you'll get up
	לֹא תָּקוּם	you won't get up
	תָּקוּמוּ	you'll (pl.) get up
	לֹא תָּקוּמוּ	you (pl.) won't get up
Examples of a request:	תָּקוּם	get up!
	אַל תָּקוּם	don't get up
	תָּקוּמוּ	get up! (pl.)
	אַל תָּקוּמוּ	don't get up! (pl.)

Notice that a *negative* prediction uses לֹא, whereas a negative request requires אַל. For making a positive request, Hebrew also has the *imperative* form (see 22). Colloquial Hebrew uses the imperative with just a handful of verbs, whereas formal Hebrew uses it more extensively and tends to avoid the future tense for positive requests.

In making requests the personal pronouns אֲנִי, אַתָּה, etc. tend not to be used at all with the future tense verb:

תָּקוּם !   Get up!

In predictions, colloquial Hebrew makes heavy use of them:

כְּשֶׁאֲנִי אָקוּם   when I get up

כְּשֶׁאַתָּה תָּקוּם   when you get up

By contrast, more formal Hebrew prefers not to use 1st and 2nd person pronouns with the future (like the past), since the prefixes already make it quite clear which pronoun is intended:

כְּשֶׁאָקוּם, כְּשֶׁתָּקוּם, כְּשֶׁהוּא יָקוּם ...

22 The imperative

a Form of the imperative

The imperative has just three forms. These involve suffixes, in fact the
same suffixes as the 2nd person future tense, but without its prefixes:

Example:

masc. sing.	*no suffix*	קוּם	get up!	(to a male)
fem. sing.	ִי	קוּמִי	get up!	(to a female)
masc. and fem. pl.	וּ	קוּמוּ	get up!	(to many)

Note: The special fem. pl. form קוֹמְנָה is so rare that we have omitted it.

Suffixes aside, what the imperative looks like depends on the binyan
involved (see under the individual binyanim in 26–32 and 50–9). As a rule
of thumb, the imperative resembles either the future or the infinitive.

b Use of the imperative

The imperative (Hebrew term: צִיוּוּי) is found only in positive requests. In
negative requests, it is replaced by the future tense (see 40(c)). For the
most part, it is *formal* in tone, inhabiting fiction, documents, instruction
manuals, cookbooks, speeches and the like.

At the same time, a handful of verbs have an imperative in *all-round
everyday use*. These are usually of one syllable. Notable examples:

בּוֹא come!	זוּז move!
חַכֵּה wait!	לֵךְ go!
סַע go!	עֲזוֹב leave off!
צֵא leave!	קוּם get up!

קַח take!   רֵד get down!

רוּץ run!   שֵׁב sit!

שִׂים put!   תֵּן give!

Note: Most such one-syllable imperatives belong to one-syllable (ע"ו) verbs or to verbs that drop their first consonant.

23 The infinitive

a Form of the infinitive

The infinitive cannot be inflected. Whether one is addressing males or females, one person or many, it is unchanged.

The infinitive's distinguishing mark is a prefixed ל, thus לָקוּם 'to get up', לְשַׁפְשֵׁף 'to rub'. All the rest depends on the type of binyan and root, as set out in section 25.

b Use of the infinitive

The infinitive covers many of the uses of English 'to . . .', including 'it's hard to . . ., I want to . . .' (see 44, 45). A further important use is in issuing lofty or 'bossy' instructions, e.g. to a child, to troops, to groups of people, thus:

קָשֶׁה לָדַעַת	It's hard to know
אֲנִי רוֹצֶה לָדַעַת	I want to know
כּוּלָם לָקוּם	Everyone get up!
לָרוּץ, יְלָדִים	Run, children

The fact that the infinitive does not inflect in gender or number almost seems to underline its loftiness and detachment from the addressee, by comparison with the inflecting future tense and imperative.

24 Root and base

Most Hebrew words are built around a root and a base. The base is the basic form of a word after we have peeled off any meaningful endings or prefixes:

Root	Base		Word *with prefixes or suffixes*	
ק־ד־ם	קִידֵם	promote	קִידַמְתִּי	I promoted
	קַדֵם		אֲקַדֵם	I will promote
ק־ם	מָקוֹם	a place	הַמָּקוֹם	the place
			מְקוֹמוֹת	places
			מְקוֹמִי	my place

Note that the root is just a string of consonants; in itself it has no pronunciation. Roots may have from two to five consonants. Thus the root of קָם 'got up' can be said to be the two consonants ק־ם.

As will be seen, roots sometimes have a precise meaning. More often they do not, just like '-fect' in English: 'infect, defect, affect, confection'. Thus ק־ד־ם is the root of the verbs קָדַם 'precede', הִקְדִּים 'anticipate' and הִתְקַדֵּם 'move forward' as well as of קִידֵם 'promote'.

So it has a distinct, but not necessarily a very precise, meaning.

Many roots have no obvious meaning at all. For example, ק־ב־ל yields קִיבֵּל 'receive', קָבַל 'complain' and הִקְבִּיל 'correspond'. Many nouns and adjectives, especially foreign imports, have no obvious root at all, thus עֵז 'goat', שָׁמַיִם 'sky', כִּימִי 'chemical'.

25 Word patterns: *binyanim* and *mishkalim*

a Introduction

As already noted, all verbs and very many adjectives and nouns have a recognizable root, on which are imposed various vowels and consonants.

There is a variety of such imposed patterns. For the verb there are seven, known as *binyanim*. For the adjective and noun, there are scores of patterns, some common and some quite infrequent, known as *mishkalim*.

What makes verbs particularly different from nouns or adjectives is that all verbs, without exception, must adhere to one of the seven verb patterns (thus, all verbs consist of a root skeleton on which is mounted a binyan), whereas many nouns and adjectives have no particular root or pattern, and indeed are regularly imported direct from some foreign source. Examples would be the nouns אִידְיוֹט 'idiot' and בַּנְק 'bank' and the adjectives קוֹנְסְטְרוּקְטִיבִי 'constructive' and אַקְטוּאָלִי 'topical'.

b | Functions of the verb patterns

There are seven *binyanim*:

1	פָּעַל	2	נִפְעַל		
3	הִפְעִיל	4	הוּפְעַל		
5	פִּיעֵל	6	פּוּעַל	7	הִתְפַּעֵל

These names are a graphic representation of the past tense form of each binyan. Thus אָכַל 'ate', לָקַח 'took', נָשַׁק 'kissed' all belong to the first binyan, פָּעַל, while הִרְבִּיץ 'hit', הִטְרִיד 'bothered', הִזְכִּיר 'reminded' all belong to the third binyan, הִפְעִיל. (The choice of the letters פ-ע-ל for the names of verb patterns is because the verb פָּעַל means 'to act'.)

As the diagram suggests, the binyanim fall into three groups. These groups are basically *grammatical* rather than *semantic*: that is, the group a verb belongs to cannot tell us much about the meaning of that verb. Take, for example, the verbs קָבַל 'complain', הִקְבִּיל 'parallel', קִיבֵּל 'receive', הִתְקַבֵּל 'be received': the root ק-ב-ל is being put through the various patterns with meanings that seem mostly arbitrary. Or take the verbs בָּטַח 'trust', הִבְטִיחַ 'assure', בִּיטֵחַ 'insure': that there is a connection is obvious, but there is no 'magic formula' to tell one what precisely the connection will be.

However, the sets of binyanim *within* these groupings do tend to be related in meaning:

1 NIF'AL is often the passive of PA'AL, e.g.

| גָּנַב | steal | ~ | נִגְנַב | be stolen |
| שָׁטַף | rinse | ~ | נִשְׁטַף | be rinsed |

2 HUF'AL is the passive of HIF'IL, e.g.

| הִסְבִּיר | explain | ~ | הוּסְבַּר | be explained |
| הִגְבִּיר | step up | ~ | הוּגְבַּר | be stepped up |

3 PU'AL is the passive of PI'EL, e.g.

| חִילֵּק | hand out | ~ | חוּלַּק | be handed out |
| שִׁיתֵּף | share | ~ | שׁוּתַּף | be shared |

4 For a PA'AL (or NIF'AL) verb denoting 'something happens', there is often a HIF'IL denoting 'cause something to happen', e.g.

| גָּדַל | grow | ~ | הִגְדִּיל | magnify |
| נִזְהַר | be careful | ~ | הִזְהִיר | warn |

And for an adjective, there is similarly often a HIF'IL denoting 'cause something to be . . .', e.g.

| נָמוֹךְ | low | ~ | הִנְמִיךְ | to lower |
| רָחָב | broad | ~ | הִרְחִיב | to broaden |

5 For PI'EL verbs denoting 'doing something to something', there is often an intransitive HITPA'EL denoting 'happening by itself', e.g.

| בִּישַׁלְתִּי פּוּדִינְג | ~ | הַפּוּדִינְג הִתְבַּשֵּׁל |
| I cooked pudding | ~ | the pudding cooked |

43

6 For an ADJECTIVE there is often a HIF'IL or HITPA'EL denoting 'becoming . . .':

צָהוֹב	yellow	~	הִצְהִיב	become yellow
יָשָׁן	old	~	הִתְיַשֵּׁן	become old-fashioned

7 For a NOUN there is often a PI'EL denoting an action typical of that noun, often equivalent to '-ize', '-ate':

קְלִיפָּה	peel	~	לְקַלֵּף	to peel
גֶּשֶׁר	a bridge	~	לְגַשֵּׁר	to bridge
סוּבְּסִידְיָה	subsidy	~	לְסַבְּסֵד	to subsidize
מַחְשֵׁב	computer	~	לְמַחְשֵׁב	to computerize

8 For PA'AL or PI'EL verbs denoting 'doing something', there is occasionally a HITPA'EL verb denoting 'doing something to oneself' (the 'reflexive') or 'doing something to one another' (the 'reciprocal'), e.g.:

לְגַלֵּחַ אֶת הָראֹשׁ to shave the head	~	לְהִתְגַּלֵּחַ to shave (oneself)
נָשַׁקְתִּי אֶת אָחִי I kissed my brother	~	הִתְנַשַּׁקְנוּ we kissed (one another)
לְחַבֵּר שְׁנֵי חֲלָקִים to join two parts	~	שְׁנֵי חֲלָקִים מִתְחַבְּרִים two parts join together

There are many false beliefs about the binyanim, such as that the PI'EL is generally intensive and the HITPA'EL generally reflexive. In fact, the PI'EL is rarely the 'intensive' of anything. Taking 100–200 dictionary verbs at random, only one in five PA'AL verbs has a causative HIF'IL or an intensive or causative PI'EL.

c Function of the noun and adjective patterns

The sheer number of noun and adjective patterns (mishkalim), and their openness to further additions, make it even harder to find meaning in them. The clearest and most numerous are the action noun and de-nominal patterns: nouns denoting action (such as בִּישׁוּל 'cooking') and adjectives based on nouns (such as יַמִּי 'marine', from יָם 'sea'). See 64–5.

26–9 ILLUSTRATING THE FOUR ACTIVE BINYANIM

The following are the chief forms for the four active binyanim, meaning that they are used in active rather than passive constructions, (that is, 'Gil ate the yoghurt' as against 'the yoghurt was eaten by Gil'): PA'AL, HIF'IL, PI'EL, and HITPA'EL

The remaining three binyanim, which are primarily *passive*, are set out in 30–2.

The illustrations that follow involve the *basic root-type*. (Deviant root-types will be illustrated in 50–9.)

26 Binyan PA'AL

a Two-syllable PA'AL

The PA'AL pattern is the only one of the seven that does not have the 'burden' of a present tense prefix or general binyan prefix. For this reason it is also known as KAL, the 'light' pattern. Using the verb כָּנַס 'to gather':

Past

Pl.	Sing.
כָּנַסְנוּ	כָּנַסְתִּי
כְּנַסְתֶּם	כָּנַסְתָּ
כְּנַסְתֶּן	כָּנַסְתְּ
כָּנְסוּ	כָּנַס
	כָּנְסָה

45

Notes:

1 The suffixes consisting of a vowel (i.e. 3rd fem. sing. ה and 3rd pl. ו) take the stress. All the other suffixes are unstressed. This is true of most verb types, in all tenses. However, for the 2nd pl. forms newscasters, teachers and their like insist on stressing the *suffix*, in accordance with the Classical rules כְּנַסְתֶּם, כְּנַסְתֶּן.

2 The last vowel in the base drops when it loses its stress: not *kanasa* but *kansa*, not *kanasu* but *kansu*.

3 Notice also that in most forms in the table the base vowels are *a-a*. In fact, in nearly all 1st or 2nd person forms of the past tense, in all binyanim, the last base vowel is likewise *a*.

Present

	Pl.	*Sing.*
masc.	כּוֹנְסִים	כּוֹנֵס
fem.	כּוֹנְסוֹת	כּוֹנֶסֶת

Notes:

1 The feminine singular is stressed כּוֹנֶסֶת.

2 In the plural, instead of the expected *konesim, konesot*, we get *konsim, konsot*. The stressed *e* has lost its stress to the ending, and drops out as a result. This is a standard rule for the *e* vowel.

Future

Pl.	*Sing.*
נִכְנוֹס	אֶכְנוֹס
תִּכְנְסוּ	תִּכְנוֹס
	תִּכְנְסִי
יִכְנְסוּ	יִכְנוֹס
	תִּכְנוֹס

Notes:

1 The vowel in the 1st person (אֶכְנֹס) is odd one out: not *i* but *e*. (Putting it technically, א 'lowers' the vowel that goes with it.)

2 In this and other binyanim, except HIF'IL, stress is shifted onto the suffix, if any, and as a result the vowel losing the stress is relegated to a brief *e* or lost, thus:

tichnosi → *tichn^{e}si,*   *tichnosu* → *tichn^{e}su*

3 When the first root consonant is ב, כ, פ, it will be soft rather than hard, i.e. it will be 'v, ch, f'. This is the result of a general rule: with certain exceptions ב, כ, פ are soft after a vowel and otherwise hard.

Infinitive	Imperative	
לִכְנֹס	masc. sing.	כְּנֹס
	fem. sing.	כְּנְסִי
	pl.	כְּנְסוּ

Notes:

1 The infinitive prefix ל here is usually לְ.

2 A general rule for virtually the entire verb system is that *the future, the infinitive and the imperative share the same vowel pattern,* thus:

יִכְנֹס ~ לִכְנֹס ~ כְּנֹס !, יָקוּם ~ לָקוּם ~ קוּם !.

Action noun

כְּנִיסָה

---

b *One-syllable PA'AL, e.g.* קָם *'get up'*

Strictly speaking, ONE-SYLLABLE verbs (e.g. קָם 'get up') are just a variant of the PA'AL binyan, arising because they have a two-consonant root. But they are sufficiently distinct to warrant separate treatment.

Note: The traditional name for such verbs with a two-consonant root is ע״ו (Ayin-Vav) verbs, meaning that in place of the usual middle letter (the so-called Ayin letter) of the root these verbs sometimes feature a vav.

Past

קַֽמְנוּ	קַֽמְתִּי
קַמְתֶּם	קַֽמְתָּ
קַמְתֶּן	קַֽמְתְּ
קַֽמוּ	קָם
	קַֽמָה

For clarity, we have marked stress by ⁀ on the first syllable: in one-syllable verbs, stress *never* falls on the past or future tense suffixes.

Present

	Pl.	*Sing.*
masc.	קַמִּֽים	קָם
fem.	קַמֹּֽות	קַֽמָה

Stress here is peculiar: although the suffixes look just like adjective suffixes, colloquial usage stresses the fem. sing. as קַֽמָה instead of קָמָֽה. The result is that 'she got up' and 'she gets up' are both הִיא קַֽמָה.

Future

נָקוּם	אָקוּם
תָּקֽוּמוּ	תָּקוּם
	תָּקֽוּמִי
יָקֽוּמוּ	יָקוּם
	תָּקוּם

Here, and on the imperative below, we have again marked stress with an accent mark to show that stress is always on the base, not on the suffix.

Exception: שָׁר 'sing', רָב 'quarrel', and שָׂם 'put' have the vowel י rather than ו in the future, imperative, and infinitive: אָשִׂים, שִׂים!, לָשִׂים.

Also, one important verb, בָּא 'come', has ו instead: אָבוֹא, בּוֹא!, לָבוֹא.

Imperative

masc. sing.	קוּם
fem. sing.	קוּ֫מִי
pl.	קוּ֫מוּ

Infinitive

לָקוּם

Action noun

קִימָה

27 Binyan HIF'IL

All the binyanim except PA'AL and ONE-SYLLABLE verbs have a distinctive *binyan prefix*. Binyan HIF'IL has a distinctive binyan prefix ה in its past tense, infinitive, and action noun. Notice that the present, future, infinitive, and action noun have something of their own in common: the use of -a- as the vowel in the prefix. Using the verb הִכְנִיס 'to insert':

Past

הִכְנַ֫סְנוּ	הִכְנַ֫סְתִּי
הִכְנַסְתֶּם	הִכְנַ֫סְתָּ
הִכְנַסְתֶּן	הִכְנַ֫סְתְּ
הִכְנִ֫יסוּ	הִכְנִיס
	הִכְנִ֫יסָה

49

Notes:

1 In the past tense, the base vowel is 'stress-dominant', like the *a* in the past tense of ONE-SYLLABLE VERBS (see 26(b)), hence, הִכְנִ֫יסָה, הִכְנִ֫יסוּ.

2 The vowels are *i-i* (3rd person) or *i-a*. Similar vowel-alternation occurs in the PI'EL binyan: *i-e, i-a.**

* Because wherever there is a consonantal suffix, the adjacent vowel (i.e. the last vowel in the base) will become 'a', הִכְנִיסָה instead of הִכְנַסְתִּי.

Present

	Pl.	*Sing.*
masc.	מַכְנִיסִים	מַכְנִיס
fem.	מַכְנִיסוֹת	מַכְנִיסָ֫ה

Notes:

1 The fem. sing. ending, ה, is *stressed*, like a regular adjective or noun such as טוֹבָה. (The verb patterns shown so far have unstressed ה or ת, and so do nearly all verb patterns.)

2 Present tense here is marked by מ, as it is for all the remaining binyanim (HUF'AL, PI'EL, PU'AL and HITPA'EL).

Future

נַכְנִיס	אַכְנִיס
תַּכְנִ֫יסוּ	תַּכְנִיס
	תַּכְנִ֫יסִי
יַכְנִ֫יסוּ	יַכְנִיס
	תַּכְנִיס

Just as in the past tense, the base of the HIF'IL is stress-dominant – the endings do not get the stress.

Imperative

הַכְנֵס, הַכְנִיסִי, הַכְנִיסוּ

Infinitive

לְהַכְנִיס

The 'binyan prefix' is ה (*h*), as in the past tense. Thus, one can view לְהַכְנִיס as *le* + *ha* + BASE (כְנִיס).

Action noun

הַכְנָסָה

28–9 BINYAN PI'EL AND HITPA'EL

The family PI'EL, HITPA'EL, and the passive PU'AL (see 32) are closely related in prefixes, vowels, and, above all, in requiring that ב, כ, פ as the middle root-letter be hard (with a few exceptions).

28 PI'EL

PI'EL has no binyan prefix. Using the verb כִּינֵס 'to convene':

Past

כִּינַסְנוּ	כִּינַסְתִּי
כִּינַסְתֶּם	כִּינַסְתָּ
כִּינַסְתֶּן	כִּינַסְתְּ
כִּינְסוּ	כִּינֵס
	כִּינְסָה

As with the *a* vowel in binyan PA'AL, the vowel *e* drops when it loses its stress, yielding not *kinesa*, *kinesu* but rather *kinsa*, *kinsu*.

Present

מְכַנְּסִים	מְכַנֵּס
מְכַנְּסוֹת	מְכַנֶּסֶת

The vowel in the present tense is מְ, and similarly for the future and infinitive.

Future

נְכַנֵּס	אֲכַנֵּס
תְּכַנְּסוּ	תְּכַנֵּס
	תְּכַנְּסִי
יְכַנְּסוּ	יְכַנֵּס
	תְּכַנֵּס

Notes:

1   Notice that the prefix vowel becomes ֲ with the א prefix.

2   Be aware of the difference between the future tense of PI'EL and that of PA'AL: on paper, in unpointed Hebrew, the PI'EL future forms תכנסי, תכנסו, יכנסו are liable to be confused with the PA'AL future.

Imperative   Infinitive

כַּנֵּס, כַּנְּסִי, כַּנְּסוּ   לְכַנֵּס

Action noun

כִּינוּס

29 HITPA'EL

Binyan HITPA'EL uses a distinctive binyan prefix. In the past tense, infinitive, and action noun, it shows up as הִת. In the present and future tense, the additional prefixes מְ, א, ת, etc. swallow up the ה and the הת. Using the verb הִתְכַּנֵּס 'to assemble':

Past

הִתְכַּנַּסְנוּ	הִתְכַּנַּסְתִּי
הִתְכַּנַּסְתֶּם	הִתְכַּנַּסְתָּ
הִתְכַּנַּסְתֶּן	הִתְכַּנַּסְתְּ
	הִתְכַּנֵּס
הִתְכַּנְסוּ	הִתְכַּנְסָה

Unlike the binyan PI'EL, the base vowels are *a-e* (3rd person) or *a-a* – not *i-e*, *i-a*.

Note: The reason: where there is a prefix, the adjacent vowel (i.e. the first vowel in the base) will become '*a*'. Here, in the HITPA'EL, there is such a prefix, הת. But in the PI'EL, the past tense has no prefix, hence '*i*'. Similarly, wherever there is a suffix, the adjacent (preceding) vowel will become '*a*', hence: הִתְכַּנַּסְתִּי ~ הִתְכַּנֵּס and כִּינַסְתָּ ~ כִּינֵס.

Present

מִתְכַּנְסִים	מִתְכַּנֵּס
מִתְכַּנְסוֹת	מִתְכַּנֶּסֶת

Future

נִתְכַּנֵּס	אֶתְכַּנֵּס
תִּתְכַּנְסוּ	תִּתְכַּנֵּס
	תִּתְכַּנְסִי
יִתְכַּנְסוּ	יִתְכַּנֵּס
	תִּתְכַּנֵּס

Imperative

הִתְכַּנֵּס, הִתְכַּנְסִי, הִתְכַּנְסוּ

Infinitive

לְהִתְכַּנֵּס

Action noun

הִתְכַּנְסוּת

30–2 THE PASSIVE BINYANIM: NIF'AL, HUF'AL, PU'AL

'The rabbi found it' is an active sentence. 'It was found by the rabbi' is a passive sentence, saying essentially the same thing as the active sentence but with a different perspective on the action – and with the subject switched around and the verb form changed.

Hebrew has three passive binyanim: NIF'AL, HUF'AL, and PU'AL. Examples:

זֶה נִגְנַב	it was stolen
הוּחְלַפְתִּי	I was replaced
הֵם בּוּטְלוּ	they were cancelled

NIF'AL is used commonly, though by no means always, as the passive of PA'AL. It has several other important functions. HUF'AL and PU'AL are used exclusively as the passive of HIF'IL and PI'EL respectively, and are distinguished by a *u–a* vowel pattern throughout.

In colloquial usage, all these passives are somewhat less common: the active binyanim are preferred.

גָּנְבוּ אֶת זֶה	It was stolen
הֶחְלִיפוּ אוֹתִי	I was replaced

However, NIF'AL is also commonly employed for several *non*-passive verbs, such as נִכְנַס 'to enter', נִתְקַל 'to trip', נִלְחַם 'to fight', נִשְׁמַט 'to slip off', נִמְנַע 'to abstain', and נִרְדָּם 'to fall asleep'. It also sometimes denotes 'happening by itself', e.g.

הָאוֹר לֹא נִדְלַק	The light didn't turn on
הַתּוֹכְנִית נִפְתַּחַת	The program is opening

30 NIF'AL

NIF'AL, unlike the other binyanim, switches between *two* binyan prefixes: הִי in the infinitive and imperative; נ in the present and past.

We illustrate NIF'AL with the verb נִכְנַס 'to enter':

Past and Present

Past		Present	
נִכְנַסְנוּ	נִכְנַסְתִּי	נִכְנָסִים	נִכְנָס
נִכְנַסְתֶּם	נִכְנַסְתָּ	נִכְנָסוֹת	נִכְנֶסֶת
נִכְנַסְתֶּן	נִכְנַסְתְּ		
נִכְנְסוּ	נִכְנַס		
	נִכְנְסָה		

Notes:

1 NIF'AL's binyan prefix in the present and past tense is נ.

2 Notice that the vowel *a* does not drop out in the present plural: נִכְנָסִים, נִכְנָסוֹת.

   The dropping of *a* as seen, for example, in PA'AL (כָּנְסוּ) never affects present tense verbs.

3 In the past tense, however, *a* drops: נִכְנְסָה, נִכְנְסוּ.

Future

נִיכָּנֵס	אֶכָּנֵס
תִּיכָּנְסוּ	תִּיכָּנֵס
	תִּיכָּנְסִי
יִיכָּנְסוּ	יִיכָּנֵס
	תִּיכָּנֵס

Notes:

1 Some omit the letter **י** in the prefix, for example תִּכָּנֵס. Written without vowel points, תכנס, this is liable to be confused with PI'EL future tense (28).

2 Observe the hard **כּ**. It is a peculiarity of the NIF'AL future, infinitive, and action noun that **פ ,כ ,ב** as the first letters of the base are hard.

3 Be aware of the difference between the future tense of PI'EL and that of NIF'AL:

(a) The PI'EL future as a whole can be confused on paper with the NIF'AL future.

(b) The PI'EL prefix has the vowel ֲ while the NIF'AL prefix has ִ.

Imperative	Infinitive
הִיכָּנֵס !, הִיכָּנְסִי !, הִיכָּנְסוּ !	לְהִיכָּנֵס

As with ONE–SYLLABLE and PA'AL verbs, the NIF'AL imperative and infinitive are like the future. However, the binyan prefix **הי** is added, one of the many ways in which NIF'AL is the odd-man-out. Many people spell this as **ה** rather than **הי**.

Action noun

הִיכָּנְסוּת

31 HUF'AL

The HUF'AL has the same prefixes and vowels as its active counterpart, the HIF'IL, except that *u-a* replaces *i-i*, *i-a*, and *a-i* throughout. Using the verb הוּכְנַס 'to be inserted':

Past		Present	
הוּכְנַ֫סְנוּ	הוּכְנַ֫סְתִּי	מוּכְנָסִים	מוּכְנָס
הוּכְנַסְתֶּם	הוּכְנַ֫סְתָּ	מוּכְנָסוֹת	מוּכְנֶ֫סֶת
הוּכְנַסְתֶּן	הוּכְנַ֫סְתְּ		
הוּכְנְסוּ	הוּכְנַס		
	הוּכְנְסָה		

Future

נוּכְנַס	אוּכְנַס
תּוּכְנְסוּ	תּוּכְנַס
	תּוּכְנְסִי
יוּכְנְסוּ	יוּכְנַס
	תּוּכְנַס

Infinitive

לִהְיוֹת מוּכְנָס

Neither HUF'AL nor PU'AL has a simple infinitive. Instead, they use the infinitive of הָיָה 'be' + the 'passive adjective' (set out in 69). There is no imperative, either.

32 PU'AL

As already noted, the binyanim PI'EL, PU'AL, and HITPA'EL form a family. They have similar prefixes and vowels and, above all, they all require that ב, כ, פ as the middle root-letter be hard (with a few exceptions). Observe in particular that PI'EL and PU'AL have the vowel ַ in their various prefixes.

PU'AL, like the other passive binyan, HUF'AL, has the vowels *u-a* throughout. It has no binyan prefix. Using the verb כּוּנַס 'to be convened':

Past

כּוּנַּסְנוּ	כּוּנַּסְתִּי
כּוּנַּסְתֶּם	כּוּנַּסְתָּ
כּוּנַּסְתֶּן	כּוּנַּסְתְּ
כּוּנְסוּ	כּוּנַס
	כּוּנְסָה

As with the *a* vowel in binyan PA'AL and *e* in PI'EL, the vowel *a* drops when it loses its stress, hence not *kunasa*, *kunasu* but rather *kunsa*, *kunsu*.

Present

מְכוּנָּסִים	מְכוּנָּס
מְכוּנָּסוֹת	מְכוּנֶּסֶת

Notice that the *a* vowel is kept even when there is a suffix; this is characteristic of the present tense of NIF'AL and HUF'AL, too.

Future

נְכוּנַס	אֲכוּנַס
תְּכוּנְסוּ	תְּכוּנַס
	תְּכוּנְסִי
יְכוּנְסוּ	יְכוּנַס
	תְּכוּנַס

Infinitive

לִהְיוֹת מְכוּנָּס

33 Direct and indirect object

In English, some verbs take a direct object ('Eat *meat'*) and some an indirect object, introduced by a preposition ('Opt for *octopus*, look at *the leopard'*). Such prepositions are 'empty' and have no meaning of their own (contrast 'for' or 'at' in 'This is for you', 'I'm at the party'). The same is true of Hebrew: some Hebrew verbs take a direct object, whereas others take an indirect object introduced by a preposition.

Which verbs take which type of object is somewhat arbitrary, in both languages. Thus חִיפֵּשׂ 'look for' (indirect object in English) takes a direct object in Hebrew, and conversely הִשְׁתַּמֵּשׁ 'use' (direct object in English) requires an indirect object with בְּ:

אֲנִי מְחַפֵּשׂ בֵּייבִּיסִיטֶר	I'm looking for a baby-sitter
תִּשְׁתַּמֵּשׁ בְּעִפָּרוֹן	Use a pencil

For more on indirect objects and their prepositions, see 34(b).

34 Object markers

a The direct object marker אֶת

The Hebrew direct object is only strictly direct when it is *indefinite*, as in:

קַח בָּשָׂר	Take meat
קַח כִּיסֵא	Take a chair

When definite (e.g. הַבָּשָׂר 'the meat'), it is generally introduced by the special preposition אֶת. This is known as the direct object marker. By 'definite', we mean (a) a noun with הַ, or (b) a name, or (c) a definite pronoun.

קַח אֶת הַבָּשָׂר   Take the meat

קַח אֶת הַכִּסֵא   Take the chair

קַח אֶת דַלְיָה לְסֶרֶט   Take Dalya to a film

קַח אֶת זֶה   Take it

אֶת מִי לָקַחְתָּ   Who did you take?

Thus, direct objects are *sometimes* introduced by an object marker. As will presently be seen, indirect objects *nearly always* are.

Note: מִי? 'who?' is considered definite, but not מה? 'what?'. Thus מַה לָקַחְתָּ? 'What did you take?', rather than אֶת מַה לָקַחְתָּ?. The reasons are too complex to be set out here.

b Indirect objects with עַל, מִ, עִם, בְּ, לְ

An indirect object is generally introduced by (governed by) one of five prepositions: עַל, מִ, עִם, בְּ, לְ, which are used not in their regular sense of 'to, in, with, from, on', but in an *abstract* sense.

Such prepositions are called indirect object markers. Examples:

הִמְתִּין ל	wait for	בָּטַח ב	trust in
הִקְשִׁיב ל	listen to	נָגַע ב	touch
הֶאֱמִין ל	believe	הִתְמַצֵּא ב	be familiar with
הִתְחַתֵּן עִם	marry	שָׁכַח מ	forget about
דִּיבֵּר עִם	speak to	מֵת מ	die of
רָב עִם	quarrel with	פָּחַד מ	be afraid of
סָמַךְ עַל	rely on		
חָזַר עַל	repeat		
שָׁמַר עַל	look after		

With these object markers, unlike אֶת, it makes no difference whether the object is definite or indefinite:

רַבְתִּי עִם נֶהָג	I quarreled with a driver
רַבְתִּי עִם הַנֶּהָג	I quarreled with the driver

Many adjectives, too, take an object, in which case there is *almost always* a preposition. For example:

שַׁיָּךְ לְ . . .	belonging to
גֵּאֶה בְּ . . .	proud of
מַבְּסוּט מִ . . .	pleased with

Which preposition goes with which verb or adjective is not completely arbitrary. Thus verbs of fear and distancing take מִ, and verbs of giving and communicating usually take לְ. But the only way to be sure is to consult a good dictionary, for example the *Even-Shoshan* Hebrew–Hebrew dictionary.

35–6 PREPOSITIONS AND OTHER PREFIXES AND SUFFIXES

35 Preposition + suffix

When the prepositions בְּ and לְ or, indeed, any of the prepositions introduce a personal pronoun ('me, you, him, her, it, us, them'), this has to be in the form of a *suffix*. In other words, Hebrew does not allow לְאַתָּה, בְּהֶם for such forms as 'to you' or 'in them'; instead of אַתָּה there will be the suffix ךְ and so on.

An exception is זֶה 'it', which does *not* change its form. Thus one has:

לְזֶה to it	מִזֶּה from it

a *Preposition + suffix: בְּ, לְ, etc.*

In the case of בְּ and לְ, the suffix is the same as with שֶׁל (see 17(b)):

1st	בָּנוּ	בִּי	לָנוּ	לִי
2nd masc.	בָּכֶם	בְּךָ	לָכֶם	לְךָ
2nd fem.	בָּכֶן	בָּךְ	לָכֶן	לָךְ
3rd masc.	בָּהֶם	בּוֹ	לָהֶם	לוֹ
3rd fem.	בָּהֶן	בָּהּ	לָהֶן	לָהּ

Notice that the stress for the 'we' form, בָּנוּ and לָנוּ, is never on the נוּ. Hardly surprisingly, the same is true of נוּ in verbs, and of אֲנַחְנוּ.

The suffixed form of לְ is אֵלַי, אֵלֶיךָ etc. (as in 35e) when using verbs of motion or connection, such as בָּא 'come', הִצְטָרֵף 'join', צִלְצֵל 'phone', דִּיבֵּר 'speak', הִתְיַיחֵס 'relate to, treat, refer to':

מָתַי אַתְּ קוֹפֶצֶת אֵלֵינוּ?   When are you popping over to us?

b *Preposition + suffix: אוֹתִי, אוֹתוֹ, etc.*

To express the direct object 'me, him', etc., the direct object marker אֶת is used with a suffix. But אֶת becomes . . . אוֹת (except for 2nd person pl.*). Suffixes are the same as in 35(a), except that 'they' is ם and ן, not הֶם and הֶן.

1st	אוֹתָנוּ	אוֹתִי
2nd masc.	אֶתְכֶם	אוֹתְךָ
2nd fem.	אֶתְכֶן	אוֹתָךְ
3rd masc.	אוֹתָם	אוֹתוֹ
3rd fem.	אוֹתָן	אוֹתָהּ

Examples:

סִילַקְתִּי אוֹתוֹ	I threw him out
קַח אוֹתָנוּ	Take us!

* Colloquial speech often sidesteps the anomaly by using אוֹתְכֶם.

c | Preposition + suffix: עִם and מ

עִם and מ, whether meaning 'with' and 'from' or merely functioning as indirect object markers, have the following suffixed forms:

1st	אִתָּנוּ	אִתִּי	מֵאִתָּנוּ/מִמֶּנּוּ מִמֶּנִּי	
2nd masc.	אִתְּכֶם	אִתְּךָ	מִכֶּם	מִמְּךָ
2nd fem.	אִתְּכֶן	אִתָּךְ	מִכֶּן	מִמֵּךְ
3rd masc.	אִתָּם	אִתּוֹ	מֵהֶם	מִמֶּנּוּ
3rd fem.	אִתָּן	אִתָּהּ	מֵהֶן	מִמֶּנָה

עִם and מ are both irregular, each in its own way:

1 עִם takes on an entirely new base, אִת (no connection with אֶת). Only in formal style are עִמִּי, עִמְּךָ, etc. sometimes found.

2 Notice, though, that the endings in אִתִּי, אִתְּךָ, etc. are the same as for אוֹתִי etc. (see 35(b)).

3 The inflection of מ is so odd as to defy simple explanation. Of the two forms for 'from us', מִמֶּנּוּ is more colloquial. It is in fact identical with the 'him' form.

d | *Preposition + suffix:* בִּשְׁבִיל

The endings for the preposition בִּשְׁבִיל 'for' are rather different from those shown so far (which all involve prepositions that have the extra function of indirect object marker): the 2nd fem. sing. and 1st pl. endings, though spelled the same way, are pronounced *-ech, -enu,* not *-aH, -anu* except in colloquial speech.

This type of ending is used by *most* Hebrew prepositions, though not by several of the most common. It is also used by nouns (see 73).

1st	בִּשְׁבִילֵנוּ	בִּשְׁבִילִי
2nd masc.	בִּשְׁבִילְכֶם	בִּשְׁבִילְךָ
2nd fem.	בִּשְׁבִילְכֶן	בִּשְׁבִילֵךְ
3rd masc.	בִּשְׁבִילָם	בִּשְׁבִילוֹ
3rd fem.	בִּשְׁבִילָן	בִּשְׁבִילָה

e | *Preposition + suffix:* אַחֲרֵי, לִפְנֵי, אֶל, עַל

The prepositions introduced so far take light suffixes. But a dozen or so prepositions take heavy suffixes, notably עַל 'on', אֶל 'to', לִפְנֵי 'before, in front of', אַחֲרֵי 'after':

1st	אֵלֵינוּ	אֵלַי	עָלֵינוּ	עָלַי
2nd masc.	אֲלֵיכֶם*	אֵלֶיךָ	עֲלֵיכֶם	עָלֶיךָ
2nd fem.	אֲלֵיכֶן	אֵלַיִךְ	עֲלֵיכֶן	עָלַיִךְ
3rd masc.	אֲלֵיהֶם	אֵלָיו	עֲלֵיהֶם	עָלָיו
3rd fem.	אֲלֵיהֶן	אֵלֶיהָ	עֲלֵיהֶן	עָלֶיהָ

Note the stress on the last-but-one syllable in the ‑ַי, ‑ֶיךָ, ‑ַיִךְ, ‑ָיו, ‑ֶיהָ, ‑ֵינוּ forms.

* Purists insist on pronouncing the 2nd and 3rd pl. אֲלֵיכֶן, אֲלֵיכֶם etc.

1st	אַחֲרֵינוּ	אַחֲרֵי	לְפָנֵינוּ	לְפָנַי
2nd masc.	אַחֲרֵיכֶם	אַחֲרֶיךָ	לִפְנֵיכֶם	לְפָנֶיךָ
2nd fem.	אַחֲרֵיכֶן	אַחֲרַיִךְ	לִפְנֵיכֶן	לְפָנַיִךְ
3rd masc.	אַחֲרֵיהֶם	אַחֲרָיו	לִפְנֵיהֶם	לְפָנָיו
3rd fem.	אַחֲרֵיהֶן	אַחֲרֶיהָ	לִפְנֵיהֶן	לְפָנֶיהָ

Notice, first, that all these suffixes have an extra letter ', except the 1st person pl.: hence the term heavy suffixes. However, its effect on actual pronunciation is quite irregular. The only regular feature is that the suffixes (and the stressed syllable) are the same for all these prepositions.

Second, the base of לִפְנֵי changes to לְפָנַ־ for all but the 2nd and 3rd pl.

Finally, as we shall see in 73, the heavy suffixes happen to be identical to the possessive suffixes ('my, your', etc.) attached to plural nouns. Thus we have דּוֹדָיו 'his uncles'. But regard this as a coincidence: there is nothing plural about the meaning of עַל, לְפָנֵי, etc.

36   Pronunciation rules

a   *בְּ, כְּ, לְ, ו and the like*

The Hebrew of broadcasters, teachers and their ilk makes certain rather complicated adjustments in pronouncing words beginning with a prefixed בְּ, כְּ, לְ and וְ. Colloquial Hebrew generally does not bother. (None of these adjustments ever apply to בַּ, כַּ, לַ.)

Adjustment (a)

If the next letter is written with the vowel ְ the prefix is pronounced בְּ, כְּ, לְ and ו. Examples:

בְּשְׁלַבִּים in stages   כִּמְנַהֵל as a manager

וּלְחִימָה and combat

Adjustment (b)

If the next letter is ב, כ or פ, it will be soft. Examples:

בְּפַחַד in fear

בְּכָל יוֹם every day

כְּבִיקוֹרֶת as criticism

לְכוֹהֵן to a priest

Adjustment (c)

If the next letter is one of the four 'lip letters' – ב, ו, מ, פ – the prefix וְ is pronounced וּ. Examples:

וּבָדְקוּ and examined

וּמַסְלוּל and a runway

וּפִיטְרוּ and dismissed

וּוִיתְּרוּ and gave in

In colloquial usage, by contrast:

בְּשְׁלַבִּים in stages

בְּפַחַד in fear

וְבָדְקוּ and examined

וְמַסְלוּל and a runway

b Which syllable is stressed in nouns and adjectives?

Most nouns are stressed on the final syllable, including when this is a plural or other inflectional ending, thus מִכְתָּב 'letter' ~ מִכְתָּבִים. One major exception among nouns are the segolates (see 7(c) and 60(c)), such as סֶרֶט 'film', טוֹפֶס 'form', פַּחַד 'fear', מַחְבֶּרֶת 'notebook', מִקְלַחַת 'shower', but note that even here the stress will fall on any plural or other inflectional ending, thus סְרָטִים, מַחְבָּרוֹת, etc.

Another kind of exception are foreign words. They fall into two types:

1 Those with a 'heavy' Latin suffix (ending in a double consonant, such as '-ent', '-ism') stress the final syllable:

סְטוּדֶ֫נְט 'student', מַרְכְּסִ֫יסְט 'Marxist', פְּרוֹיֶ֫קְט 'project'

2 Most others stress the syllable before last:

אִי־מֶ֫ייל 'e-mail', וִ֫יזָה 'visa', אִינְסְטַלָ֫טוֹר 'plumber'

3   Some exceptions:

אוּנִיבֶּ֫רְסִיטָה 'university', אִ֫ינְטֶרְנֶט 'internet', טֶ֫לֶפוֹן 'telephone', מִיקְרוֹפוֹ֫ן 'microphone'

In any event, the stress in foreign words rarely falls on a plural or other inflectional ending, hence:

פְּרוֹיֶ֫קְטִים, סְטוּדֶ֫נְטִים, אוּנִיבֶּ֫רְסִיטוֹת, אִינְסְטַלָ֫טוֹרִים, לְיזוֹת, אִ֫י־מֵיילִים

Stress tends to fall on the *syllable before last* in children's words, as well as in many given names and old-time Israeli localities:

גֻּ֫לוֹת marbles	(סָ֫בְתָה grandmother (pl.: סָ֫בְתוֹת
מֹ֫שֶׁה Moshe	רִ֫בְקָה Rivka
יָ֫פָּה Yafa	רְחֹ֫בוֹת Rehovot
רַ֫מְלֶה Ramle	זִ֫כְרוֹן Zichron

Most adjectives, too, are stressed on the final syllable. The major exception: when a foreign-sourced adjective ends in -*i*, this -*i* is not stressed, thus:

לִיבֶּ֫רְלִי 'liberal', פְּרַקְטִ֫י 'practical', דֶמוֹקְרַ֫טִי 'democratic', נָאִ֫יבִי 'naive', יַפָּ֫נִי 'Japanese', נְיוּ־יוֹ֫רְקִי 'New Yorker'

The same happens when -*i* is added to most names of towns in Israel and the region:

תֵּל־אֲבִ֫יבִי, יְרוּשַׁ֫לְמִי, רְחוֹבֹ֫תִי, חַדֵ֫רָתִי, בַּגְדָ֫דִי

But note that for these purposes, the names of most major foreign nationalities that were on the Jewish 'Radar screen' in the early twentieth century do stress a final -*i*, e.g.

גֶּרְמַנִ֫י 'German', אַנְגְּלִ֫י 'English', צָרְפָתִ֫י 'French', רוּסִ֫י 'Russian', מִצְרִ֫י 'Egyptian', עֲרָבִ֫י 'Arab'

37 יֵשׁ 'there is, there are'

For 'there is . . ., there are . . .' (i.e. 'there exists'), Hebrew uses the verbal particle יֵשׁ. It generally precedes its noun, like English 'there is', and is unchanged for feminine or plural:

יֵשׁ בְּעָיָה	There's a problem
יֵשׁ בְּעָיוֹת	There are problems

For 'there isn't . . ., there aren't . . .', one uses the verbal particle אֵין. It is positioned and inflected just like יֵשׁ:

אֵין וִידֵאוֹ	There isn't a video
אֵין עוֹזְרוֹת	There aren't any cleaning ladies

For other tenses, Hebrew simply uses the verb הָיָה, preceding the noun and generally *agreeing* with it:

הָיָה פְּקָק	There was a jam
הָיְתָה תְּאוּנָה	There was an accident
לֹא יִהְיֶה וִידֵאוֹ	There won't be a video
לֹא יִהְיוּ עוֹזְרוֹת	There won't be any cleaners

Similar to יֵשׁ is the particle הִנֵּה 'here is, here are':

הִנֵּה הַכַּפְתּוֹר	Here's the switch
הִנֵּה הוּא !	Here he is!
הִנֵּה הֵם	Here they are

38 'I have': יֵשׁ לִי

For 'have' (present tense), Hebrew again makes use of the verb יֵשׁ (see 37). The construction יֵשׁ . . . לְ ('to x there is . . .') denotes 'x has . . .':

לְרִבְקָה יֵשׁ עוֹזֶרֶת	Rivka has a cleaning lady

Notice that, as in English, the possessor (Rivka) comes before the verb, and the possessed (a cleaning lady) comes after. יֵשׁ itself does not inflect.

For 'I have, you have', etc., one uses לִי, לְךָ, etc., generally placed *after* יֵשׁ, but always preceding the possessed:

יֵשׁ לִי עוֹזֶרֶת	I have a cleaning lady
יֵשׁ לָהּ חוּצְפָּה	She has nerve!
יֵשׁ לָנוּ עוֹזֶרֶת	We have a cleaning lady
יֵשׁ לָהֶם חוּצְפָּה	They have nerve!

For 'don't have', one uses . . . אֵין . . . לְ, thus:

לַשְׁכֵנִים אֵין וִידֵאוֹ	The neighbors don't have a video
אֵין לִי עוֹזֶרֶת	I don't have a cleaning lady

Colloquial Hebrew treats the possessed as a sort of direct object (rather than as a subject), hence the use of אֶת when the possessed is definite:

יֵשׁ לְךָ אוֹתָם ?	Do you have them?
אֵין לִי אֶת הַמִּסְפָּר	I don't have the number

For 'have' in other tenses, Hebrew simply uses the verb הָיָה in place of יֵשׁ, keeping the word order and everything else the same. Notice that the verb agrees with the thing possessed, literally 'to me were pains':

לַשְׁכֵנִים יִהְיֶה וִידֵיאוֹ	The neighbors will have a video
הָיְתָה לִי עוֹזֶרֶת	I had a cleaning lady
הָיוּ לִי כְּאֵבִים	I had pains

39 Questions

a Questions of the type ‏יוֹרָם בְּתֵל־אָבִיב?‏

For questions that expect the answer 'yes' or 'no' (as against 'what, when, where' questions), everyday spoken Hebrew simply uses *tone of voice* to distinguish the question from a statement. Word order is unchanged:

‏יוֹרָם בְּתֵל־אָבִיב?‏	Is Yoram in Tel Aviv?

In writing, it is important to remember the question mark. In formal usage, one can also start a question with the particle ‏הַאִם‏. See 101 for details.

b 'What, where, when'

In questions of the 'what, where, when, how?' sort, the 'question word' (‏מַה, מִי, אֵיפ'ֹה‏, etc.) usually comes first, as in English. But, unlike English, the rest of the sentence can remain unchanged: the verb need not leapfrog over the subject:

‏מִי צוֹעֵק?‏	Who's shouting?
‏מַה הַבּוֹס אוֹמֵר?‏	What does the boss say?
‏אֵיפ'ֹה הוּא גָר?‏	Where is he living?
‏לָמָה הָאַרְגָז נָעוּל?‏	Why is the trunk locked?

But observe that if there is a preposition (as in ‏עִם סַכִּין‏ 'with a knife', ‏לְדָנִי‏ 'for Danny'), it must remain *in front* of its noun; it cannot go to the end of the question as in English.

‏עִם מַה נָעַלְתָּ?‏	What did you lock up with?
‏אֵצֶל מִי הֵם אָכְלוּ?‏	Whose place did they eat at?
‏בִּשְׁבִיל מִי בֵּירַרְתָּ?‏	Who were you checking for?

40 Negation or how to say 'no'

a *'I'm not . . ., he isn't . . ., they didn't'*

To negate most types of sentence, colloquial Hebrew simply inserts לֹא
after the subject (or, more accurately, in front of the predicate):

הַמֵּיכָל לֹא רֵיק	The tank isn't empty
הוּא לֹא פֹּה	He's not here
אַתָּה לֹא מַדְלִיק אֶת הָאוֹר ?	You aren't turning on the light?
לֹא שָׁאַלְתִּי	I didn't ask

Formal Hebrew, as we shall see in 99, sometimes uses אֵין instead of לֹא.

b *אֵין as the opposite of יֵשׁ*

For 'there isn't . . ., there aren't . . .', 'I haven't . . .', Hebrew uses the
verbal particle אֵין. This word is the opposite of יֵשׁ. See 37, 38, e.g.:

אֵין זְמָן	There isn't time

c *Negative instructions*

When using the infinitive to issue an instruction (in 'lofty' requests), use
לֹא in the normal way to make it negative:

לֹא לָזוּז	No moving, Don't move!

However, the commonest form of negative request is to use אַל (not לֹא)
plus the future tense. (The imperative form of the verb is not used in the
negative.)

אַל תָּזוּז	Don't move
אַל תִּשְׁפְּכִי	Don't spill

By contrast, לֹא תָּזוּז would mean 'you won't move', i.e. a prediction rather than a request.

41 'The cake in the fridge, stamps from Israel'

For phrases such as 'the cake in the fridge, some stamps from Israel', Hebrew closely resembles English:

הָעוּגָה בַּמְקָרֵר הִיא לְשַׁבָּת
The cake in the fridge is for Shabbat

יֵשׁ לְךָ בּוּלִים מִיִּשְׂרָאֵל?
Do you have some stamps from Israel?

אֵיפֹה הָאָדוֹן עִם הַשְׁטְרַיימֶל?
Where's the gentleman in the shtreimel?

Elegant Hebrew often prefers to insert שֶׁ, thus:

הַפְּגָם שֶׁבַּתּוֹכְנִית   the flaw (*lit.* that is) in the plan

42 Degree words: מְאֹד, כָּל-כָּךְ, דַי, etc.

Degree words ('very, a bit, quite, so, more') usually *come before* their adjective in colloquial usage:

מְאֹד קָשֶׁה	very hard	דַי יָפֶה	quite nice
קְצָת קָשֶׁה	a bit hard	כָּל-כַּךְ יָפֶה	so nice
יוֹתֵר קָשֶׁה	harder	נוֹרָא יָפֶה	real nice

מְאֹד 'very' equally well follows its adjective: יָפֶה מְאֹד. Similarly, מִדַי 'too': יָפֶה מִדַי 'too nice'. In formal Hebrew, most degree words tend to follow the adjective, e.g. קָשֶׁה יוֹתֵר 'harder'.

Degree words also go with verbs:

אֲנִי מְאֹד מִצְטַעֵר	I very much regret it
זֶה קְצָת מַפְרִיעַ לִי	It bothers me a little
זֶה מִתְחַכֵּךְ יוֹתֵר מִדַי	It's rubbing too much

The pattern
אֲנִי רוֹצֶה
לְהִתְעַטֵשׁ:
'I want to sneeze'

43 Adverbs of time and place in the sentence

Adverbs of time and place can safely be placed in the same position as in English: first, last or (for some time adverbs) right after the subject. The only difference this usually makes to the meaning is a nuance in emphasis.

עַכְשָׁיו הוּא יָשֵׁן	Now he's asleep
הוּא עַכְשָׁיו יָשֵׁן	He's now asleep
הוּא יָשֵׁן עַכְשָׁיו	He's asleep now
שָׁם אֲנִי קוֹנֶה בַּד	There I buy cloth
אֲנִי קוֹנֶה בַּד שָׁם	I buy cloth there

Unlike English, Hebrew adverbs can also come between verb and object:

אֲנִי קוֹנֶה שָׁם בַּד	(*lit.* 'I buy there cloth')

44–9 EMBEDDED CLAUSES

44 The pattern אֲנִי רוֹצֶה לְהִתְעַטֵשׁ: 'I want to sneeze'

Many Hebrew verbs take an infinitive, just like English 'want to' – for example, רוֹצֶה 'want', מְסָרֵב 'refuse', מְנַסֶה 'try':

אֲנִי רוֹצֶה לְהִתְעַטֵשׁ	I want to sneeze

In fact, Hebrew commonly has an infinitive even where English has *-ing*:

לִפְעָמִים הֵם מְנַסִּים לַחֲלֹק
Sometimes they try sharing

הוּא מִתְעַקֵּשׁ לִשְׁרוֹק
He insists on whistling

הוּא אוֹהֵב לָטוּס אָז הוּא הִפְסִיק לָדוּג
He loves flying so he's stopped fishing

יִשְׂרְאֵלִים מַרְבִּים לִנְסוֹעַ לְחוּ"ל
Israelis do a lot of traveling overseas

נֶהָגִים מְמַעֲטִים לְהַבִּיט לַצְּדָדִים
Drivers look very little to the sides

45 The pattern טוֹב לְחַיֵּיךְ: 'It's good to smile'

Where English has 'it is good [or other adj.] to . . .', Hebrew often leaves out 'it is':

מְסוּכָּן לִגְלֹשׁ	It is dangerous to ski
קָשֶׁה לָנוּחַ	It's hard to rest

Similarly for the construction 'it's good that . . .':

טוֹב שֶׁבָּאתָ	It's good you've come
מוּזָר שֶׁאֵין לוֹ	It's weird that he doesn't have

46 Reported thoughts and object clauses

To lead into reported statements, beliefs, feelings, etc., one generally inserts שֶׁ, which is equivalent to 'that'. (For the tense, see 82(c).)

הוּא אָמַר שֶׁיֵּשׁ עוֹד זְמָן	He said that there's still time
אֲנִי חוֹשֵׁב שֶׁזֶּה בְּסֵדֶר	I think it's O.K.

With a verb or adjective that would normally require an indirect object marker, e.g. פָּחַד מִ or בָּטוּחַ בְּ (see 34(b)), the object marker is normally omitted when a שֶׁ or לְ is going to follow:

אֲנִי מְפַחֵד שֶׁהוּא יִבְרַח	I'm afraid he might run away
אֲנִי בָּטוּחַ שֶׁזֶה יַצְלִיחַ	I'm certain it'll work out

Some verbs and prepositions cannot take a clause beginning with שֶׁ. Instead, one has to use שֶׁ כַּךְ or זֶה שֶׁ, thus:

דִּבַּרְנוּ עַל כַּךְ שֶׁהַלְחִימָה נִמְשֶׁכֶת
We talked about the fact that the fighting is going on

הַשְׂמֹאל בְּעַד זֶה שֶׁנִּיסּוֹג מִכָּל הַשְׁטָחִים
The Left is in favor of us withdrawing from all the territories

אֲנִי לְגַמְרֵי מִתְנַגֵּד לְכָךְ שֶׁיַּתְחִילוּ קוּנץ כָּזֶה
I'm totally against them starting such a gimmick

In journalistic or formal Hebrew, כִּי is sometimes used in place of שֶׁ. This כִּי does not mean 'because':

הָעִתּוֹן מְדַוּוַח כִּי בָּאַחֲרוֹנָה נִרְאוּ בָּאָרֶץ שְׁנֵי כּוֹכְבֵי סַיינְפֶלד
The paper reports that the two Seinfeld stars were recently sighted in Israel

47 Relative clauses with שֶׁ

Relative clauses ('the guy *who called*, the room *that I painted*') are commonly introduced by the conjunction שֶׁ. It is always prefixed to the next word. For the moment, regard שֶׁ as the equivalent of 'who, which, that':

הִנֵּה הָאוֹטוֹבּוּס שֶׁנּוֹסֵעַ לְגִילֹ'ה	Here's the bus that goes to Gilo
אֵיפֹה הַלַּחְמָנִיָּה שֶׁאָכַלְתִּי?	Where's the roll I was eating?
מִי הַגְּבֶרֶת שֶׁפָּגַשְׁתָּ קוֹדֶם?	Who's the lady whom you met earlier?

48 Adverbial clauses: ‏אַחֲרֵי שֶׁ, בִּגְלַל שֶׁ, אִם, כִּי‎, etc.

Adverbial clauses – clauses expressing time, cause, purpose, etc. – generally require the insertion of a conjunction ‏שֶׁ‎:

‏אַחֲרֵי שֶׁהַתֻּכִּי אָכַל, הוּא פִּיהֵק‎
After the parrot ate, it yawned

‏אֵיפֹה אַתְּ גַּרְתְּ לִפְנֵי שֶׁבָּאת לְכָאן?‎
Where did you live before you came here?

‏אֲנִי הוֹלֵךְ לַמְרוֹת שֶׁגַּם הוּא הוֹלֵךְ‎
I'm going despite the fact that he's also going

‏זֶה נִדְפַּק לְךָ בַּדֶּרֶךְ בִּגְלַל שֶׁלֹּא אִכְפַּת לְךָ!‎
It got ruined on the way because you just don't care

However, ‏כִּי‎, a common word for 'because', has no ‏שֶׁ‎. Nor does ‏אִם‎ 'if':

‏אֲנִי מְצַלְצֵל כִּי יֵשׁ תַּקָּלָה‎
I'm calling because there's a hitch

‏אִם הַנְּיָיר לֹא יוֹצֵא, אָז זֶה דָּפוּק‎
If the paper won't come out, it's broken

A quite distinct, two-word conjunction is ‏אִם כִּי‎, which has nothing to do with either ‏אִם‎ or ‏כִּי‎. It means 'although' in the sense of 'though admittedly':

‏יֵשׁ לָנוּ חֲנוּיוֹת נֶהֱדָרוֹת, אִם כִּי לֹא כְּמוֹ בְּפָּרִיז‎
We have great stores, though not like in Paris

As for ‏כְּשֶׁ‎, the usual word for 'when, while', treat it as one word (not as ‏כְּ + שֶׁ‎):

‏כְּשֶׁעָצַרְתִּי, הָאוֹר הַשְּׂמָאלִי לֹא נִדְלַק‎
When I stopped, the left-hand light didn't come on

Even for English 'after eating . . .', 'while watching . . .', Hebrew regularly uses a whole clause (or an 'action noun', see 64):

הוּא יָשֵׁן אַחֲרֵי שֶׁהוּא אוֹכֵל
He sleeps after eating

לַמְרוֹת שֶׁנִּיצַּחְנוּ חָתַרְנוּ לִפְשָׁרָה
Despite winning, we worked for a compromise

מֵאָז הִתְפַּטְּרוּתוֹ לֹא נִרְאָה בַּטֶּלֶוִיזְיָה
Since resigning he hasn't been seen on TV

לִפְנֵי עֲלִיָּיתֵנוּ לַמָּטוֹס, עָבַרְנוּ עוֹד בְּדִיקוֹת
Before boarding the plane, we went through more checks

There are several other prepositions that take שֶׁ or לְ where English might
use -ing, thus:

עָשִׂינוּ אֶת זֶה בְּלִי לַחֲשׁוֹב
We did it without thinking

נִכְנַסְתִּי בְּלִי שֶׁהִבְחִינוּ בִּי
I went in without them spotting me

חַכֵּה שְׁנִיָּה בִּמְקוֹם לַחֲטוֹף
Wait a second instead of grabbing

and in colloquial Hebrew:

הָיִיתִי עָסוּק בְּלַעֲשׂוֹת סְפוֹנְזָ'ה
I was busy (with) mopping

Contrast the use of שֶׁ to denote 'so' in the sense of 'in order that' with the
use of כָּךְ שֶׁ meaning 'so' in the sense of 'and as a result':

שׁוֹמְרִים אֶת זֶה בְּסוֹד, שֶׁלֹּא תִּהְיֶה פָּאנִיקָה
They're keeping it secret so there won't be a panic

פִּסְפַּסְתִּי אֶת הַטְּרֶמְפּ, כָּךְ שֶׁלֹּא אֶהְיֶה בַּשִּׂיחָה
I missed the lift, so I won't be at the talk

The counterpart of an English equivalence clause with 'as' or 'like'
generally employs כְּפִי שֶׁ or כְּמוֹ שֶׁ:

אֲנִי מוּדְאָג, כְּפִי שֶׁכּוּלָם מוּדְאָגִים הַיּוֹם
I'm worried, like everyone's worried today

זֹאת כִּיתָה קָשָׁה, כְּמוֹ שֶׁאַתָּה יוֹדֵעַ
This is a difficult class, as you know

כְּפִי שֶׁצִיַּינְתִּי, חֶבְרוֹן הָיְתָה בִּירָתוֹ הָרִאשׁוֹנָה שֶׁל דָּוִד
As I noted, Hebron was David's first capital

77

For hypothetical 'like' and 'as if', use כְּאִלּוּ:

הִיא רוֹעֶדֶת כְּאִלּוּ חָטְפָה שׁוֹק
She's shaking as if she had a shock

Note that שֶׁ is the same conjunction as that used in relative clauses and reported thoughts (46, 47). It has the very broad task of marking where a subordinate (i.e. embedded) clause begins.

49 Sentences without a subject

a *The 'general' plural:* שֶׁקֶט, חוֹשְׁבִים! *'Quiet, people are thinking!'*

To express *'one forgets, people forget, you forget'* – that is, an open-ended, non-specific subject – Hebrew has a special construction: the verb (or adjective) is used in the masculine plural, without a subject:

אֵיךְ הוֹלְכִים?   How does one go?

הֶחְלִיפוּ אֶת הָרַמַטְכַּ"ל   They've changed the Chief of Staff

b צָרִיךְ, כְּדַאי, אֶפְשָׁר *without a subject*

Several adjectives, verbs and other words need not (and some even cannot) have a subject, including כְּדַאי 'you'd better', צָרִיךְ 'it's necessary', אֶפְשָׁר 'you may, it's possible', חֲבָל 'it's a pity', חַם 'it's hot', קַר 'it's cold'.

אֲנִי חוֹשֵׁב שֶׁאֶפְשָׁר   I think you can

עַכְשָׁיו כְּבָר אִי־אֶפְשָׁר   By now it's impossible

צָרִיךְ פָּשׁוּט חוּשׁ   One just needs an instinct

בֶּטַח שֶׁצָּרִיךְ!   Sure one must!

בָּרוּר שֶׁחֲבָל!   It's obvious that it's a shame!

אַתְּ לֹא רוֹאָה שֶׁקַּר בַּחוּץ?   Can't you see that it's cold outside?

78

Level Two

50–9 | SPECIAL ROOT-TYPES

Many roots contain a weak letter which sometimes mutates or simply drops out. They are thus 'problem roots'.

The two-consonant verb has already been introduced (26(b)). At this level, we now introduce the other main types of problem root (traditionally known as the 'weak *gezarot*').

50 | ל'ה roots

a | Introduction

Roots ending in the letter ה are a problem: the ה can mutate or just vanish. There are many common roots of this type. Verbs built out of such roots are pronounced *kana*, *hikna*, *gila* and so on; that is, orally, they lack a third consonant and just end in a vowel. In writing, however, ה or י generally serve to mark where the 'missing consonant' should have been. Examples of verbs affected:

בָּנָה build	שָׁתָה drink
הִשְׁוָוה compare	הִפְנָה refer
חִיכָּה wait	רִימָה cheat
הִתְמַנָה be appointed	הִתְמַחָה specialize

Note: We shall call these root-types by the traditional name: ל'ה roots – 'roots whose final consonant is (often) ה'. Such terminology sets up an abstract root פ.ע.ל and refers to any first consonant as פ, any second consonant as ע and any third consonant as ל. So ל'ה means 'whose third consonant is ה'.

b | ל'ה in PA'AL and PI'EL

We first give verb tables, using the root ג.ל.ה. Following this, we offer explanations for these forms.

PA'AL: גָּלָה 'go into exile'

Past גָּלִיתִי, גָּלִיתָ, גָּלִית, גָּלָה, גָּלְתָה
גָּלִינוּ, גָּלִיתֶם, גָּלִיתֶן, גָּלוּ

Present גּוֹלֶה, גּוֹלָה, גּוֹלִים, גּוֹלוֹת

Future אֶגְלֶה, תִּגְלֶה, תִּגְלִי, יִגְלֶה, תִּגְלֶה
נִגְלֶה, תִּגְלוּ, יִגְלוּ

Imperative גְּלֵה   Infinitive לִגְלוֹת

Action noun גְּלִיָּה

PI'EL: גִּילָה 'to discover'

Past גִּילִיתִי, גִּילִיתָ, גִּילִית, גִּילָה, גִּילְתָה
גִּילִינוּ, גִּילִיתֶם, גִּילִיתֶן, גִּילוּ

Present מְגַלֶּה, מְגַלָּה, מְגַלִּים, מְגַלּוֹת

Future אֲגַלֶּה, תְּגַלֶּה, תְּגַלִּי, יְגַלֶּה, תְּגַלֶּה
נְגַלֶּה, תְּגַלּוּ, יְגַלּוּ

Imperative גַּלֵּה   Infinitive לְגַלּוֹת

Action noun גִּילּוּי

The system behind these verb tables is as follows:

1 To form the present fem. sing. and the past 3rd fem. sing. from the corresponding masc. sing., the rule is -e → -a and -a → -ta, thus present גּוֹלָה, past גָּלְתָה. Compare this tricky state of affairs with a normal verb:

	PA'AL	PI'EL
Present fem. sing.	קוֹבֶלֶת	מְקַבֶּלֶת
Past	קָבְלָה	קִיבְּלָה

2 In most cases where there is no suffix, the ל'ה verb will end in the vowel *-e* (written ־ֶה), for example:

Present PA'AL גוֹלֶה Present PI'EL מְגַלֶה

1st Future PA'AL אֶגְלֶה 2nd Future PI'EL תְגַלֶה

Exceptions: (1) 3rd masc. sing. past will end in *-a* (still written ה); and (2) the infinitive will end in וֹת, thus:

1 נִגְלָה, גִילָה, הִתְגַלָה

2 לִגְלוֹת, לְהַגְלוֹת, לְהִתְגַלוֹת

3 In the past 1st and 2nd sing. and pl. these verbs will end in *-i* (written י), for example:

PA'AL גָלִיתִי, גָלִיתָ PI'EL גִילִינוּ, גִילִיתֶם

c | ל'ה *in HITPA'EL and HIF'IL*

We again give verb tables, using the root ג.ל.ה.

HITPA'EL: הִתְגַלָה 'be discovered'

Past	הִתְגַלֵיתִי, הִתְגַלֵיתָ, הִתְגַלֵית, הִתְגַלָה, הִתְגַלְתָה הִתְגַלֵינוּ, הִתְגַלֵיתֶם, הִתְגַלֵיתֶן, הִתְגַלוּ
Present	מִתְגַלֶה, מִתְגַלָה, מִתְגַלִים, מִתְגַלוֹת
Future	אֶתְגַלֶה, תִתְגַלֶה, תִתְגַלִי, יִתְגַלֶה, תִתְגַלֶה נִתְגַלֶה, תִתְגַלוּ, יִתְגַלוּ
Imperative	הִתְגַלֵה Infinitive לְהִתְגַלוֹת
Action noun	הִתְגַלוּת

HIF'IL: הִגְלָה 'banish'

Past	הִגְלֵיתִי, הִגְלֵיתָ, הִגְלֵית, הִגְלָה, הִגְלְתָה
	הִגְלֵינוּ, הִגְלֵיתֶם, הִגְלֵיתֶן, הִגְלוּ

Present	מַגְלֶה, מַגְלָה, מַגְלִים, מַגְלוֹת

Future	אַגְלֶה, תַּגְלֶה, תַּגְלִי, יַגְלֶה, תַּגְלֶה
	נַגְלֶה, תַּגְלוּ, יַגְלוּ

Imperative	הַגְלֵה	Infinitive	לְהַגְלוֹת

Action noun	הַגְלָיָיה

The system behind these verb tables is as follows:

1   The feminine is identical to PA'AL and PI'EL in 50(b)(1) above.

2   Where there is no suffix, the rule is identical to 50(b)(2) above.

3   In the PAST 1st and 2nd sing. and pl. these verbs will end in -*e*, not -*i* (still written י). HUF'AL and PU'AL ל/ה verbs belong to this group, too. Examples:

HITPA'EL	הִתְגַּלֵּיתֶם	you were discovered
HIF'IL	הִגְלֵיתִי	I have banished
PU'AL	גוּלֵיתֶם	you were discovered
HUF'AL	הוּגְלֵיתִי	I was banished

d *ל/ה in* NIF'AL

נִגְלָה 'be revealed'

Past	נִגְלֵיתִי, נִגְלֵיתָ, נִגְלֵית, נִגְלָה, נִגְלְתָה
	נִגְלֵינוּ, נִגְלֵיתֶם, נִגְלֵיתֶן, נִגְלוּ

Present	נִגְלֶה, נִגְלֵית, נִגְלִים, נִגְלוֹת

Future   אֶגָּלֶה, תִּגָּלֶה, תִּגָּלִי, יִגָּלֶה, תִּגָּלֶה
נִגָּלֶה, תִּגָּלוּ, יִגָּלוּ

Imperative   הִגָּלֵה   Infinitive   לְהִיגָּלוֹת

Action noun   הִיגָּלוּת

The system behind this verb table is as for the other binyanim, except that:

1   The fem. sing. in the present is not the expected נִגְלָה but נִגְלֵית.

2   Where there is no suffix, the rule is as in the other binyanim – except that colloquially one tends to say נִגְלָה rather than נִגְלֶה in the present masc. sing., in keeping with the vowels in the regular NIF'AL (30). For this reason, everyday usage has זֶה נִרְאָה טוֹב 'It looks good' rather than . . . נִרְאֶה . . . .

51   Roots with 'gutturals'

a   Introduction

'Gutturals' are the letters ע, ח, ה. These were all once pronounced throatily and involved such an effort that they affected the form of neighboring vowels, giving them the quality of an *a* (the most 'throaty' of vowels).

Nowadays, in the dominant ('Europeanized') Israeli accent, ע is usually pronounced like א, i.e. with a quick catch in the throat rather than with guttural friction. In the same way, ה is commonly pronounced like א: it is not usually heard as 'h'. As for ח, it is usually simply like כ. Yet ע, ח, ה still cause neighboring vowels to vary their form, a kind of historical echo that still causes considerable complications for modern Hebrew grammar. So we are entitled to talk of abstract 'gutturals', in inverted commas.

Two other letters, א and ר, have 'guttural' effects sometimes, the latter very occasionally.

The overall effect of 'gutturals' is on *pronunciation*, involving scores of common verbs. The written text itself is unaffected.

b *When the first letter is a 'guttural'*

When a root has an *initial guttural*, i.e. a 'guttural' as first root letter, this affects the pronunciation of particular forms of the verb: for example, particular binyanim or tenses. Examples of verbs affected:

אָרַז pack   הֶאֱמִין believe

הָרַס destroy   חָשַׁב think

הֶחְלִיט decide   הֶעֱבִיר transfer

עָזַר help   נֶעֱדַר be absent

נֶעֱלַם vanish

1   'Gutturals' cannot tolerate a preceding *i* vowel in their verbal prefix. They lower it to *a* (in binyan PA'AL) or to *e* (in HIF'IL and NIF'AL). Taking the root ח.שׁ.ב:

PA'AL

     Future: אֶחְשׁוֹב*, תַּחְשׁוֹב, תַּחְשְׁבִי, יַחְשׁוֹב ... etc.

     Infinitive: לַחְשׁוֹב

HIF'IL

     Past: הֶחְשַׁבְתִּי, הֶחְשַׁבְתָּ, הֶחְשַׁבְתְּ, הֶחְשִׁיב ... etc.

NIF'AL

     Past**:   נֶחְשַׁבְתִּי, נֶחְשַׁבְתָּ, נֶחְשַׁבְתְּ, נֶחְשַׁב ... etc.

     Future: אֶחָשֵׁב, תֵּיחָשֵׁב, תֵּיחָשְׁבִי, יֵיחָשֵׁב, תֵּיחָשֵׁב ... etc.

     Infinitive: לְהֵיחָשֵׁב

*   This particular form needs no adjustment, as the regular 1st person form would in any case be אֶרְשׁוֹם with an -e- vowel. But colloquially one often hears אַחְשׁוֹב.

** An important exception in the NIF'AL is the verb נַעֲשָׂה 'become' (rather than נֶעֱשָׂה).

2   A further adjustment is made to strengthen an initial ע and ה (but not ח): a second *a* or *e* vowel is inserted between them and the following consonant (in slow, deliberate speech). For example:

PA'AL   תַּהֲרוֹס, תַּעֲרוֹךְ

HIF'IL   הֶהֱדַרְתִּי, הֶעֱרַכְתִּי, תַּעֲרִיךְ

NIF'AL   נֶהֱרַס, נֶעֱרַךְ

3   As for א, it behaves like ע and ה, except that in careful speech it converts *i* in the PA'AL to *e* rather than to *a*, e.g. יֶאֶגְרוּ, תֶּאֱרוֹז.

None of the other binyanim or tenses needs to be adjusted for 'initial gutturals'.

| c | *When the middle letter is a 'guttural'*

Examples of verbs affected:

תָּאַם be compatible	נִשְׁאַר remain
גִּיהֵץ iron	נִזְהַר be careful
בָּחַן test	בָּעַר burn
שִׁיעֵר assess	הִתְנַעֵר shake oneself off
בֵּירֵךְ congratulate	

1   Where ע, ה, א are middle letters, Hebrew bolsters them by giving
    them 'more breathing space', that is, by preventing another consonant
    from following immediately. The problem arises mainly in verbs with
    a stressed ending, e.g. ־ִים ,־ָה ,־וּ. The remedy is to insert a 'helping' *a*
    vowel:

	Past	*Present*	*Future*
PA'AL	זָהֲרָה, זָהֲרוּ	זוֹהֲרִים, זוֹהֲרוֹת	תִּזְהֲרִי, תִּזְהֲרוּ
NIF'AL	נִזְהֲרָה, נִזְהֲרוּ		תִּיזָהֲרִי, תִּיזָהֲרוּ
HUF'AL	הוּזְהֲרָה, הוּזְהֲרוּ		תּוּזְהֲרִי, תּוּזְהֲרוּ
PI'EL	נִיהֲלָה, נִיהֲלוּ	מְנַהֲלִים, מְנַהֲלוֹת	תְּנַהֲלִי, תְּנַהֲלוּ
PU'AL	נוּהֲלָה, נוּהֲלוּ	מְנוּהֲלִים, מְנוּהֲלוֹת	תְּנוּהֲלִי, תְּנוּהֲלוּ
HITPA'EL	הִתְנַהֲלָה . . .	מִתְנַהֲלִים, מִתְנַהֲלוֹת	תִּתְנַהֲלִי, תִּתְנַהֲלוּ

However, the letter ה is somewhat anomalous (recall 51(b)(2)) and
tends not to require a 'helping -*a*-', particularly in casual speech.
Hence שִׂיחֲקָה, שִׂיחֲקוּ 'play'.

2   In the PA'AL future of some middle guttural verbs, -*o*- becomes -*a*-,
    e.g. אֶבְחַר, תִּבְחַר 'choose' etc. and אֶשְׁאַל, תִּשְׁאַל 'ask' etc. – whereas
    in some other verbs -*o*- holds its ground: אֶדְחוֹס, תִּדְחוֹס 'squeeze' etc.
    There is no simple rule. Consult a major dictionary or ask an Israeli.

3   Where the PI'EL has a middle א or ר, the vowels in the respective
    action noun will commonly be *e-u*, not *i-u*. Thus:

תֵּיאוּר description   פֵּירוּט detail

גֵּירוּשׁ expulsion   יֵאוּשׁ despair

4 A peculiar adjustment, more commonly found in formal than in colloquial Hebrew, involves PI'EL past and PU'AL: when there is a middle א or ר, any preceding *-i-* is lowered to *-e-* and any preceding *-u-* is lowered to *-o-*. Thus:

תֵּאֵר described   תּוֹאַר, מְתוֹאָר, יְתוֹאַר was, is, will be described

גֵּירֵשׁ divorced   גּוֹרַשׁ, מְגוֹרָשׁ, יְגוֹרַשׁ was, is, will be divorced

---

d *When the final letter is a 'guttural'*

Examples of verbs affected:

הִגְבִּיהַ raise   צָרַח yell

נִפְתַּח open   נִיצֵּחַ defeat

הִתְקַלֵּחַ take a shower   יָדַע know

נִשְׁמַע sound   הִפְתִּיעַ surprise

1 Whenever a verb, or any other word, ends in ח or ע (or root ה, which is a rarity by comparison with suffixed ה), the last vowel must be *-a*. This is an invariable rule of Hebrew. To achieve this, verb patterns whose last vowel would ordinarily be, say, *-e-* or *-i-* add a helping *-a-*. This happens in *nearly all binyanim and tenses*.

Examples from selected binyanim and tenses:

PA'AL	Present	שׁוֹמֵעַ, סוֹלֵחַ	Infinitive	לִשְׁמוֹעַ, לִסְלוֹחַ
PI'EL	Infinitive	לְשַׁוֵּעַ, לְשַׁבֵּחַ	Future	יְשַׁוֵּעַ, יְשַׁבֵּחַ
HIF'IL	Past	הִשְׁמִיעַ, הִבְטִיחַ	Present	מַשְׁמִיעַ, מַבְטִיחַ
NIF'AL	Future	יִישָׁמֵעַ, יִיסָלֵחַ	Infinitive	לְהִישָׁמֵעַ, לְהִיסָלֵחַ
1-SYLLABLE	Future	אָנוּעַ, אָנוּחַ	Infinitive	לָנוּעַ, לָנוּחַ

The one major exception is the PA'AL Future. Here, -a- is not added but *substituted*. Thus:

Not יִסְלוֹחַ or יִסְלוֹח   . . . but rather יִסְלַח

Not יִשְׁמוֹעַ or יִשְׁמוֹע   . . . but rather יִשְׁמַע

A similar but minor exception: particularly in formal style, the future of PI'EL and NIF'AL is sometimes יְיסָלַח, יְשַׁוַּע, יְשֻׁבַּח, etc., i.e. -a- is again *substituted* rather than added.

2   Once a feminine suffix has been added, the 'final guttural' is, of course, no longer final. Yet the vowels are still affected provided the feminine suffix is ־ת, i.e. in all but HIF'IL and ONE-SYLLABLE verbs. The guttural gives rise to the endings עַת_ or חַת_. For example:

שׁוֹמַעַת, סוֹלַחַת   נִשְׁמַעַת, נִרְצַחַת

מוּשְׁמַעַת, מוּבְטַחַת   מְשַׁוַּעַת, מְשַׁבַּחַת

52   Roots with ב, כ, פ: 'soft' or 'hard'?

Virtually without exception, ב, כ or פ as the first letter of a verb will have a hard pronunciation (b, k, p), i.e. pointed texts would insert a 'dagesh': בּ, כּ, פּ. Conversely, as the last letter of a verb they nearly always receive a soft pronunciation (v, ch, f): ב, כ, פ. Thus:

First letter	בִּיקֵשׁ asked	כָּתַב wrote	פָּטַר exempted
Last letter	חִישֵׁב calculated	שָׁפַךְ spilled	שָׂרַף burned

But when the very same verbs take on prefixes, so that the ב, כ, פ are no longer the first letter, or when ב, כ, פ are from the outset the *middle consonants* of the root, there are various rules affecting whether the ב, כ, פ are hard or soft. These are given in 52(a), (b) and (c).

a Usually soft

פ, כ, ב directly following the verbal prefix are usually soft, thus:

PA'AL	Future	אֶבְדּוֹק, תִּבְדּוֹק ...	Infinitive	לִבְדּוֹק		
NIF'AL	Present	נִבְדָּק	Past	נִבְדַּק		
PI'EL	Present	מְפַטֵּר	Future	אֲפַטֵּר, תְּפַטֵּר ...	Infinitive	לְפַטֵּר
PU'AL	Present	מְפוּטָר	Future	אֲפוּטַר, תְּפוּטַר ...		
HIF'IL	Present	מַכְנִיס	Past	הִכְנַסְתִּי, הִכְנַסְתָּ ...		
	Future	אַכְנִיס, תַּכְנִיס ...	Infinitive	לְהַכְנִיס		
HUF'AL	Present	מוּכְנָס	Past	הוּכְנַסְתִּי, הוּכְנַסְתָּ ...	Future	אוּכְנַס, תּוּכְנַס

The only major exceptions are that after the HITPA'EL prefixes (יִת, מִת,
etc.), פ, כ, ב are hard, thus מִתְכַּנֵּס, and similarly after the NIF'AL future
and infinitive prefixes, e.g. אֶבָּדֵק, תִּיבָּדֵק and לְהִיבָּדֵק.

b Usually hard

פ, כ, ב as the middle root consonant are mostly hard. This nearly always
holds for the *entire set* of HIF'IL, HUF'AL, PI'EL, PU'AL and HITPA'EL
forms, hence the hard כ in:

PI'EL	to delay	עִיכֵּב, מְעַכֵּב, יְעַכֵּב, לְעַכֵּב ...
HIF'IL	to put to bed	הִשְׁכִּיב, מַשְׁכִּיב, יַשְׁכִּיב, לְהַשְׁכִּיב ...

91

But there are two kinds of exception:

1   In PA'AL present and past, middle ב, כ, פ are soft, while in the future and infinitive they are best classified as hard, though colloquially in many verbs middle ב and פ are kept soft throughout:

PA'AL	Present	שׁוֹבֵר	Past	שָׁבַר
	Future	יְשָׁבּוֹר but יִתְפֹּס	Infinitive	לִשְׁבּוֹר but לִתְפֹּס

2   In NIF'AL present and past, middle ב, כ, פ are hard, while in the future and infinitive they are soft:

NIF'AL	Present	נִשְׁבָּר	Past	נִשְׁבַּר
	Future	יִישָׁבֵר	Infinitive	לְהִישָׁבֵר

c *Always soft*

When a *suffix* is added to a verb, it does not affect final ב, כ, פ. They remain soft. For example, הָלַךְ 'go': הָלַכְתִּי, הָלְכוּ, הוֹלְכִים.

53 Four-consonant roots

Many verbs and their corresponding action nouns are formed with roots of *four* or even *five* consonants, but only in three (related) binyanim: PI'EL, PU'AL and HITPA'EL. Examples:

שִׁפְשֵׁף rub   בִּזְבֵּז waste

פִּסְפֵּס miss   שִׁכְפֵּל duplicate

הִתְבַּלְבֵּל get confused   הִתְפַּרְנֵס earn a living

הִתְחַשְׁמֵל get electrocuted

Most such roots repeat the same two consonants (reduplicative roots), e.g. ק־ל־ק־ל, or are based on nouns that have four consonants, e.g. מַחְשֵׁב 'computer' → מ־ח־ש־ב, yielding the verb מִחְשֵׁב 'computerize'. Hebrew finds it particularly convenient to turn foreign nouns into verbs in this way, thus:

טוֹרְפֶּדוֹ torpedo → טִרְפֵּד torpedoed, טוּרְפַּד was torpedoed

Such verbs and action nouns have the same vowel pattern as if they had three consonants. Using the verbs קִלְקֵל 'ruined', קוּלְקַל 'was ruined', הִתְקַלְקֵל 'became ruined':

PI'EL: קִלְקֵל, קִלְקַלְתִּי . . . ,, מְקַלְקֵל, מְקַלְקְלִים . . . ,, אֲקַלְקֵל, תְּקַלְקְלִי . . . ,, לְקַלְקֵל

PU'AL: קוּלְקַל, קוּלְקַלְתִּי, קוּלְקְלוּ . . . ,, מְקוּלְקָל, מְקוּלְקָלִים . . . ,, אֲקוּלְקַל, תְּקוּלְקְלִי . . .

HITPA'EL: הִתְקַלְקֵל, הִתְקַלְקַלְתִּי . . . ,, מִתְקַלְקֵל, מִתְקַלְקְלִים . . . ,, אֶתְקַלְקֵל, תִּתְקַלְקְלִי . . . ,, לְהִתְקַלְקֵל

Action nouns: הִתְקַלְקְלוּת, קִלְקוּל ruination

Note: Where the middle letters (root consonant 2 and 3) involve פ, כ, ב, 'schoolbook Hebrew' usually requires consonant 2 to be soft and consonant 3 to be hard. But there are numerous exceptions, particularly in foreign-origin words like טִלְפֵּן 'telephoned', סִבְּסֵד 'subsidized'.

54 פ״י roots

Roots whose first consonant is י are called פ״י roots (פ standing for the first consonant of any root). Examples of verbs with פ״י roots:

יָשַׁב sit	יָרַד go down
יָלַד give birth	יָשֵׁן sleep
נוֹעַד (root י.ע.ד.) hold a meeting	נוֹתַר remain
הוֹצִיא (root י.צ.א.) bring out	הוֹבִיל transport
יִיצֵא export	הִתְיַשֵׁב settle

a | Regular פ״י verbs

פ״י roots are perfectly regular in PI'EL, PU'AL and HITPA'EL, thus יִיצֵא 'to export' and הִתְיַשֵׁב 'to settle':

יִיצוּא	לְיַיצֵא . . .	יְיַצֵא . . .	מְיַיצֵא . . .	יִיצֵא
לְהִתְיַשֵׁב	יִתְיַשֵׁב . . .	מִתְיַשֵׁב . . .	הִתְיַשֵׁב	

As for PA'AL, some פ״י roots are anomalous (see 54(b)), while others are quite regular except for slight adjustment in 1st sing. future, e.g. יָזַם 'initiate', יָצַר 'form':

Past . . . יָזַמְתִּי	Present . . . יוֹזֵם	Future . . . אִיזוֹם, תִּיזוֹם
		Infinitive לִיזוֹם

b | Deviant פ״י verbs

In some PA'AL verbs, and wherever there is a NIF'AL, HIF'IL or HUF'AL available, פ״י roots upset the normal pattern:

1 Several verbs, some very common, lose their י in the PA'AL future, infinitive and imperative. Moreover, as if to compensate for their missing י:

(a) they adopt the vowel -e-; and

(b) rather like ל״ה verbs (50), they add a suffix ת in the infinitive.

For example, יָשַׁב 'sit':

Past	...יָשַׁבְתִּי	Present	...יוֹשֵׁב
Future	אֵשֵׁב, תֵּשֵׁב, תֵּשְׁבִי, יֵשֵׁב, תֵּשֵׁב, נֵשֵׁב, תֵּשְׁבוּ, יֵשְׁבוּ		
Infinitive	לָשֶׁבֶת	Imperative	שֵׁב, שְׁבִי שְׁבוּ

2 In HIF'IL the root letter י is eliminated and in compensation the prefix is given the vowel וֹ throughout, thus הוֹשִׁיב 'sit (someone) down':

Past	...הוֹשַׁבְתִּי, הוֹשַׁבְתָּ, הוֹשִׁיב	Present	...מוֹשִׁיב, מוֹשִׁיבָה
Future	...אוֹשִׁיב, תּוֹשִׁיב, תּוֹשִׁיבִי	Infinitive	לְהוֹשִׁיב

3 A few פ״י roots also yield a peculiar NIF'AL, again with וֹ in place of י. Thus the NIF'AL counterpart of יָצַר 'created' is נוֹצַר 'was created':

Present   נוֹצַר

Future   יִיוָּצֵר   Infinitive   לְהִיוָּצֵר

Similarly נוֹעַד 'met':

Present   נוֹעַד

Future   יִיוָּעֵד   Infinitive   לְהִיוָּעֵד

Other common verbs of the anomalous פ״י type include יָרַד 'go down':

Future   ...אֵרֵד, תֵּרֵד, תֵּרְדִי

Infinitive   לָרֶדֶת   Imperative   רֵד, רְדִי, רְדוּ

The guttural יָדַע 'know':

Future   ...אֵדַע, תֵּדַע, תֵּדְעִי

Infinitive   לָדַעַת   Imperative   דַּע, דְּעִי, דְּעוּ

And a verb with a final א (see 58(d)), יָצָא 'go out':

Future   . . . אֵצֵא, תֵּצֵא, תֵּצְאִי

Infinitive   לָצֵאת   Imperative   צֵא, צְאִי, צְאוּ

These roots also yield הוֹרִיד 'take down', הוֹדִיעַ 'let know', נוֹדַע 'be known' and הוֹצִיא 'take out'.

55 'Cross-over': roots with initial שׁ, שׂ, צ, ס, ז

Sibilants are the consonants that 'hiss': ז, ס, צ, שׂ, שׁ. Where a root begins with a sibilant (e.g. שׁ-ג-ע), Hebrew does not allow the binyan HITPA'EL to create forms like הִתְשַׁגֵעַ. Instead, to make the הת prefix more distinct phonetically from the שׁ of the root, the שׁ crosses in front of the ת of the prefix: הִשְׁתַּגֵעַ 'go crazy'. Similarly for ס and שׂ:

ROOT: ס-כ-ן

    HITPA'EL: not הִתְסַכֵּן   . . . but הִסְתַּכֵּן endanger oneself

ROOT: שׂ-ר-ט

    HITPA'EL: not הִתְשָׂרֵט   . . . but הִשְׂתָּרֵט scratch oneself

This phenomenon, called 'sibilant cross-over', similarly affects four-consonant roots:

ROOT: שׁ-ע-מ-ם

    HITPA'EL: not הִתְשַׁעְמֵם   . . . but הִשְׁתַּעְמֵם get bored

Cross-over applies to all forms, thus:

הִשְׁתַּגַעְתִּי, הִשְׁתַּגַעְתָּ, הִשְׁתַּגֵעַ, . . . , מִשְׁתַּגֵעַ . . . אֶשְׁתַּגֵעַ, תִּשְׁתַּגְעִי . . . לְהִשְׁתַּגֵעַ

and the corresponding action nouns:

הִסְתַּכְּנוּת   endangering oneself

Further examples:

הִשְׁתַּתֵּף participate   הִשְׁתַּעֵל cough

הִשְׁתַּכְנֵעַ be convinced   הִסְתַּכֵּל look

הִסְתַּנְוֵר be blinded   הִשְׂתָּרֵעַ stretch

Where the initial sibilant is ז or צ, additional adjustments are made. With צ the *-t-* of the prefix is spelled ט, though with no effect on pronunciation:

ROOT: צ־ע־ר

HITPA'EL: not הִתְצַעֵר   but הִצְטַעֵר   be sorry

Further examples:

הִצְטַלֵּם be photographed   הִצְטַיֵּין excel

הִצְטַמְצֵם diminish

With ז there is an adjustment to pronunciation. ת is replaced by ד, thus:

ROOT: ז־ק־ן

HITPA'EL: not הִתְזַקֵן   ... but הִזְדַקֵן   grow old

Further examples:

הִזְדַהָה identify oneself   הִזְדָרֵז hurry

הִזְדַמֵן happen to come

56 Maverick verbs

Several common verbs belong to particularly small groups; and some are a law unto themselves.

a פ"נ roots

A few verbs lose an initial נ. The commonest are:

1 נָפַל 'fall', which loses נ in the future and infinitive:

Future	. . . אֶפּוֹל, תִּפּוֹל, תִּפְּלִי, יִפּוֹל
Infinitive	לִיפּוֹל

2 נָסַע 'travel' and נָגַע 'touch', which lose נ in the future and imperative (notice also that their last letter is a guttural, hence אֶסַע just like אֶשְׁמַע):

Future	אֶסַע, תִּסַּע, תִּסְעִי, יִסַּע, תִּסַּע, נִסַּע, תִּסְּעוּ, יִסְּעוּ
	אֶגַּע, תִּגַּע, תִּגְּעִי, יִגַּע, תִּגַּע, נִגַּע, תִּגְּעוּ, יִגְּעוּ
Imperative	סַע, סְעִי, סְעוּ
	גַּע, גְּעִי, גְּעוּ

Notice the 'nun' in the infinitive: **לִנְסוֹעַ, לִנְגּוֹעַ**

3 נָשָׂא 'bear', which loses נ in the future, infinitive and imperative. (Notice that its last letter is א, hence אֶשָׂא just like אֶקְרָא in 58(d) below. Notice also the ת in the infinitive just like לָצֵאת.)

Future	. . . אֶשָׂא, תִּשָׂא, תִּשְׂאִי, יִשָׂא
Infinitive	לָשֵׂאת
Imperative	שָׂא, שְׂאִי, שְׂאוּ

4 נָתַן 'give', which is altogether odd: besides losing its first נ in the future, infinitive and imperative, it also loses its second נ in part of the past tense:

Past	נָתַתִּי, נָתַתָּ, נָתַתְּ, נָתַן, נָתְנָה, נָתַנּוּ, נְתַתֶּם, נְתַתֶּן, נָתְנוּ
Present normal	נוֹתֵן, נוֹתֶנֶת, נוֹתְנִים, נוֹתְנוֹת
Future	. . . אֶתֵּן, תִּתֵּן, תִּתְּנִי, יִתֵּן
Infinitive	לָתֵת
Imperative	תֵּן, תְּנִי, תְּנוּ

5 נָגַשׁ 'walk up to', another law unto itself: the past and present belong to binyan NIF'AL (the root is נ־ג־שׁ, but instead of נִנְגַשׁ we get נִגַּשׁ), while the future and infinitive belong to PA'AL (and again the נ drops).

Past	נָגַשְׁתִּי, נָגַשְׁתָּ, נָגַשְׁתְּ, נָגַשׁ, נָגְשָׁה, נָגַשְׁנוּ, נָגַשְׁתֶּם, נָגַשְׁתֶּן, נָגְשׁוּ
Present	נִגָּשׁ, נִגֶּשֶׁת, נִגָּשִׁים, נִגָּשׁוֹת
Future	אֶגַּשׁ, תִּגַּשׁ, תִּגְּשִׁי, תִּגַּשׁ, יִגַּשׁ, נִגַּשׁ, תִּגְּשׁוּ, יִגְּשׁוּ
Infinitive	לָגֶשֶׁת

b לָקַח

לָקַח 'take' is the only verb to lose a ל. It loses it in the future, infinitive and imperative:

Future	אֶקַּח, תִּקַּח, תִּקְּחִי, יִקַּח, תִּקַּח, נִקַּח, תִּקְּחוּ, יִקְּחוּ
Infinitive	לָקַחַת
Imperative	קַח, קְחִי, קְחוּ

c הָלַךְ

הָלַךְ 'go' is the only verb to lose an initial ה. It loses it in the future, infinitive and imperative. Comparison with יָשַׁב in 54 will show that הָלַךְ is behaving as if it were a פ״י verb:

Future	אֵלֵךְ, תֵּלֵךְ, תֵּלְכִי, יֵלֵךְ, תֵּלֵךְ, נֵלֵךְ, תֵּלְכוּ, יֵלְכוּ
Infinitive	לָלֶכֶת
Imperative	לֵךְ, לְכִי, לְכוּ

d *יָכוֹל and צָרִיךְ*

יָכוֹל 'can' and צָרִיךְ 'must' not only look unlike any other verb to start with but even switch binyanim in some tenses, and worse. Here are the basic forms (other alternatives exist):

יָכוֹל

Present	יָכוֹל, יְכוֹלָה, יְכוֹלִים, יְכוֹלוֹת
Past	יָכוֹלְתִּי, יָכוֹלְתָּ, יָכוֹלְתְּ, הָיָה יָכוֹל, יָכְלָה, יָכוֹלְנוּ, יָכוֹלְתֶּם, יָכוֹלְתֶּן, יָכְלוּ
Future	אוּכַל, תּוּכַל, תּוּכְלִי, יוּכַל, תּוּכַל, נוּכַל, תּוּכְלוּ, יוּכְלוּ
Infinitive	None

צָרִיךְ

Present	צָרִיךְ, צְרִיכָה, צְרִיכִים, צְרִיכוֹת
Past	הָיִיתִי צָרִיךְ, הָיִיתָ צָרִיךְ, הָיִית צְרִיכָה . . .
Future	אֶצְטָרֵךְ, תִּצְטָרֵךְ, תִּצְטָרְכִי, יִצְטָרֵךְ, תִּצְטָרֵךְ, נִצְטָרֵךְ, תִּצְטָרְכוּ, יִצְטָרְכוּ
Infinitive	לְהִצְטָרֵךְ

e *Some verbs beginning with א*

אָמַר 'say, tell', אָכַל 'eat' and אָהַב 'like' have a strange future tense. אָמַר is peculiar in other ways, too:

Future	אוֹמַר, תֹּאמַר, תֹּאמְרִי, יֹאמַר, תֹּאמַר, נֹאמַר, תֹּאמְרוּ, יֹאמְרוּ
	אוֹכַל, תֹּאכַל, תֹּאכְלִי, יֹאכַל, תֹּאכַל, נֹאכַל, תֹּאכְלוּ, יֹאכְלוּ
	אֹהַב, תֹּאהַב, תֹּאהֲבִי, יֹאהַב, תֹּאהַב, נֹאהַב, תֹּאהֲבוּ, יֹאהֲבוּ

אָמַר has the infinitive לוֹמַר but, in fact, in colloquial usage the future and infinitive for אָמַר are borrowed from another verb entirely, הִגִּיד:

Past	אָמַר
Present	אוֹמֵר
Future	אַגִּיד, תַּגִּיד, תַּגִּידִי, . . .
Infinitive	לְהַגִּיד

Note: אומר, אוכל, אוהב could thus be read as present or as future tense: אוֹמֵר or אוֹמַר etc.

f The verb הָיָה 'be'

The verb הָיָה 'be' has no present tense. So in 'Yoram is tough, Yoram is a he-man' etc., Hebrew either drops the verb or inserts הוּא, הִיא, etc. (particles of being). See 2.

g The verbs חַי 'live' and מֵת 'die'

חַי 'live' and מֵת 'die' are maverick two-consonant verbs.

Unlike קָם 'get up' (26(b)), מֵת has the vowel ֵ in the past 3rd person and in the present tense:

Past	מֵת, מֵתָה, מֵתוּ
Present	מֵת, מֵתָה, מֵתִים, מֵתוֹת
Future	אָמוּת, תָּמוּת . . .
Infinitive	לָמוּת

חַי is even odder. It is basically a ל"ה verb (recall 50), but in the 3rd person past and in the present tense it becomes a two-consonant (ע"ו) verb:

Past	חָיִיתִי, חָיִיתָ, חָיִית, חַי, חַּיָה, חָיִינוּ, חָיִיתֶם, חָיִיתֶן, חַּיוּ
Present	חַי, חַּיָה, חַיִּים, חַיּוֹת
Future	אֶחְיֶה, תִּחְיֶה, תִּחְיִי, יִחְיֶה . . .
Infinitive	לִחְיוֹת

h ע״ע *roots*

Roots whose second and third consonants are identical are traditionally called ע״ע (ayin-ayin) roots, since the middle letter (represented by 'ayin') is repeated as the third letter. These roots can on occasion cause special difficulties: one of the repeated consonants can drop, triggering changes from the normal verb and noun patterns.

The HIF'IL of a few ע״ע roots favors the vowel -*e*-. It has -*e-e*- (not -*i-i*-) in both the present and past tense; and -*a-e*- (not -*a-i*-) in the future and infinitive:

הֵגֵן 'defend'

Past	הֵגֵן
Present	מֵגֵן
Future	יָגֵן
Infinitive	לְהָגֵן

and likewise הֵקֵל 'alleviate', הֵעֵז 'dare', הֵחֵל 'commence'.

In place of the normal PI'EL, PU'AL and HITPA'EL, these roots sometimes use the forms PO'EL, PO'AL and HITPO'EL. See 59.

57 HIF'IL verbs with two-consonant stems: הִכִּיר, הֵכִיל

Several HIF'IL verbs have *two* consonants showing in their base rather than three. They are of two types, the הִכִּיר 'recognize' type and the הֵכִיל 'contain' type. Disregarding the HIF'IL prefix ה, we have here the consonants כ־ר and כ־ל.

a הִכִּיר verbs

הִכִּיר verbs behave just like other HIF'IL verbs in terms of vowels and ב, כ, פ behavior: there is just a missing consonant:

Past	הִכַּרְתִּי, הִכַּרְתָּ, הִכַּרְתְּ, הִכִּיר, הִכִּירָה, הִכַּרְנוּ, הִכַּרְתֶּם, הִכַּרְתֶּן, הִכִּירוּ
Present	מַכִּיר, מַכִּירָה, מַכִּירִים, מַכִּירוֹת
Future	אַכִּיר, תַּכִּיר, תַּכִּירִי, יַכִּיר, תַּכִּיר, נַכִּיר, תַּכִּירוּ, יַכִּירוּ
Infinitive	לְהַכִּיר

More examples:

הִגִּיד say, tell	הִצִּיג present
הִפִּיל drop	הִבִּיט look
הִצִּיעַ suggest	הִצִּיל rescue
הִתִּיר undo	הִזִּיק harm

b הֵכִיל verbs

הֵכִיל verbs behave quite differently, with -e- in the past and present tense prefix rather than -ia-, and with a soft פ, כ, ב (if any):

Past	הֵכַלְתִּי, הֵכַלְתָּ, הֵכַלְתְּ, הֵכִיל, הֵכִילָה, הֵכַלְנוּ, הֵכַלְתֶּם, הֵכַלְתֶּן, הֵכִילוּ
Present	מֵכִיל, מְכִילָה, מְכִילִים, מְכִילוֹת
Future	אָכִיל, תָּכִיל, תָּכִילִי, יָכִיל, תָּכִיל, נָכִיל, תָּכִילוּ, יָכִילוּ
Infinitive	לְהָכִיל

103

More examples:

הֵבִין understand   הֵכִין prepare

הֵגִיב react   הֵצִיץ peep

הֵרִים lift   הֵבִיא bring

הֵשִׁיב reply   הֵעִיר awaken

הֵזִיז shift

Similarly for related nouns: type a: הַכָּרָה 'recognition'; type b: הֲכָנָה 'preparation'.

c What are the roots of these verbs?

Although most modern dictionaries list such verbs under ה, traditional grammars insist that type a are from roots with initial נ (thus נ־כ־ר → הכיר), while type b are from one-syllable roots (thus כ־ל → הכיל). However, it is simplest to regard *both* as having one-syllable roots*.

* In fact, the only notable connection between type a and initial נ verbs is הִפִּיל 'drop' ~ נָפַל 'fall' and הִסִיעַ 'give a lift' ~ נָסַע 'travel'.

58 PA'AL verbs with -i-a- in the future: 'grow'

A few PA'AL verbs do not have -i-o- in the future but -i-a- without any guttural being to blame. There are three types:

a גָּדַל, גָּדֵל, יִגְדַּל

A small group of intransitive verbs have -i-a- in the future (and imperative) and -a-e- in the present, e.g.:

גָּדַל 'grow'

Past   גָּדַל . . .

Present   גָּדֵל, גְּדֵלָה, גְּדֵלִים, גְּדֵלוֹת

| Future | אֶגְדַל, תִּגְדַל, תִּגְדְלִי, יִגְדַל, תִּגְדַל, נִגְדַל, תִּגְדְלוּ, יִגְדְלוּ |
| Infinitive | לִגְדֹל |

More examples:

יָשֵׁן sleep	חָדַל cease
חָסֵר be absent	שָׂמַח be glad
תָּמַהּ wonder	

Traditionally these have been called stative verbs, but this is not an accurate label.

b שָׁכַב, יִשְׁכַּב, לִשְׁכַּב

Two verbs have -i-a- in the future (and imperative) and in the infinitive too, but a regular present: שָׁכַב 'lie down' and רָכַב 'ride':

שָׁכַב 'lie down'

Past	שָׁכַב . . .
Present	שׁוֹכֵב . . .
Future	אֶשְׁכַּב, תִּשְׁכַּב, תִּשְׁכְּבִי, יִשְׁכַּב, תִּשְׁכַּב, נִשְׁכַּב, תִּשְׁכְּבוּ, יִשְׁכְּבוּ
Infinitive	לִשְׁכַּב

c לָבַשׁ, יִלְבַּשׁ

A handful have -i-a- in the future (and imperative) and are otherwise regular:

לָבַשׁ 'wear'

| Past | לָבַשׁ . . . |
| Present | לוֹבֵשׁ . . . |

Future   ... אֶלְבַּשׁ, תִּלְבַּשׁ, תִּלְבְּשִׁי, יִלְבַּשׁ

Infinitive   לִלְבּוֹשׁ

and likewise לָמַד 'study' and שָׁאַל 'ask'.

d *ל"א verbs:* מָצָא, יִמְצָא

A few verbs have a final א and are termed ל"א verbs. Notably: מָצָא 'find', יָצָא 'leave', קָרָא 'read, call', שָׂנָא 'hate'.

Although this א is not usually sounded, it does (like the other gutturals) create -*i-a*- in the future and imperative, though not in the infinitive. Notice also the present fem. sing.:

Past   ... מָצָא

Present   מוֹצֵא, מוֹצֵאת, מוֹצְאִים, מוֹצְאוֹת

Future   אֶמְצָא, תִּמְצָא, תִּמְצְאִי, יִמְצָא, תִּמְצָא,
              נִמְצָא, תִּמְצְאוּ, יִמְצְאוּ

Infinitive   לִמְצוֹא

Observe that יָצָא 'leave' acts in the future and infinitive like a פ"י verb (54):

לָצֵאת   ... אֵצֵא, תֵּצֵא

It has a related HIF'IL, הוֹצִיא 'take out', which has past tense vowels slightly different from the regular HIF'IL:

הוֹצֵאתִי, הוֹצֵאתָ, הוֹצֵאת, הוֹצִיא, הוֹצִיאָה,   הוֹצֵאנוּ, הוֹצֵאתֶם, הוֹצִיאוּ

Similarly, הֵבִיא 'bring' has the vowel *e* in the past tense:

הֵבֵאתִי, הֵבֵאתָ, הֵבֵאת, הֵבִיא, הֵבִיאָה,   הֵבֵאנוּ, הֵבֵאתֶם, הֵבִיאוּ

59 A minor binyan: the PO'EL and HITPO'EL

We have described the one-syllable verb, e.g. קָם, as having a two-consonant root: קֿ־ם. We have shown such roots in two binyanim: the PA'AL (26(b)) and HIF'IL, e.g. הֵקִים (57(b)).

These roots frequently also have a PI'EL, PU'AL and HITPA'EL form, but a special variety thereof, namely the PO'EL, PO'AL and HITPO'EL. This involves:

1 adding the letter ו; and

2 creating a *third consonant*. This is done by repeating the second.

Moreover, middle ב, כ, פ are soft. Take for example, קוֹמֵם 'arouse':

Past	קוֹמַמְתִּי, קוֹמַמְתָּ, קוֹמַמְתְּ, קוֹמֵם, קוֹמְמָה,
	קוֹמַמְנוּ, קוֹמַמְתֶּם, קוֹמַמְתֶּן, קוֹמְמוּ
Present	מְקוֹמֵם, מְקוֹמֶמֶת, מְקוֹמְמִים, מְקוֹמְמוֹת
Future	אֲקוֹמֵם, תְּקוֹמֵם, תְּקוֹמְמִי, יְקוֹמֵם,
	נְקוֹמֵם, תְּקוֹמְמוּ, יְקוֹמְמוּ
Infinitive	לְקוֹמֵם

The PO'AL is like the PU'AL except that instead of -*u-a*- the vowels are -*o-a*-:

קוֹמַם . . . מְקוֹמָם . . . יְקוֹמַם . . .

The HITPO'EL is like HITPA'EL except (as in PO'EL) for the ו and the repeated third consonant:

הִתְקוֹמֵם . . . מִתְקוֹמֵם . . . יִתְקוֹמֵם . . . לְהִתְקוֹמֵם . . . הִתְקוֹמְמוּת

Further examples of such verbs corresponding to two-consonant PA'AL:

רָץ	run	~	הִתְרוֹצֵץ	run about
שָׂח	say	~	שׂוֹחֵחַ	chat
גָּר	live	~	הִתְגּוֹרֵר	stay
הֵכִין	make ready	~	הִתְכּוֹנֵן	get oneself ready
הֵבִין	understand	~	הִתְבּוֹנֵן	contemplate

A further source of PO'EL and HITPO'EL: some three-consonant roots with an *identical second and third consonant* have a regular PI'EL and HITPA'EL, whereas others (for no obvious reason) instead have a PO'EL and HITPO'EL:

פּוֹצֵץ blow up (transitive)	הִתְפּוֹצֵץ blow up (intransitive)
סוֹבֵב turn (transitive)	הִסְתּוֹבֵב turn (intransitive)
הִשְׁתּוֹלֵל run wild	הִתְלוֹנֵן complain
שׁוֹטֵט roam	הִתְמוֹדֵד confront

אֲנִי מְסוֹבֵב אֶת זֶה אֲבָל זֶה לֹא מִסְתּוֹבֵב טוֹב !
I'm turning it but it isn't turning properly!

60 More plurals of nouns

a Plurals ending in ـַיִּם

While most nouns form their plural with ים or וֹת, a few (including some very common nouns) use ـַיִּם (stress -áyim). These are of two types:

1 Many nouns for objects that typically involve a pair of things, notably parts of the body. Note, however, that this ـַיִּם denotes the *plural*, not necessarily two of something, thus:

אַרְבַּע רַגְלַיִּם   four legs

Examples:

אוֹזְנַיִים ears   שִׁינַיִים teeth

מוֹתְנַיִים hips   מִשְׁקָפַיִים spectacles

אוֹפַנַיִים bicycle   גַרְבַּיִים socks

כִּירַיִים cooking range

2   A few miscellaneous nouns include:

שָׁמַיִים sky   מַיִים water

שׁוּלַיִים margin   צוֹהֳרַיִים lunchtime

The construct form is simply יֵ, as with ordinary plurals:

רַגְלֵי הַסַּפָּה the legs of the couch   גַרְבֵּי נַיילוֹן nylon socks

b   Duals ending in יִים

A handful of time units and numerals form a *dual* form by adding יִים, namely:

שָׁעֲתַיִים two hours   יוֹמַיִים two days

שְׁבוּעַיִים two weeks   חוֹדְשַׁיִים two months

שְׁנָתַיִים two years   פַּעֲמַיִים twice

מָאתַיִים 200   אַלְפַּיִים 2000

c   Plural of segolate nouns with ת־ (e.g. מָסוֹרֶת 'tradition')

Typical segolate nouns and their plural, בְּגָדִים:בֶּגֶד, were introduced in 7(c). But special note should be taken of segolates ending in feminine ת. These usually have three syllables, and all form their plural by essentially the same method. Notice that the stress in the plural falls on the plural ending:

Type 1:   *-e-et* or *a-at*   →   *-a-ót*

מְקַלַּחַת or מִפְלֶצֶת   →   מְקַלְחֹת, מִפְלָצֹת

Type 2:   *-o-et*   →   *-o-ót*

מַלְכֹּדֶת   →   מַלְכֹּדֹת

Examples:

Type 1:   דַּיֶּלֶת air-hostess   כַּוֶּרֶת bee-hive

             מַחְבֶּרֶת exercise-book   מִשְׁלַחַת delegation

             מִגְבַּעַת hat   טַבַּעַת ring

Type 2:   תִּסְפּוֹרֶת hair-do   מָסוֹרֶת tradition

             מַחְלוֹקֶת dispute

Note: Many 'segolate' nouns ending in ת belong in fact to a different category: nouns based on present tense verbs. For example: מְטַפֶּלֶת 'child-minder', עוֹזֶרֶת 'cleaning lady'. See 72.

d *Plural nouns: some exceptions*

Numerous masculine nouns form their plural with וֹת. Many of these nouns already have -o- as their last vowel; adding וֹת rather than יׁם thus creates a vowel harmony. Examples:

בּוֹר:בּוֹרוֹת	pit	חוֹל:חוֹלוֹת	sand(s)
מָקוֹם:מְקוֹמוֹת	place	מָלוֹן:מְלוֹנוֹת	hotel
יִתְרוֹן:יִתְרוֹנוֹת	advantage	חֲלוֹם:חֲלוֹמוֹת	dream
שׁוּלְחָן:שׁוּלְחָנוֹת	table	קִיר:קִירוֹת	wall
חֶרֶב:חֲרָבוֹת	sword	שֵׁם:שֵׁמוֹת	name
אָב:אָבוֹת	father		

Many nouns ending in הָ take the ending וֹת, e.g.

מַחֲזֶה:מַחֲזוֹת	play	מַחֲנֶה:מַחֲנוֹת	camp

Conversely, some thirty feminine nouns take יִם, including about half of the feminine nouns that have no feminine ending in their singular – and several words for flora and fauna. (Consult a good dictionary.)

אֶבֶן:אֲבָנִים	stone	דֶּרֶךְ:דְּרָכִים	route
אֲפוּנָה:אֲפוּנִים	pea	יוֹנָה:יוֹנִים	pigeon
שׁוֹשַׁנָה:שׁוֹשַׁנִים	lily	נְמָלָה:נְמַלִים	ant

And there are plurals that are unique, or nearly so, such as:

שָׁנָה:שָׁנִים	year	אִשָּׁה:נָשִׁים	woman
אִישׁ:אֲנָשִׁים	person	מַעֲשֶׂה:מַעֲשִׂיוֹת	tale
בַּיִת:בָּתִּים	house	עִיר:עָרִים	city
בֵּן:בָּנִים	son	בַּת:בָּנוֹת	daughter
אֵם:אִמָּהוֹת	mother	אָחוֹת:אַחָיוֹת	sister
רַב:רַבָּנִים	rabbi	לַיְלָה:לֵילוֹת	night
קוּפְסָה:קוּפְסוֹת/ קוּפְסָאוֹת	can	דֻּגְמָה:דֻּגְמוֹת/ דֻּגְמָאוֹת	pattern
יוֹם:יָמִים	day	עִפָּרוֹן:עֶפְרוֹנוֹת	pencil
חִסָּכוֹן:חִסְכוֹנוֹת	saving	שׁוֹר:שְׁוָורִים	bull
שׁוּק:שְׁוָקִים	market	רְאִי:מַרְאוֹת	mirror
אוֹת:אוֹתִיוֹת	letter	רֹאשׁ:רָאשִׁים	head
צַד:צְדָדִים	side	צֵל:צְלָלִים	shadow

111

61 Vowel raising: כָּל-כֻּלּוֹ, אָדוֹם-אֲדוּמִים

A few important words, when given an inflectional suffix, 'raise' their vowels: they change -o- to -u- and -e- to -i- (if they have such a vowel) and sometimes even -a- to -i-. In addition, they 'harden' their last letter if it is פ, כ, ב.

1 *o* to *u*

אֲדוּמָה, אֲדוּמִים, אֲדוּמוֹת ← אָדוֹם   red

רוּבּוֹ, רוּבָּה, . . ., רוּבָּם ← רוֹב   most: most of it . . . most of them

2 *e* to *i*

חִיצַי, חִיצֶיךָ . . . ← חֵץ   arrow: arrows ~ my, your . . . arrows

3 *a* to *i*

מִיסַי, מִיסֶיךָ . . . ← מַס   tax: taxes ~ my, your . . . taxes

4 A few harden the last letter without raising the vowel, thus:

גַּבִּים : גַּבִּי, גַּבְּךָ . . . ← גַּב   back: backs ~ my, your . . . back

and similarly:

דַּף page   כַּף spoon

שְׁלָב stage   רַךְ soft

זַךְ pure   רַב much, many

o → *u* applies

(a) to most color adjectives;

(b) to a few other adjectives and one-syllable nouns; and

(c) to the quantifiers כָּל 'all' and רוֹב 'most'

$e \rightarrow i$ and $a \rightarrow i$ apply to some twenty one-syllable nouns. Examples:

וָרֹד pink	כָּחֹל dark blue
יָרֹק green	צָהֹב yellow
מָתוֹק sweet	עָגֹל round
אָיֹם awful	תֹּף drum
חֹק law	שֵׁן tooth
עֵז goat	

62 Generic plurals: 'I hate cockroaches'

To express the generic (i.e. something in general), one simply uses the plural of the noun:

אֲנִי שׂוֹנֵא גּ׳וּקִים	I hate cockroaches
שׁוֹאֲבֵי־אָבָק תָּמִיד מִתְקַלְקְלִים	Vacuum-cleaners always go wrong

63 Plural loss: עֶשְׂרִים אִישׁ 'twenty persons'

Instead of עֶשְׂרִים יָמִים, Hebrew requires עֶשְׂרִים יוֹם 'twenty days'. Such loss of the plural ending occurs with certain *units of time* and with most *units of quantity*. The following may be taken as rules of thumb:

1 Where the numeral itself ends in a plural ending, e.g. שְׁלוֹשִׁים '30', אַרְבַּע מֵאוֹת '400', שֵׁשֶׁת אֲלָפִים '6000', any unit of time that would ordinarily have ים in the plural has to lose this ים. Thus:

שְׁלוֹשִׁים יוֹם, שְׁלוֹשִׁים חוֹדֶשׁ, שְׁלוֹשִׁים שָׁנָה
30 days, 30 months, 30 years

By contrast, שְׁלוֹשִׁים דַּקוֹת, שְׁלוֹשִׁים שָׁבוּעוֹת '30 minutes, 30 weeks' (the unit of time ends in וֹת).

113

2 Most other types of *unit of quantity* lose their ‑ים when combined with *any* numeral (except in pedantic style), thus:

שְׁלוֹשָׁה דוֹלָר, שְׁלוֹשָׁה מֶטֶר, שְׁלוֹשָׁה קִילוֹ,
שְׁלוֹשָׁה מַייל, שְׁלוֹשָׁה מִלְיוֹן, שְׁלוֹשָׁה אָחוּז
three dollars, meters, kilos, miles, million, percent

The word אִישׁ 'person' is treated in the same way: שְׁלוֹשָׁה אִישׁ 'three persons'. However, שֶׁקֶל is heard in both the masculine plural and the feminine singular:

שְׁלוֹשָׁה שְׁקָלִים, שָׁלוֹשׁ שֶׁקֶל   three shekels

64–8 NOUN TYPES (MISHKALIM)

64 Action nouns, e.g. חִידוּשׁ 'renewal'

To form nouns denoting actions ('destruction, confinement, playing . . .'), Hebrew is generally able to use five fixed noun patterns, corresponding closely and fairly systematically to five of the seven binyanim. These action nouns have already been listed in the verb inflection tables:

Noun pattern	Example		Corresponding verb (and binyan)	
PE'ILA	שְׁבִירָה a breakage	←	שָׁבַר break	(PA'AL)
HIPA'ALUT	הִיבָּדְלוּת segregation		נִבְדַּל become segregated	(NIF'AL)
HAF'ALA	הַבְדָּלָה distinction		הִבְדִּיל distinguish	(HIF'IL)
PI'UL	עִיכּוּב a delay		עִיכֵּב delay	(PI'EL)
HITPA'ALUT	הִתְבַּדְּלוּת self-segregation		הִתְבַּדֵּל segregate oneself	(HITPA'EL)

Note that ל"ה action nouns (recall 50) insert י for their 'missing letter', except for the two וּת- patterns (HIPA'ALUT and HITPA'ALUT):

בָּנָה	← בְּנִיָּיה	building
נִשְׁנָה	← הִישָּׁנוּת	repetition
כִּיסָה	← כִּיסוּי	cover
הִתְכַּסָּה	← הִתְכַּסוּת	covering oneself
הִפְלָה	← הַפְלָיָה	discrimination

Sometimes, nouns of these patterns have further or simply other meanings. Thus:

כְּרִיכָה	(action of) binding	or	(physical) binding of a book
קִיבּוּץ	(action of) gathering	or	a kibbutz

Sometimes an unexpected pattern is used, e.g.:

רָקַד	← רִיקוּד	dancing
הִתְחַתֵּן	← חֲתוּנָה	wedding
חִילֵּק	← חֲלוּקָה	distribution
קִיבֵּל	← קַבָּלָה	acceptance
נִלְחַם	← לְחִימָה	fighting

Unfortunately, few dictionaries list the action noun under the verb.

65 Nouns from adjectives, e.g. אִיטִיוּת 'slowness'

Abstract nouns can often be formed from adjectives, just like English 'vast → vastness'.

For adjectives with the suffix י (8(a), 69), simply add וּת:

אִיטִי	slow	→	אִיטִיוּת	slowness
נוֹרְמָלִי	normal	→	נוֹרְמָלִיוּת	normality

115

For most other adjectives, take the plural stem. This is often different from the singular, thus the plural stem of שָׁמֵן 'fat' is שְׁמֵן (recall 8(c): שְׁמֵנִים vs. שָׁמֵן). Then add וּת:

שָׁמֵן	fat	→	שְׁמֵנוּת	fatness
מָהִיר	quick	→	מְהִירוּת	speed
יָעִיל	efficient	→	יְעִילוּת	efficiency

And where the adjective has וּ for its last vowel, the noun will have י instead:

| רָטוֹב | wet | → | רְטִיבוּת | wetness |
| מָתוּן | moderate | → | מְתִינוּת | moderation |

A few adjectives require other patterns. One important one is the segolate pattern for measurement nouns:

| גָדוֹל | big | → | גּוֹדֶל | size |

Similarly עוֹמֶק 'depth', אוֹרֶךְ 'length', רוֹחַב 'width', גּוֹבַה 'height', עוֹבִי 'thickness', שׁוֹוִי 'worth', עוֹמֶס 'load'.

66 The noun patterns פַּעָל and פַּעְלָן

The noun pattern PA'AL (פַּעָל), with a hard middle פ, כ, ב, commonly denotes someone doing a particular job. It is often based on verbs and sometimes even on nouns:

כַּתָּב	reporter	(כָּתַב write)
טַיָּס	pilot	(טָס fly)
טַבָּח	cook	(טָבַח slaughter)
חַיָּט	tailor	(חוּט thread)
חַיָּל	soldier	(חַיִל corps)

The noun pattern PA'ALAN (פַּעְלָן) has several functions, again based on verbs or nouns:

1 someone doing a job, e.g. צַנְחָן 'paratrooper' (הִצְנִיחַ 'to parachute'), חַבְּלָן 'saboteur' (חִבֵּל 'to damage'), יַצְרָן 'manufacturer' (יִיצֵר 'to manufacture').

2 someone engaged in some voluntary activity, e.g. שַׂחְיָין 'swimmer' (שָׂחָה 'swim'), קַלְפָן 'card-player' (קְלָף 'card').

3 a device, e.g. רַעֲשָׁן 'rattle' (רַעַשׁ 'noise'), לַוְיָין 'satellite' (לִיוָּה 'accompany').

4 a personality type, e.g. חַנְפָן 'flatterer' (הֶחֱנִיף 'flatter'), קַמְצָן 'miser' (קָמַץ 'close'), דַּיְיקָן 'punctual person' (דִּיֵּיק 'to be punctual').

The Hebrew noun and adjective – unlike the Hebrew verb – have a multitude of patterns, many of which have no clear-cut meaning. So it is difficult to say, on the basis of its pattern, what a noun or adjective means. Conversely, it is just as difficult to anticipate which pattern to use for expressing a given concept.

67 Nouns with the suffix ָן and ַאי

a The suffix ָן

The suffix ָן is often added to an existing word to denote an activity, a personality, or even an object:

1 תּוֹתְחָן 'gunner' (תּוֹתָח 'big gun'), יְבוּאָן 'importer' (יְבוּא 'imports'), כַּלְכְּלָן 'economist' (כַּלְכָּלָה 'economics'), סוֹלָן 'soloist' (סוֹלוֹ 'solo'), לוּלָן 'poultry-keeper' (לוּל 'hen-house')

2 חוּצְפָן 'cheeky person' (חוּצְפָה 'cheek'), גִּזְעָן 'racist' (גֶּזַע 'race'), הַרְפַּתְקָן 'adventurer' (הַרְפַּתְקָה 'adventure'), תּוֹקְפָן 'aggressor' (תּוֹקֵף 'attacking')

3 יוֹמָן 'diary' (יוֹם 'day'), פּוֹתְחָן 'can-opener' (פּוֹתֵחַ 'opens'), מֵימָן 'hydrogen' (מַיִם 'water')

b The suffix אִי

The suffix אִי is often added to an existing word to denote someone engaged in an activity, especially to words ending in הָ. Purists insist that it be pronounced אִי (as one syllable) but it is often pronounced אָי (two syllables), thus קוּפָּאי. Examples:

עִתּוֹנַאי journalist   קוּפַּאי cashier

טֶנִיסַאי tennis-player   שַׁחְמָטַאי chess-player

יַמַּאי seaman

68   Some other noun patterns

Here are some more common noun patterns that tend to have a characteristic meaning or meanings. In some cases, they are based on another noun or a verb.

1   מַפְעֵל: usually a device of some kind:

מַגְהֵץ iron   מַחְשֵׁב computer

מַקְדֵּחַ drill   מַפְתֵּחַ key

מַזְלֵג fork   מַשְׁפֵּךְ funnel

2   מַפְעֵלָה: usually a device – or the location on an activity:

מַצְלֵמָה camera   מַחְרֵשָׁה plough

מַמְטֵרָה sprinkler   מַכְבֵּסָה laundry

מַחְלֵבָה dairy

3   מִפְעָל: commonly denotes an action or its product, or a location:

מִצְעָד parade   מִשְׁדָּר broadcast

מִבְחָן exam   מִשְׂרָד office

מִקְדָּשׁ temple   מַעֲגָן anchorage (notice the -a-a-vowels caused by the 'guttural' ע)

4 מִפְעָלָה: commonly denotes a location or an organization:

מִדְרָכָה sidewalk   מִפְקָדָה headquarters

מִסְעָדָה restaurant   מַעֲבָּדָה lab (notice the -a-a- vowels caused by the 'guttural' ע)

מִשְׁטָרָה police   מִכְלָלָה college

מַעֲצָמָה a power

5 פַּעֶלֶת: usually an illness – or a grouped object:

דַלֶּקֶת inflammation   צַהֶבֶת jaundice

טַיֶּסֶת squadron   נַיֶּדֶת patrol

6 תַּפְעִיל: usually the outcome or physical product of an action:

תַּסְבִּיךְ a (psychological) complex (סִיבֵּךְ complicate)

תַּקְדִּים precedent (הִקְדִּים precede)

תַּקְלִיט disc (הִקְלִיט record)

תַּקְרִית 'incident' (קָרָה happen; notice the ת in lieu of the root-letter ה)

7 תִּפְעוֹלֶת: usually the outcome or physical product of an action, typically something elaborate:

תִּסְרוֹקֶת hair-do (סִירֵק comb)

תִּלְבּוֹשֶׁת costume (לָבַשׁ wear)

תִּסְמוֹנֶת syndrome (סִימֵן signify)

תִּשְׁלוֹבֶת a complex (שִׁילֵב integrate)

תִּקְשׁוֹרֶת communications (הִתְקַשֵּׁר communicate)

8 פְּעַלְעַל: commonly a diminutive. The final syllable in the source noun is reduplicated, while itself changing its vowel to -a-:

כְּלַבְלַב puppy (כֶּלֶב)   חֲתַלְתּוּל kitten (חָתוּל)

זְקַנְקַן small beard (זָקָן beard)

9 The suffix וֹן has a variety of meanings: often 'a place for', 'a publication for', 'a mini-something':

פָּעוֹטוֹן crèche   שְׁבוּעוֹן weekly magazine

שְׁנָתוֹן yearbook   מְחִירוֹן pricelist

תַּקְלִיטוֹן computer diskette   סִרְטוֹן short film

דִּגְלוֹן small flag   טִפְּשׁוֹן little fool

10 The suffix יְסְט: added to words ending in a vowel or in –n: someone belonging to a group or engaged in an activity:

תִּיכוֹנִיסְט high school student   שְׁמִינִיסְט eighth-grader

שַׁבָּתוֹנִיסְט person on sabbatical   בַּלְגָנִיסְט messy person

פָּשִׁיסְט Fascist   סוֹצִיאָלִיסְט Socialist

11 The suffix נִיק: similar function to יְסְט, but attached to words ending in a consonant:

מוֹשַׁבְנִיק moshav member   קִיבּוּצְנִיק kibbutz member

לִיכּוּדְנִיק Likud member   ג'וֹבְנִיק shirker

12 The suffix ית: a mini-something, or simply an object related to something, particularly a vehicle or a brand-name (and of course the regular feminine of nouns like אָמֶרִיקָאִי 'American'). It also denotes languages, basing itself on the feminine of nationality adjectives, e.g. אַנְגְלִית 'English', סִינִית 'Chinese':

כַּפִּית teaspoon   כּוֹסִית small glass

שַׂקִית bag   מְכוֹנִית car

מוֹנִית cab   חֲלָלִית space-ship

פֶּזִית Pazit (a brand of cookie)   סוּכְּרָזִית Sucrazit (a brand of sweetener)

13 The suffix יָה ְ : simply an object related to something, particularly apparel, plants, stores and workshops, collections and ensembles:

כְּתֵפִיָּה cape   גּוּפִיָּה undershirt

חָזִיָּה bra   שְׁקֵדִיָּה almond-tree

סְטֵיקִיָּה steak-house   מִגְדָּנִיָּה patisserie

מַסְגֵּרִיָּה metal workshop   שְׁלִישִׁיָּה trio

סִפְרִיָּה library   כַּרְטִיסִיָּה season-ticket

צִמְחִיָּה vegetation

14 Compounds: Hebrew likes to compound two words together to create a new word, sometimes with a little trimming of unwanted letters. Compounds are treated as a single word in terms of plural endings etc.

כַּדּוּר + רֶגֶל ball + foot	→	כַּדּוּרֶגֶל soccer
תַּקְלִיט + אוֹר disc + light	→	תַּקְלִיטוֹר CD
מִדְרָכָה + רְחוֹב sidewalk + street	→	מִדְרְחוֹב pedestrian-only street
מָדַד + חֲנָיָה to measure + parking	→	מַדְחָן parking meter
רָם + קוֹל loud + sound	→	רַמְקוֹל loudspeaker (pl.: רַמְקוֹלִים)

Acronyms: rather like 'NATO' and 'AIDS' in English, Hebrew often creates new words out of initials or abbreviations. The vowels are generally -a-a- or, if the middle letter is vav, -o-. A double apostrophe (Hebrew: גֵּרְשַׁיִים) is placed before the last letter:

תּוֹרָה נְבִיאִים כְּתוּבִים	→	תַּנַ"ך	Bible
צָבָא הֲגָנָה לְיִשְׂרָאֵל	→	צַהַ"ל	Israeli Defense Forces
ראשׁ מַטֶּה כְּלָלִי	→	רַמַטְכָּ"ל	Chief of Staff
דִּין וְחֶשְׁבּוֹן	→	דוּ"ח	report
שֶׁקֶל חָדָשׁ	→	שַׁ"ח	New Sheqel

15 Nouns from problem roots: even where a noun pattern gives no clear indication of a word's meaning, to connect the noun with some root may give useful clues as to the meaning – or at least help with memorization. But where the root is a 'problem root' (see 50–9) with weak letters, making the connection can be difficult.

The pattern תְּפוּלָה is commonly based on Ayin-Vav verbs (recall 26(b)):

תְּשׁוּבָה response ~ שׁ.ב (cf. הֵשִׁיב respond)

תְּבוּאָה (farm) produce ~ ב.א (cf. הֵבִיא bring)

תְּעוּדָה certificate ~ ע.ד (cf. עֵד a witness)

תְּלוּנָה complaint ~ ל.ן (cf. הִתְלוֹנֵן complain)

Roots with an initial נ (פ"נ roots, see 56) often drop the נ in nouns, e.g.:

מַגָּב windshield wiper and מַגֶּבֶת towel from נ.ג.ב (cf. נִיגֵּב wipe)

מַפָּל־מַיִם waterfall and מַפּוֹלֶת landslide from נ.פ.ל (cf. נָפַל fall)

מַסָּע campaign from נ.ס.ע (cf. נָסַע travel)

Roots with an initial י (פ"י roots, see 54) often provide nouns with the letter ו instead of י, thus:

מוֹלֶדֶת homeland and יוֹם הוּלֶדֶת birthday from י.ל.ד (cf. יָלַד give birth)

מוֹשָׁב seat and תּוֹשָׁב inhabitant from י.שׁ.ב (cf. יָשַׁב sit)

מוֹדָעָה notification and תּוֹדָעָה consciousness from י.ד.ע (cf. יָדַע know)

Roots with an identical second and third letter (ע"ע roots, see 56) often drop one of these letters:

חוֹק law (cf. חָקַק legislate)

גַּן garden (cf. גַּנָּן gardener)

שַׂר minister (cf. שָׂרַר rule)

דּוֹם stand to attention (cf. דּוֹמֵם inanimate)

חֵן grace (cf. חָנַן to pardon)

כָּל all (cf. כָּלַל include)

צַד ~ צְדָדִים side, צֵל ~ צְלָלִים shadow

תְּפִילָה prayer (cf. הִתְפַּלֵּל pray)

מְסִילָה track (cf. סָלַל pave)

מְחִיצָה partition (cf. חָצַץ to come between)

69–71 ADJECTIVE TYPES

69 Passive adjectives (כָּנוּס, מוּכְנָס, מְכוּנָס)

Three of the verb patterns (binyanim) are capable of a direct object: PA'AL, HIF'IL and PI'EL. And each usually has a corresponding *passive adjective*, expressing a 'state of having been done' (also known as the passive participle). Example:

פָּתַחְתִּי אֶת הַדֶּלֶת   →   הַדֶּלֶת פְּתוּחָה
I opened the door   The door is open
Verb   Passive adj.

Using our model root כ־נ־ס:

1 Corresponding to PA'AL   כָּנַס   'to draw in': כָּנוּס 'drawn in'*

כָּנוּס, כְּנוּסָה, כְּנוּסִים, כְּנוּסוֹת

2 Corresponding to HIF'IL   הִכְנִיס   'to insert': מוּכְנָס 'inserted'

מוּכְנָס, מוּכְנֶסֶת, מוּכְנָסִים, מוּכְנָסוֹת

123

3 Corresponding to PI'EL   כִּינֵס 'to convene': מְכוּנָס 'convened'

מְכוּנָס, מְכוּנֶסֶת, מְכוּנָסִים, מְכוּנָסוֹת

* For ל"ה verbs, the letter yod is added for the 'missing' final consonant; for example:

אָפָה bake   →   דָג אָפוּי baked fish

Examples:

1 זֶה שָׁבוּר it's broken   רְכוּשׁ גָּנוּב stolen property

הַגִ'ינְס מָכוּר the jeans are sold

2 שִׂיחָה מוּקְלֶטֶת a recorded talk   שֶׁטַח מוּזְנָח a neglected area

זֶה מוּכָן it's ready

3 הוּא מְקוּפָּח he's deprived   טִיּוּל מְאוּרְגָן an organized trip

מְאֹד מְבוּקָשׁ in big demand

The PI'EL and HIF'IL passive adjectives are identical with the present tense forms of the passive binyanim, PU'AL and HUF'AL. The PA'AL passive adjective, on the other hand, is to be distinguished (usually) from the present tense NIF'AL, which does the job of a *verb*:

זֶה נִשְׁבָּר   It's breaking, it breaks   (verb)

זֶה שָׁבוּר   It's broken   (passive adjective)

70 Adjectives from nouns

Many adjectives are created from nouns, by adding the suffix י:

יָם   sea   →   יַמִּי   marine

חִינוּךְ   education   →   חִינוּכִי   educational

Where the noun ends in ה, this may often first be removed:

| כַּלְכָּלָה | economics → | כַּלְכָּלִי | economic |
| הַנְדָּסָה | engineering → | הַנְדְּסִי | engineering |

But, particularly where the ending is יָה ., the ה will often convert to ת. This is none other than the construct ending (recall 17(d)):

בְּעָיָה	problem →	בְּעָיָיתִי	problematic
תַּעֲשִׂיָּה	industry →	תַּעֲשִׂיָּיתִי	industrial
אוֹפְנָה	fashion →	אוֹפְנָתִי	fashionable
זְוָוָעָה	horror →	זְוָוָעָתִי	hideous

The adjective will often appear at first sight to be a noun + possessive suffix יִ־, e.g. יַמִּי 'my sea'. But true ambiguity is unlikely.

Note: Sometimes adjustments have to be made to the vowels of the noun, e.g. לָשׁוֹן 'language' → לְשׁוֹנִי 'linguistic', בַּיִת 'house' → בֵּיתִי 'domestic'. Similar vowel adjustments are made to construct nouns (see 76); they can be learned together.

71 Other meaningful adjective patterns

1 פַּעֲלָן

Using the noun pattern PA'ALAN (66) denoting personality types, Hebrew creates many *adjectives of personality*:

פָּעוֹט בַּכְיָן	a crybabyish infant
מוֹרֶה קַפְדָן	a fussy teacher
אִינְסְטַלָטוֹר פַּטְפְּטָן	a talkative plumber
יֶלֶד חַיְכָן	a smiling child

2 פַּעֲלָנִי

Some adjectives have the pattern PA'ALANI, mostly based on verbs and denoting *personality* or *emotion*:

סַבְלָנִי	patient
עַצְבָּנִי	uptight
קַטְלָנִי	murderous
חַשְׁדָנִי	suspicious
לַמְדָנִי	scholarly

3 The suffix ־נִי

Often, the adjectival suffix נִי is just added to a noun or verb as it stands, without changing the vowels to -a-a-, thus:

קוֹלָנִי	vociferous	(קוֹל	voice)
חוֹלְמָנִי	dreamy	(חוֹלֵם	dreaming)
חוּצְפָּנִי	cheeky	(חוּצְפָּה	cheek)
עוֹקְצָנִי	stinging	(עוֹקֶץ	sting)

Besides personality and emotion, it can also denote ideology:

שְׂמֹאלָנִי	leftist	(שְׂמֹאל	left)
לְאוּמָנִי	nationalistic	(לְאוֹם	nation)
מַהְפְּכָנִי	revolutionary	(מַהֲפֵּכָה	revolution)

4 פָּעִיל

The pattern PA'IL has two characteristic meanings: often (a) 'capable of being (washed, fixed, believed, etc.)' and sometimes (b) 'tending to do something'. In many cases, however, there is no predictable meaning (c):

(a) קָרִיא 'legible' (קָרָא 'read'), חָדִיר 'permeable' (חָדַר 'permeate'),
כָּבִיס 'washable' (כִּיבֵּס 'wash'), אָמִין 'credible' (הֶאֱמִין 'believe')

(b) סָבִיל 'passive' (סָבַל 'suffer'), פָּעִיל 'active' (פָּעַל 'act'), רָגִישׁ
'sensitive' (הִרְגִּישׁ 'feel'), זָהִיר 'careful' (נִזְהַר 'take care')

(c) גָּמִישׁ 'flexible', סָדִיר 'regular', בָּרִיא 'healthy', יָעִיל 'efficient'

5 פָּעוֹל

The pattern PA'OL is used for most colors and a few other adjectives.
NB: When there is a feminine or plural ending, the -o- vowel usually
changes to -u-, and צָהוֹב acquires a 'hard' final consonant: צָהוּבָּה,
צָהוּבִּים (see 61):

אָדוֹם red	צָהוֹב yellow
יָרוֹק green	כָּחוֹל dark blue
וָרוֹד pink	שָׁחוֹר black
אָפוֹר gray	מָתוֹק sweet
אָיוֹם terrible	עָגוֹל round

שחור and אפור do not change their -o- to -u-. Colors that do not use
this pattern include לָבָן 'white', תְּכֵלֶת 'light blue', חוּם 'brown'.

6 פְּעַלְעַל

The pattern PE'AL'AL supplies several diminutives for adjectives (cf.
English 'ish'), as it does for nouns – recall 68(8). It normally works by
reduplicating a 'base' adjective. The vowels will always be -a-a-.
Notice the 'hard' fourth letter in לבנבן and הפכפך. Examples:

greenish	יָרוֹק ← יְרַקְרַק	pinkish	וָרוֹד ← וְרַדְרַד
whitish	לָבָן ← לְבַנְבַּן	flighty	הָפַךְ ← הֲפַכְפַּךְ
plumpish	שָׁמֵן ← שְׁמַנְמַן	slightly sour	חָמוּץ ← חֲמַצְמַץ

7 עַל־קוֹלִי, תַּת־יַמִי etc.

Hebrew has some twenty short prefixes which can be hyphenated to a noun, after which the noun is given the suffix ־י, creating a phrasal adjective. The whole phenomenon is reminiscent of European terminology like 'supersonic', 'subterranean', and is much used in technical Hebrew. Examples:

עַל־קוֹלִי	supersonic (קוֹל sound)
תַּת־יַמִי	submarine
אַנְטִי־מִלְחַמְתִּי	anti-war
בֵּין־לְאוּמִי	international
חַד־סִטְרִי	one-way, unidirectional
דוּ־לְשׁוֹנִי	bilingual
רַב־תַּכְלִיתִי	multi-purpose

72 Present tense 'verbs' as nouns and adjectives

Many nouns corresponding to the 'seller', 'runner', 'inspector', 'consultant' type (agent nouns) are simply formed by utilizing present tense verbs.

שׁוֹפֵט judge		מוֹכֶרֶת salesgirl	
תּוֹפֶרֶת seamstress		קוֹנָה customer	
בּוֹנֶה builder		מַתְחִיל beginner	
מַשְׁקִיעַ investor		מְבַקֵּר visitor	
מְהַגֵּר migrant		מִתְנַחֵל settler	

There are, however, several other patterns for agent nouns (see 66–7).

Similarly, many adjectives of the 'frightening', 'refreshing', 'shining' type utilize present tense verbs. Among them are many that have a NIF'AL or PU'AL passive present tense form (recall 69) without being passive at all:

זוֹהֵר shining		לוֹהֵט ardent	
נִרְגָּשׁ emotional		נִזְעָם furious	
נֶהְדָּר gorgeous		מַשְׁמִין fattening	
מַגְעִיל revolting		מְרַתֵּק exciting	
מִתְפַּתֵּל twisting		מְיוּחָד special	
מְשׁוּנֶה strange		מְסוּרְבָּל clumsy	

Nearly all* such nouns and adjectives form their feminine and plural as if they were verbs, thus:

מוֹכֵר, מוֹכֶרֶת, מוֹכְרִים, מוֹכְרוֹת

מַשְׁמִין, מַשְׁמִינָה, מַשְׁמִינִים, מַשְׁמִינוֹת

מְיוּחָד, מְיוּחֶדֶת, מְיוּחָדִים, מְיוּחָדוֹת

* Notable exceptions: נִפְלָא 'wonderful', נוֹרָא 'frightful', נֶחְמָד 'nice' add הַ in the feminine.

73–7 CONSTRUCTS AND POSSESSIVES

73 The construct as a possessive

In 17 we introduced possessive שֶׁל 'of', as in הָאָח שֶׁל רוֹנִית 'the brother of Ronit', הָאָח שֶׁלִּי 'my brother'. Hebrew can also use the *construct* for the possessive, particularly in formal style. And here we are talking not only about placing two *nouns* side by side, as in אֲחֵי הַמֶּלֶךְ 'the king's brothers', but also about combining a noun with a possessive *suffix*, as in אָחִי 'my brother'. In both cases, אָח is construct.

129

a *Noun + noun, e.g.* הוֹרֵי הַכַּלָּה *'the bride's parents'*

Formal Hebrew often uses possessive construct phrases such as:

סוֹף הַסִּיפּוּר	the end of the story
הַחְלָטַת הַוַּעֲדָה	the committee's decision
נוֹשֵׂא הַתּוֹכְנִית	the subject of the program
אִיגְרוֹת הָרַב קוּק	the letters of Rav Kook
הוֹרֵי הַכַּלָּה	the bride's parents

For possessives – as against set expressions – there is nothing wrong with using שֶׁל 'of'; the use of the construct just tends to be more succinct and elegant.

Similarly, for phrases equivalent to 'the closing of the gate, rearing turkeys' with an action noun, formal Hebrew tends to use a construct, while colloquial style uses שֶׁל, thus:

סְגִירַת הַשַּׁעַר	or	סְגִירָה שֶׁל הַשַּׁעַר	the closing of the gate
טִיפּוּחַ הוֹדוּ	or	טִיפּוּחַ שֶׁל הוֹדוּ	rearing of turkeys

b–c *Possessive suffixes:* ... דּוֹדִי, דּוֹדְךָ

Possessive suffixes are generally favored in – and limited to – formal style: literature, lectures, officialese, journalese and the like. Thus תַּרְבּוּתֵנוּ 'our culture', אִישׁוּרָם 'their approval'.

However, even colloquial Hebrew may often use possessive suffixes with certain words, notably kinship terms such as אָח 'brother', אֵם 'mother', and הוֹרִים 'parents'; indeed, there is a general preference for ... בַּעֲלִי, בַּעֲלֵךְ 'my, your ... husband' and ... אִשְׁתִּי, אִשְׁתֵּךְ 'my, your ... wife' (rather than הַבַּעַל שֶׁלִי, הָאִשָּׁה שֶׁלִי and so on).

b | With singular nouns

We first illustrate the suffixes with singular nouns. Notice that they are identical to the light suffixes used with the preposition בִּשְׁבִיל 'for' (35(d)) and that there is no difference in spelling between 'your' (masc. sing.) and 'your' (fem. sing.) except for the nikkud.

Notice too that the feminine noun has the ת ending associated with the *construct form* (recall 17(d)); it is advisable, in fact, to regard noun + possessive suffix as a kind of construct phrase, amounting to: *dod* + *o* 'uncle-of-him', *dodat* + *o* 'aunt-of-him'.

דּוֹד uncle			
דּוֹדֵנוּ	our uncle	דּוֹדִי	my uncle
דּוֹדְכֶם	your (masc. pl.) uncle	דּוֹדְךָ	your (masc. sing.) uncle
דּוֹדְכֶן	your (fem. pl.) uncle	דּוֹדֵךְ	your (fem. sing.) uncle
דּוֹדָם	their (masc. pl.) uncle	דּוֹדוֹ	his uncle
דּוֹדָן	their (fem. pl.) uncle	דּוֹדָהּ	her uncle

דּוֹדָה aunt			
דּוֹדָתֵנוּ	our aunt	דּוֹדָתִי	my aunt
דּוֹדַתְכֶם	your (masc. pl.) aunt	דּוֹדָתְךָ	your (masc. sing.) aunt
דּוֹדַתְכֶן	your (fem. pl.) aunt	דּוֹדָתֵךְ	your (fem. sing.) aunt
דּוֹדָתָם	their (masc. pl.) aunt	דּוֹדָתוֹ	his aunt
דּוֹדָתָן	their (fem. pl.) aunt	דּוֹדָתָהּ	her aunt

c | With plural nouns

Plural nouns take a slightly different set of suffixes, identical to the heavy suffixes used with the preposition עַל 'on' (recall 35(e)). The important point is that the extra letter *yod* in all these suffixes can be explained as a *plural ending* of the noun – the *construct* ending (17(d)). Thus, דּוֹדָיו really amounts to a construct phrase: *dodey* + *o* 'uncles-of-him'.

Observe, however, that this *yod* also shows up with *feminine plural* nouns, as in דּוֹדוֹתֵיהֶם 'their aunts (aunts-of-them)', i.e. *dodot* + *ey* + *hem* 'aunts + PL + them', even though their 'plural-hood' is already marked by their ending וֹת.

Purists insist on distinguishing the pronunciation of נוּ and ינוּ as *-énu* vs. *-éynu*, but both are commonly pronounced *-éynu*.

דּוֹדִים uncles			
דּוֹדֵינוּ	our uncles	דּוֹדַי	my uncles
דּוֹדֵיכֶם	your (masc. pl.) uncles	דּוֹדֶיךָ	your (masc. sing.) uncles
דּוֹדֵיכֶן	your (fem. pl.) uncles	דּוֹדַיִךְ	your (fem. sing.) uncles
דּוֹדֵיהֶם	their (masc. pl.) uncles	דּוֹדָיו	his uncles
דּוֹדֵיהֶן	their (fem. pl.) uncles	דּוֹדֶיהָ	her uncles

דּוֹדוֹת aunts			
דּוֹדוֹתֵינוּ	our aunts	דּוֹדוֹתַי	my aunts
דּוֹדוֹתֵיכֶם	your (masc. pl.) aunts	דּוֹדוֹתֶיךָ	your (masc. sing.) aunts
דּוֹדוֹתֵיכֶן	your (fem. pl.) aunts	דּוֹדוֹתַיִךְ	your (fem. sing.) aunts
דּוֹדוֹתֵיהֶם	their (masc. pl.) aunts	דּוֹדוֹתָיו	his aunts
דּוֹדוֹתֵיהֶן	their (fem. pl.) aunts	דּוֹדוֹתֶיהָ	her aunts

Note the stress: dodáy, dodécha, dodáyich, dodáv, dodéha, dodéynu, dodeychém, dodeychén, dodeyhém, dodeyhén.

d *Construct adjective + noun, e.g.* אֲרוּכֵּי־שֵׂעָר *'long-haired'*

Hebrew makes adjectival phrases from a construct adjective and a noun. The construct form of adjective functions rather like the *-ed* in English 'long-haired'. (Note that the construct form of an adjective is sometimes indistinguishable from the absolute form.) These constructs denote a specially close kind of (1) possession or (2) make-up:

1   To describe someone's or something's appearance or clothing or nature, by a kind of transfer of the adjective to the person themselves. The phrase is hyphenated. Some of them are rather bookish. Examples:

בַּחוּרִים רַחֲבֵי־כְּתֵפַיִים	broad-shouldered fellows
פּוֹלִיטִיקָאִים יְפֵי־נֶפֶשׁ	high-minded politicians
תּוֹכְנִית אֲרוּכַּת־טְווָח	a long-term program

2   To describe the make-up of something, certain adjectives such as מָלֵא 'full' can be used in the construct:

חֶדֶר מָלֵא עָשָׁן	a smoke-filled room
חֲדָרִים מְלֵאֵי עָשָׁן	smoke-filled rooms
שְׁטִיחִים מְכוּסֵּי אָבָק	dust-covered carpets
מְדִינָה עֲשִׁירַת נֵפְט	an oil-rich country
מַרְגָּרִינָה דַלַת שׁוּמָן	low-fat margarine

Making a whole sentence (as against a phrase), use בְּ rather than the construct:

הַחֲדָרִים מְלֵאִים בְּעָשָׁן

3   In addition, formal Hebrew uses בַּעַל and חֲסַר in the construct for describing the appearance or characteristics of someone or something:

יְלָדִים בַּעֲלֵי שֵׂיעָר אָרוֹךְ וּמְתוּלְתָּל
children with long, curly hair

הַתּוֹכְנִית הַזֹּאת בַּעֲלַת חֲשִׁיבוּת מְיוּחֶדֶת
this program is of particular importance

קְבוּצָה חַסְרַת זֶהוּת אֶתְנִית
a group lacking an ethnic identity

74 לְ of possession: הִסְתַּכַּלְתִּי לָהּ בָּעֵינַיִים 'I looked into her eyes'

When referring to a part of the body, colloquial Hebrew tends to use הַ
and even לְ rather than שֶׁל:

יוֹרָם סֵירֵק אֶת הַשֵּׂיעָר	Yoram combed his hair *(combed the hair)*
סָגַרְתִּי אֶת הָעֵינַיִים	I closed my eyes *(closed the eyes)*
יוֹרָם סֵירֵק לְאֶפְרָת אֶת הַשֵּׂיעָר	Yoram combed Efrat's hair *(combed to Efrat the hair)*
הִסְתַּכַּלְתִּי לָהּ בָּעֵינַיִים	I looked into her eyes *(I looked to her into the eyes)*
מַה אַתָּה מַרְבִּיץ לוֹ בַּבֶּטֶן !	Why are you hitting him in the stomach!

Study the construction just illustrated: instead of a possessive with the
body part, one simply uses הַ. If it is a person other than the subject that is
being affected, that person becomes a kind of indirect object, requiring לְ-,
and is mentioned *before* the part of the body.

More formal Hebrew, however, prefers:

יוֹרָם סֵירֵק אֶת הַשֵּׂיעָר שֶׁל אֶפְרָת

הִסְתַּכַּלְתִּי בְּעֵינֶיהָ

75–6 CONSTRUCT NOUNS – VOWEL CHANGES

75 Construct segolates

Apart from the possibility of a construct suffix (17(d)), construct nouns
are sometimes distinguished by internal vowel changes, depending largely
on the noun pattern involved.

A notable case is the construct plural of segolate nouns; segolates were
introduced in 7(c). (The singular itself does *not* have a distinct construct
form, hence בֶּגֶד 'garment': בֶּגֶד־יָם 'swimsuit'.) There are three main
types:

a *The* פֶּרַח/בֶּגֶד *type (initial ֶ)*

בְּגָדִים garments → בִּגְדֵי   בִּגְדֵי־יָם   swimsuits

                                  סִרְטֵי־מֶתַח   thrillers

פְּרָחִים flowers → פִּרְחֵי   פִּרְחֵי־בָּר   wild flowers

                                  צִבְעֵי־הַקֶּשֶׁת   colors of the rainbow

b *The* בַּעַל *type (initial ַ)*

בְּעָלִים owners → בַּעֲלֵי   בַּעֲלֵי־רֶכֶב   vehicle owners

                                  יַעֲרוֹת קק"ל   JNF forests

c *The* טוֹפֶס *type (initial וֹ)*

טְפָסִים forms → טוֹפְסֵי   טוֹפְסֵי הַפְקָדָה   deposit forms

                                  חוֹדְשֵׁי הַשָּׁנָה   months of the year

Observe that in each case the construct plural is reminiscent of the singular.

There are three groups of exceptions to 75(a):

1 Some nouns have ִ in the construct plural, e.g. מֶלֶךְ, יַלְדֵי 'child' ~ יֶלֶד
'king' ~ כַּלְבֵי, כֶּלֶב 'dog' ~ כַּלְבֵי, מַלְכֵי

2 Nouns with an initial 'guttural' similarly have ַ, e.g. עֶרֶב 'evening' ~
חַסְדֵי חֶסֶד 'kindness' ~ חַסְדֵי, עַרְבֵי

3 A sub-exception to 2: several common nouns keep their *e* (in terms of
nikkud, ֶ changes to ֱ): עֵבֶר, חֶפְצֵי 'article' ~ חֵפֶץ, חֶלְקֵי, חֵלֶק 'part' ~
'side' ~ עֶבְרֵי

76 Some other vowel changes in constructs

a | Loss of a: מָקוֹם~מְקוֹם

A vowel *a* in the last-but-one syllable commonly drops in the construct of masculine singular nouns, thus:

מָקוֹם	place	~	מְקוֹם־מְגוּרִים	place of residence
שָׁלוֹם	peace	~	שְׁלוֹם־הַמְּדִינָה	peace of the realm
צָבָא	army	~	צְבָא עִירַאק	the army of Iraq

This 'second-from-the-end rule' has much in common with the 'third-from-the-end rule', which removes the vowel *a* where an ending has been added (compare 7(b)). In both rules, the exceptions are the same:

1   *a* does not drop if this would produce a run of three consonants, hence:

מַכְשִׁיר	~	מַכְשִׁיר וִידֵאוֹ	video set
תַּלְמִיד	~	תַּלְמִיד יְשִׁיבָה	Yeshiva student

2   *a* does not drop in words where the dictionary spells it with ָ rather than ַ:

טַייָס	~	טַייַס אֶל־עַל	El Al pilot
כַּתָּב	~	כַּתַּב סְפּוֹרְט	sports correspondent

b | Inserting an -i-: בְּרָכָה, דְּבָרִים, etc.

We just saw (in 75(a)) that the construct of בְּגָדִים is בִּגְדֵי, with an -*i*-inserted and the loss of the -*a*-. The same thing occurs in the construct of two other, less numerous types of noun that happen to have a similar vowel pattern: (1) feminines of the type שְׂמָלוֹת ~ שִׂמְלָה or בְּרָכוֹת ~ בְּרָכָה, and (2) masculine plurals of the type דְּבָרִים or זְקֵנִים.

1 Construct of בְּרָכָה: בִּרְכַּת (notice also the hardened כ)

בְּרָכוֹת: בִּרְכוֹת

Similarly: חֲרָדָה ~ חֶרְדַּת, נְקָמָה ~ נִקְמַת 'revenge', קְלָלָה ~ קִלְלַת 'curse', שְׂמָלוֹת ~ fear' (the -e- is due to the ח), הֲלָכוֹת ~ הִלְכוֹת 'regulations', שְׂמָלוֹת 'dresses'.

2 Construct of דְּבָרִים: דִּבְרֵי

זְקֵנִים: זִקְנֵי

כְּתָבִים: כִּתְבֵי

Similarly: מְשָׁלִים ~ מִשְׁלֵי 'proverbs', צְבָאוֹת ~ צִבְאוֹת 'armies'. Examples:

בִּרְכַּת נִישׂוּאִין wedding greeting   דִּבְרֵי הַשָּׂר the minister's speech

יְלְלַת תַּנִים howling of jackals   חֶרְדַּת טִיסָה fear of flying

כִּתְבֵי־עֵת periodicals

c Some important oddments

Other notable construct forms, found in common phrases, are:

בַּיִת ~ בֵּית (בֵּית חוֹלִים hospital)

חַיִּל ~ חֵיל (חֵיל־שִׁרְיוֹן armored corps)

מִשְׁפָּחָה ~ מִשְׁפַּחַת (note the stress on the last-but-one vowel: מִשְׁפַּחַת לֵוִי the Levy family)

מֶמְשָׁלָה ~ מֶמְשֶׁלֶת (מֶמְשֶׁלֶת יַרְדֵן the government of Jordan)

מִפְלָגָה ~ מִפְלֶגֶת (מִפְלֶגֶת שַׁ״ס the Shass party)

עֵצִים ~ עֲצֵי (עֲצֵי־זַיִית olive trees)

שָׁנָה ~ שְׁנַת (שְׁנַת לִימוּדִים academic year)

שֵׁמוֹת~שְׁמוֹת (שְׁמוֹת־מִשְׁפָּחָה last names)

Any good dictionary lists the construct forms of a noun.

77 Double possessives: בֵּיתָהּ שֶׁל שָׂרָה

In addition to the two possessive constructions already introduced – using שֶׁל (17(a)) and the construct (73(a)) – a third construction is employed in *formal* Hebrew: the *double possessive*. This is the שֶׁל construction with the addition of a possessive suffix on the first noun, referring ahead to (anticipating) the second noun. Thus compare:

שֶׁל possessive:	הַתְּשׁוּבָה שֶׁל יָאִיר	Yair's reply
	הַתְּשׁוּבָה שֶׁל שָׂרָה	Sara's reply
double possessive:	תְּשׁוּבָתָהּ שֶׁל שָׂרָה	Sara's reply
		(*lit.* her reply of Sara)
	תְּשׁוּבָתוֹ שֶׁל יָאִיר	Yair's reply
		(*lit.* his reply of Yair)

Either noun may be singular or plural, thus:

| פָּרוֹתָיו שֶׁל אִיכָּר | the cows of a farmer |
| תְּשׁוּבוֹתֵיהֶם שֶׁל חֲבֵרִים | the replies of friends |

There is no semantic difference between the two possessives. Sometimes the double possessive is preferred for reasons of rhythm or elegance and occasionally for grammatical reasons: even in colloquial usage, the double construction אִשְׁתּוֹ שֶׁל ... is preferred to the single construction הָאִישָׁה שֶׁל ... for saying 'the wife of ...'.

78 Preposition + suffix: בְּלִי, בֵּין, כְּמוֹ

The suffixed forms of כְּמוֹ 'like', בֵּין 'between' and בְּלִי 'without' are as follows:

```
כָּמֹּונִי, כָּמֹוךָ, כָּמֹוךְ, כָּמֹוהוּ, כָּמֹוהָ,
כָּמֹונוּ, כְּמֹוכֶם, כְּמֹוכֶן, כְּמֹוהֶם, כְּמֹוהֶן

בֵּינִי, בֵּינְךָ, בֵּינֵךְ, בֵּינוֹ, בֵּינָהּ,
בֵּינֵינוּ, בֵּינֵיכֶם, בֵּינֵיכֶן, בֵּינֵיהֶם, בֵּינֵיהֶן

בִּלְעָדַי, בִּלְעָדֶיךָ, בִּלְעָדַיִךְ, בִּלְעָדָיו, בִּלְעָדֶיהָ,
בִּלְעָדֵינוּ, בִּלְעָדֵיכֶם, בִּלְעָדֵיכֶן, בִּלְעֲדֵיהֶם, בִּלְעֲדֵיהֶן
```

All three are irregular in their own way:

1 כְּמוֹ changes its vowels to כָּמוֹ, with stress on -מוֹ-, except in 2nd and
   3rd plural.

2 For its plural suffixes, בֵּין switches to the 'heavy' (plural-like) endings
   just like עַל and אֶל in 35(e).

3 בְּלִי has the special stem בִּלְעַד throughout, taking 'heavy' endings.

79–81   NUMERALS

79   Definite numerals: 'the three idiots'

Besides the numerals for 2–10 (listed in (14(a)), Hebrew has some special
numerals for use with *definite* nouns. Contrast:

שְׁלוֹשָׁה אִידְיוֹטִים	three idiots	~	שְׁלוֹשֶׁת הָאִידְיוֹטִים
			the three idiots
שָׁלוֹשׁ מוֹרוֹת	three teachers	~	שְׁלוֹשׁ הַמּוֹרוֹת
			the three teachers

Notice that ה 'the' follows the numeral, as with construct nouns: recall
אֲרוּחַת-הָעֶרֶב 'the supper' in 17(e). (In casual speech, ה *precedes* the
numeral on occasion.)

Such numerals are traditionally called construct numerals because of their similarity in form and syntax to construct nouns, but it is better to call them definite numerals.

The full set of definite numerals is as follows. Observe that in the feminine only '3' has a special 'definite' form in actual pronunciation. We give two forms for feminine 3, 5, 6 and 10: here colloquial speech tends to prefer the masculine form, e.g. שְׁלוֹשֶׁת הַמּוֹרוֹת rather than שְׁלוֹשׁ הַמּוֹרוֹת. Notice also the place of stress for 3, 4, 5, 6 and 10:

	Masc.	Fem.
2	שְׁנֵי	שְׁתֵּי
3	שְׁלוֹשֶׁת	שְׁלוֹשֶׁת/שְׁלוֹשׁ
4	אַרְבַּעַת	אַרְבַּע
5	חֲמֵשֶׁת	חֲמֵשֶׁת/חָמֵשׁ
6	שֵׁשֶׁת	שֵׁשֶׁת/שֵׁשׁ
7	שִׁבְעַת	שֶׁבַע
8	שְׁמוֹנַת	שְׁמוֹנֶה
9	תִּשְׁעַת	תֵּשַׁע
10	עֲשֶׂרֶת	עֲשֶׂרֶת/עֶשֶׂר

Beyond ten, Hebrew just uses the regular numbers, e.g. עֶשְׂרִים הַשְׁלַבִּים 'the twenty stages'.

Construct *suffixes*, too, are possible, for 2, 3, 4 as with nouns, thus:

שְׁנֵינוּ, שְׁנֵיכֶם, שְׁנֵיהֶם	the two of us, of you, of them
שְׁלוֹשְׁתֵּנוּ . . .	the three of us
אַרְבַּעְתֵּנוּ . . .	the four of us

80 Ordinals: 'first, second, third . . .'

The words for 'first, second, third . . .' up to 'tenth' are regular adjectives.
Notice that from 'third' to 'tenth' they share the same vowel pattern:

	Masc.	*Fem.*
1st	רִאשׁוֹן	רִאשׁוֹנָה
2nd	שֵׁנִי	שְׁנִיָּה
3rd	שְׁלִישִׁי	שְׁלִישִׁית
4th	רְבִיעִי	רְבִיעִית
5th	חֲמִישִׁי	חֲמִישִׁית
6th	שִׁשִּׁי	שִׁשִּׁית
7th	שְׁבִיעִי	שְׁבִיעִית
8th	שְׁמִינִי	שְׁמִינִית
9th	תְּשִׁיעִי	תְּשִׁיעִית
10th	עֲשִׂירִי	עֲשִׂירִית

From 'eleventh' on, Hebrew uses the regular numerals, which agree for
gender where appropriate, e.g.

הַתְּלוּנָה הָעֶשְׂרִים	the twentieth complaint
הַתְּלוּנָה הָעֶשְׂרִים וְאַחַת	the twenty-first complaint
הַתְּלוּנָה הָעֶשְׂרִים וּשְׁתַּיִם	the twenty-second complaint

81 Hundreds and thousands

Hundreds have the following forms, for both masculine and feminine
nouns:

100	מֵאָה	600	שֵׁשׁ־מֵאוֹת
200	מָאתַיִם	700	שְׁבַע־מֵאוֹת
300	שְׁלוֹשׁ־מֵאוֹת	800	שְׁמוֹנֶה־מֵאוֹת
400	אַרְבַּע־מֵאוֹת	900	תְּשַׁע־מֵאוֹת
500	חֲמֵשׁ־מֵאוֹת		

Stress is on the first word, as marked. The form of the first word is the same as for '13–19' (recall 14(b)). The second word is reduced to *mot* in fast speech, e.g. *tsha-mot* '900'.

Thousands are as follows. They, too, are neutral in gender:

1,000	אֶלֶף	6,000	שֵׁשֶׁת־אֲלָפִים
2,000	אַלְפַּיִים	7,000	שִׁבְעַת־אֲלָפִים
3,000	שְׁלוֹשֶׁת־אֲלָפִים	8,000	שְׁמוֹנַת־אֲלָפִים
4,000	אַרְבַּעַת־אֲלָפִים	9,000	תִּשְׁעַת־אֲלָפִים
5,000	חֲמֵשֶׁת־אֲלָפִים	10,000	עֲשֶׂרֶת־אֲלָפִים

Again, stress is on the first word, which is the same as the construct masculine form (79), although it is casually pronounced *shlosht*, *chamesht*, etc. rather than *shloshet*, *chameshet*, etc., thus *shlosht-alafim*.

82 Tense

a Past habitual tense: 'I used to . . .'

One way of expressing 'used to' (i.e. 'to have been in the habit of doing something') is to add the *past* tense of היה 'be' to the *present* tense of the verb in question. This is the *compound past* tense:

בְּשַׁבָּת הָיִיתִי קָם בִּשְׁמוֹנֶה
On Shabbat I was in the habit of getting up at eight

הָיִיתִי קָם does *not* mean 'I was getting up (when, e.g., the alarm rang)'. For this, Hebrew uses the simple past tense, perhaps with the addition of בְּדִיּוּק 'just'. See 19(c).

b | *Unreal conditionals: 'If I were . . .'*

A second use of the compound past is in the *unreal conditional*. The English 'unreal conditional' generally involves two clauses, the 'if' clause and the 'would' clause: 'If we knew, we would say'. In English, the 'if' clause has the simple past tense and the 'would' clause has the conditional tense. Hebrew, by contrast, likes to use the compound past in both the 'if' clause *and* the 'would' clause:

אִם הָיִינוּ יוֹדְעִים, הָיִינוּ אוֹמְרִים
If we knew, we would say

לֹא הָיִיתִי סוֹמֶכֶת עָלָיו אִם הָיִיתִי מַכִּירָה אוֹתוֹ
I wouldn't have relied on him if I'd known him

מַה הָיִית אוֹמֶרֶת בִּמְקוֹמִי?
What would you say in my place?

The only exception is when 'if' is לוּ or אִלּוּ. (Formal or elegant Hebrew disapproves of אִם in unreal conditionals.) Then, instead of compound past, the 'if' clause can be in the *simple past*:

אִלּוּ יָדַעְנוּ, הָיִינוּ אוֹמְרִים   If we knew, we would say

Note that such sentences can signify *two* unreal tenses: 'If we'd gone, we would have said', 'If we went, we'd say'. Hebrew has no simple way of making such distinctions.

For the conditional of the verb היה ('would be'), one simply uses the simple past of היה: there is no such thing as הָיָה הוֹיֶה:

אִם זֶה הָיָה מַעֲשִׂי, הַאִם הָיִיתָ מְעוּנְיָין?
If it were feasible, would you be interested?

c | *Tense in reported thought*

The tense of reported speech or thought is as if one were transported to the moment of reporting: it is thus quite unlike English:

הָרוֹפְאִים קָבְעוּ שֶׁהוּא יָמוּת, אַךְ הֵם טָעוּ

The doctors stated that he would die (*lit.* that he will die . . .), but they were wrong

חָשַׁבְתִּי שֶׁאֲנִי מִשְׁתַּגֵּעַ

I thought I was (*lit.* I am . . .) going crazy

d | *Tense with* אִם, כְּשֶׁ *and* תּוֹךְ שֶׁ

אִם 'if', כְּשֶׁ 'when' and תּוֹךְ שֶׁ 'while' commonly take the *future* tense for a future event:

אִם אֵרָדֵם, תָּעִיר אוֹתִי, אוֹ־קֵיי?	If I fall asleep, wake me, OK?
אֲנִי אֲכַבֶּה כְּשֶׁאֲנִי אֵצֵא	I'll turn off when I go out

A quite distinct use of כְּשֶׁ and כַּאֲשֶׁר is for 'while'. Here, formal Hebrew commonly uses the *present* tense even when the whole setting is the past or future:

הַקְּבוּצוֹת צָעֲדוּ עַל־פְּנֵי הַצּוֹפִים, כְּשֶׁהֵן שָׁרוֹת וּמְנוֹפְפוֹת בְּדִגְלוֹנִים

The teams marched past the spectators, while singing and waving flags

הַקּוֹנְסוּל יַחֲזוֹר בְּקָרוֹב לִירוּשָׁלַיִם, תּוֹךְ שֶׁהוּא מוֹתִיר מֵאַחוֹרָיו הַמוֹנֵי מַכָּרִים וַחֲבֵרִים

The consul will soon return to Jerusalem, leaving behind him hosts of acquaintances and friends

Note that English often simply uses a participle (a verb ending in '-ing') to denote 'while'. In Hebrew, this is often just rendered by וְ, thus:

הִיא תָּמִיד יוֹשֶׁבֶת מֵאֲחוֹרָה וּמְקַשְׁקֶשֶׁת

She always sits in the back scribbling

83 The object suffix: לִבְנוֹתוֹ 'to build it'

A fairly common mark of official and literary Hebrew is the suffix to the *verb*, denoting an object pronoun 'it, them, us', etc. meaning exactly the same as אוֹתוֹ, אוֹתִי, etc. Here are two examples:

Suffixed infinitive:

הַאִם כְּדַאי *לְחַנְּכָם* כָּךְ ?
Is it worthwhile to educate them thus?

Suffixed past tense:

לְאַחַר *שֶׁהוֹצִיאוֹ* הַחוּצָה . . .
After he brought him outside . . .

The infinitive is the most commonly suffixed form of the verb. (Many other forms of the verb cannot be suffixed in this way; consult a traditional grammar.)

84 Reflexives: 'myself, yourself . . .'

'Myself, yourself' and so on are usually rendered by the pronoun עַצְמ־ with a suffix:

עַצְמִי, עַצְמְךָ, עַצְמֵךְ, עַצְמוֹ, עַצְמָהּ,
עַצְמֵנוּ, עַצְמְכֶם, עַצְמְכֶן, עַצְמָם, עַצְמָן

Thus:

הִבְטַחְתִּי לְעַצְמִי	I promised myself
לַמֵּד אֶת עַצְמְךָ	teach yourself

The use of אֶת is optional, hence also: לַמֵּד עַצְמְךָ 'teach yourself'.

However, many HITPA'EL and NIF'AL verbs of *physical action* are reflexive in themselves and do not use עַצְמִי etc.:

הִתְלַבֵּשׁ dress oneself   הִתְפַּשֵּׁט get undressed

הִסְתָּרֵק comb one's hair   הִתְקַלֵּחַ take a shower

הִתְנַעֵר shake oneself off   נֶחְתַּךְ cut oneself

נִשְׂרַט scratch oneself

85 'One another'

'One another' is usually expressed by a pair of pronouns:

זֶה . . . זֶה or (more colloquially) אֶחָד . . . הַשֵּׁנִי

The word order is slightly different from English:

דִּיבַּרְנוּ זֶה עִם זֶה   We spoke with one another
                                    (one with another)

הֵם אָהֲבוּ אֶחָד אֶת הַשֵּׁנִי   They loved one another

Thus the first pronoun stands separate from the second, the preposition coming between them.

If the subject noun is feminine, the pronouns will be feminine:

הַחוּלְצָה וְהַחֲצָאִית לֹא מַתְאִימוֹת אַחַת לַשְּׁנִיָּה
The blouse and skirt don't match

אֵין שְׁתֵּי הַמֶּמְשָׁלוֹת מַכִּירוֹת זוֹ בָּזוֹ
The two governments do not recognize one another

86 Experience adjectives: נוֹחַ לִי, קַר לִי 'I'm comfortable, I'm cold'

In 45 we met the constructions טוֹב לְ . . . 'It's good to . . .' and טוֹב שֶׁ . . . 'It's good that . . .' without זֶה, and in 49(b) we saw predicates that can stand completely alone, such as אֶפְשָׁר 'it's possible'.

A third phenomenon, involving many though not all of the same words, is the use of an adjective with an 'experiencer phrase', introduced by לְ. Here, too, no word for 'it' is normally used, thus:

קַר לַחַיֶּלֶת   The soldier's cold
            (cold to the soldier)

טוֹב לִי   I feel fine

לֹא נָעִים לִי   I feel uncomfortable

(הַחַיֶּלֶת קָרָה might signify 'cold to the touch', and אֲנִי טוֹב would mean 'I'm good'.)

87–90   COMPARATIVES

87   Comparative phrases

a יוֹתֵר מ 'more than'

'More successful, more quickly, taller, kinder' and so on are usually rendered by יוֹתֵר, either before or after the adjective. (After the adjective sounds somewhat more elegant.)

יוֹתֵר מְתוּחְכָּם or מְתוּחְכָּם יוֹתֵר   more sophisticated

יוֹתֵר חַם or חַם יוֹתֵר   warmer

Similarly, 'more (dollars)' is יוֹתֵר before the noun: יוֹתֵר דוֹלָרִים.

'Than' in such phrases is usually מ. 'Than me, you' and so on is מִמֶּנִּי, מִמְּךָ, etc., using the normal suffixes set out in 35(c):

יַפָּן צוֹרֶכֶת יוֹתֵר דָּג מִיִשְׂרָאֵל
Japan consumes more fish than Israel

הוּא יוֹתֵר טוֹב מִמֶּנִּי
He's better than me

הוּא מַרְוִויחַ פָּחוֹת מֵאַבָּא
He earns less than Daddy

147

In elegant Hebrew, 'more [adjective] than' is sometimes expressed without יוֹתֵר, by relying just on מְ:

הוּא יִהְיֶה גָּבוֹהַּ מִשְּׁאָר אֶחָיו

He will be taller than the rest of his brothers

b מֵאֲשֶׁר 'than'

For introducing a whole clause or a heavy phrase, one generally uses מֵאֲשֶׁר (or more stylishly: מִשֶּׁ), thus:

הַמְּחִיר גָּבוֹהַּ יוֹתֵר מֵאֲשֶׁר צִיפִּינוּ

The price is higher than we anticipated

זֶה הִצְלִיחַ יוֹתֵר מִשֶּׁבַּפַּעַם הַקּוֹדֶמֶת

It was more successful than last time

c מַסְפִּיק 'too', מִדַי 'enough'

When the words for 'too', מִדַי and יוֹתֵר מִדַי, introduce a clause with 'to', Hebrew uses לְ. Sometimes the לְ is reinforced by בִּשְׁבִיל or מִכְדֵי, thus:

אֲנִי עָיֵף מִדַי לִשְׁמוֹעַ

I'm too tired to listen

יֵשׁ לִי יוֹתֵר מִדַי עֲבוֹדָה בִּשְׁבִיל (or מִכְדֵי) לָצֵאת

I've got too much work to go out

Much the same happens when מַסְפִּיק is followed by a clause. Use בִּשְׁבִיל, כְּדֵי or לְ.

הוּא לֹא מַסְפִּיק אָדִיב כְּדֵי לְפַנּוֹת כֵּסֵא לָעוֹמְדִים בַּתּוֹר

He isn't polite enough to vacate a seat to people standing in line

d *'the more that . . ., the more . . .'*

Hebrew uses שֶׁ כְּכֹל or שֶׁ כָּל כַּמָה to denote 'the more that . . .'. The
ensuing clause may be introduced by כָּךְ or (colloquially) by אָז:

כָּל כַּמָה שֶׁהוּא מִתְעַכֵּב יוֹתֵר, כָּךְ יַעֲלֶה לוֹ הַדָּבָר בְּיוֹקֶר
The more he delays, the more it will cost him

88 'The most . . .'

For *'the most* successful, the tall*est*', colloquial Hebrew uses הֲכִי in front
of the adjective:

הַטִיל הֲכִי מְתוּחְכָּם	the most sophisticated missile
הַיוֹם הֲכִי חַם	the warmest day
הוּא הֲכִי טוֹב	he is the best

Formal Hebrew prefers בְּיוֹתֵר, following the adjective:

הַשַׁדְרָנִית הַמְנוּסָה בְּיוֹתֵר
the most experienced woman broadcaster

To express 'the most money' etc., one uses הֲכִי הַרְבֵּה, as in לִי יֵשׁ הֲכִי
הַרְבֵּה נִסָיוֹן 'I have the most experience'.

89 'As big as': . . . כְּמוֹ

For *'as* big *as, as* clumsy *as'*, Hebrew uses the single word כְּמוֹ:

הִיא כְּבָר גְדוֹלָה כָּמוֹךְ !	She's already as big as you (big like you)
נַיילוֹן אֵינוֹ בָּרִיא כְּמוֹ עוֹר	Nylon is not as healthy as leather

149

90 Measurement: . . . מַה גּוֹדֶל 'How big is . . .'

'How high is it?', 'it's two meters high' and similar measurements are generally rendered in Hebrew not by an adjective but by the *abstract noun* derived from it, using a construct phrase or suffix:

מַה גּוֹבַה הַחֶדֶר ?

How high is the room?
(*what's the height of the room*)

גּוֹבַה הַחֶדֶר שְׁנֵי מֶטֶר

The room's 2 meters high
(*the height of the room is 2 meters*)

Similarly for אוֹרֶךְ 'length', רוֹחַב 'width', שׁוִוי 'worth' and the like.

But when the measurement *qualifies* the noun, one uses . . . בְּגוֹבַה שֶׁל and so on:

זֶה עוֹמֵד בְּחֶדֶר בְּגוֹבַה שֶׁל שְׁנֵי מֶטֶר   It stands in a room 2 meters high

סַמִּים בְּשׁוִוי שֶׁל מִילְיַארְד דוֹלָר   drugs worth a billion dollars

For *comparative* measurement, use בְּ. Word order is flexible:

הַחֶדֶר הַזֶּה בְּשִׁבְעָה מֶטֶר יוֹתֵר אָרוֹךְ מֵהַחֶדֶר הַשֵּׁנִי
This room's 7 meters longer than the other room

שָׁמָה הַבְּגָדִים זוֹלִים יוֹתֵר בְּעֶשְׂרִים אָחוּז !
There the clothes are 20 percent cheaper!

91–6 ADVERBIALS

91 Adverbs of manner: e.g. בִּמְהִירוּת 'quickly'

Hebrew has no automatic way of converting adjectives into adverbs of manner, like 'quick → quickly'. Most commonly, it uses phrases of various types:

(1a)	בְּאוֹפֶן אוֹטוֹמַטִי
(1b)	בְּצוּרָה אוֹטוֹמָטִית automatically *(in an automatic way)*
(2)	בִּזְהִירוּת cautiously *(with caution)*

Type (1) is based directly on the adjective, type (2) on the adjectival noun introduced in 65. Generally speaking, type (1) relates to the action itself and type (2) to the person acting (thus, people are cautious but actions are automatic). As for אוֹפֶן and צוּרָה, there is no significant difference between them. Further examples:

| סְגוֹר בַּעֲדִינוּת ! | Close gently |
| זֶה לֹא מְקוּלְקָל בְּאוֹפֶן קָבוּעַ | It isn't permanently out of order |

A few common adverbs are simply adjectives, used in their masc. sing. form without agreement:

הִיא מַדְפִּיסָה טוֹב	She types well
הֵם הִתְנַהֲגוּ יָפֶה	They behaved nicely
תִּמְשׁוֹךְ חָזָק	Pull hard
תַּעֲבוֹד קָשֶׁה	Work hard
סַע יָשָׁר	Go straight

And also (colloquially)

| גָּרוּעַ or לֹא טוֹב badly | נוֹרָא awfully |
| מְצוּיָּין excellently | |

A few other common adverbs of manner are special one-word forms: מַהֵר 'fast', הֵיטֵב 'well', לְאַט 'slowly'. These cannot be used as adjectives.

92 Echo phrases: e.g. נִיצַח נִצָחוֹן מוּחְלָט 'won decisively'

Where English would use a 'manner adverb', elegant Hebrew sometimes uses an 'echo phrase', i.e. an abstract noun *echoing* the verb, to which is added an adjective of manner:

הַגּוּפוֹת נִקְבְּרוּ שָׁם *קְבוּרָה זְמַנִּית*
The bodies were buried there *temporarily*

נֶאֱנַחְתִּי שָׁלוֹשׁ אֲנָחוֹת אֲרוּכּוֹת
I sighed three long sighs

93 בְּ of time, place and means

Location in time and space is nearly always denoted by בְּ, thus:

בְּשָׁעָה שֵׁשׁ	at 6 o'clock
הִיא לֹא בָּאָה בִּימֵי שֵׁנִי	She doesn't come Mondays
אֵיפֹה הָיִיתָ בַּשָּׁנָה שֶׁעָבְרָה?	Where were you last year?

Similarly:

זֶה בְּבֵית־הַסֵּפֶר	It's at the school
זֶה בְּסַעוּדִיָה	It's in Saudi Arabia

The chief exceptions are the הַ expressions in 94 below, and time phrases with כָּל 'every':

שָׂחִיתִי כָּל יוֹם	I swam every day
כָּל פַּעַם שֶׁ . . .	every time that . . .

'With' (i.e. by means of) is commonly בְּ, but spoken Hebrew also uses עִם:

תְּנַסֶּה בְּשְׁוֵונְדִי	Try with a spanner
תֹּאכַל עִם מַזְלֵג	Eat with a fork

94 הַשָּׁנָה, הַיּוֹם 'today, this year'

הָ denotes not only 'the' but also 'this', with most units of time:

הַיּוֹם	today	הַבּוֹקֶר	this morning
הָעֶרֶב	this evening	הַפַּעַם	this time
הַשָּׁבוּעַ	this week	הַחוֹדֶשׁ	this month
הַקַּיִץ	this summer		

אֵיפֹה הָיִיתָ הַבּוֹקֶר?	Where were you this morning?

95 הָ of destination: e.g. צָפוֹנָה 'northwards'

The normal marker of movement is לְ or suffixed אֶל (e.g. אֵלַי, אֵלֶיךָ ...)
for saying 'to me, to him' etc. (see 35(a) for details). אֶל with no suffix can
be found in higher styles, particularly with other positional prepositions,
e.g. אֶל תּוֹךְ, אֶל מִתַּחַת, אֶל מֵעֵבֶר.

Instead of using לְ for 'to', a handful of words can take the suffix הָ:
צָפוֹנָה 'northwards'. Notice our stress-mark; this הָ is unstressed, and thus
distinct from feminine הָ. And similarly:

דָּרוֹמָה	southwards *(and the other points of the compass)*

יָמִינָה	rightwards	שְׂמֹאלָה	leftwards
הַצִּידָה	to the side		
קָדִימָה	forwards	אֲחוֹרָה	backwards
פְּנִימָה	inside	הַחוּצָה	out
הַבַּיְתָה	home	הָעִירָה	to town
אַרְצָה	to Israel		

The suffix הָ can also colloquially denote position rather than motion:
שָׁמָּה 'there', קָדִימָה 'in front', קְצָת דָּרוֹמָה 'a little to the South'.

96 מְ of location: e.g. מִשְׂמֹאל 'on the left'

מְ ordinarily means 'from'. However, with various prepositions and adverbs of place it means 'at', notably:

עָמַדְנוּ מִסָּבִיב, מִשְׂמֹאל, מִיָּמִין
We stood round about, on the left, on the right

מִשְׂמֹאל לַבַּיִת, מִיָּמִין לַבַּיִת
on the right of, on the left of the house

מִסָּבִיב לַבַּיִת	around the house
מֵעֵבֶר לַבַּיִת	on the other side of the house
מִתַּחַת לַבַּיִת	under the house
מֵעַל לַבַּיִת	above the house

97 The gerund: בְּהַגִּיעוֹ 'on his arrival'

For forming adverbial clauses, particularly 'when' clauses, official or literary Hebrew sometimes uses the *gerund*. This is generally simply the infinitive without לְ. Instead of לְ comes בְּ denoting 'when' or 'while'. Notice the word order. Using the verb לְהַגִּיעַ 'to arrive':

בְּהַגִּיעַ הַנּוֹסְעִים לַמָּסוֹף . . .
When the passengers arrived at the terminal . . .
 (on arrival of the passengers at the terminal . . .)

Most often, the gerund takes a suffixed pronoun:

בְּהַגִּיעֲךָ לַמָּסוֹף, עָלֶיךָ לָרֶדֶת
On arriving at the terminal, one must alight

הִכַּרְתִּי אוֹתוֹ הֵיטֵב בִּהְיוֹתוֹ בְּשַׁבָּתוֹן
I got to know him well when he was on sabbatical

98 Where to position גַם and רַק

גַם 'also, even' and רַק 'only' are 'focus words': they serve to put the focus on a particular noun or phrase. They usually precede the *focused* word(s):

גַם אַרְצוֹת־הַבְּרִית מִתְנַגֶּדֶת	The USA objects, too *(also the USA objects)*
תֵּן לִי רַק שְׁתַּיִם	Just give me two *(give me just two)*

A colloquial alternative to גַם is גַם־כֵּן, at the end of the sentence:

אַרְצוֹת־הַבְּרִית מִתְנַגֶּדֶת גַם־כֵּן	The USA objects, too

99–100 NEGATIVES

99 Inflexion of אֵין

Besides its use as the negative of יֵשׁ (i.e. 'there aren't'), אֵין can mean 'not': in present tense sentences it is a more formal or 'correct' equivalent to לֹא. In this role, אֵין usually has to agree with the subject, by means of a *suffix*:

הַמִּמְשָׁל אֵינוֹ מִתְעָרֵב	The regime does not intervene
הַשִּׁלְטוֹנוֹת אֵינָם מִתְעָרְבִים	The authorities do not intervene
אֲנִי אֵינֶנִּי מוּמְחֶה	I am not an expert

Where the subject is a personal pronoun (אֲנִי, אַתָּה . . .), it can be omitted and אֵינֶנִּי, אֵינְךָ, etc. by themselves can represent 'I do not, I am not' and so on:

אֵינֶנִּי מוּמְחֶה	I am not an expert
אֵינְכֶם אֲשֵׁמִים	You are not at fault

The suffixes of אֵין are generally as follows:

> אֵינֶנִּי, אֵינְךָ, אֵינֵךְ, אֵינוֹ, אֵינָהּ,
> אֵינֶנּוּ, אֵינְכֶם, אֵינְכֶן,אֵינָם, אֵינָן

An alternative to אֵינֶנִּי is אֵינִי. Do not confuse this אֵינִי with אֲנִי.

Note: In elevated style, אֵין can stand in front of the subject rather than after it. In such cases it never inflects:

אֵין הַשִּׁלְטוֹנוֹת מִתְעָרְבִים   The authorities do not intervene

100 'No one, nothing, nowhere, non-, un-, neither'

No one   אַף אֶחָד (colloquial) or אִישׁ (formal)

Nothing   שׁוּם דָּבָר (colloquial), דָּבָר (formal) or כְּלוּם (general)

Never   אַף פַּעַם (colloquial) or formally מֵעוֹלָם, for *past*, and לְעוֹלָם, for *present* and *future*

Nowhere   בְּשׁוּם מָקוֹם

When these negative words are part of a sentence, there also has to be a negator, i.e. אֵין, לֹא or similar:

אַף אֶחָד לֹא שִׁילֵם	No one paid *(no one didn't pay)*
מֵעוֹלָם לֹא הִכַּרְתִּי אוֹתוֹ	I never got to know him
לְעוֹלָם לֹא אַכִּיר אוֹתוֹ	I'll never get to know him
לֹא פִּיסְפַּסְתֶּם כְּלוּם	You didn't miss anything

The same goes for אַף 'a single' and שׁוּם 'no':

לֹא מָצָאתִי אַף טָעוּת   I didn't find a single mistake

But used by themselves, the negative words are intrinsically negative and do not need a לֹא:

מַה יֵּשׁ שָׁמָה ? – כְּלוּם	What's over there? – Nothing
מִי צִילְצֵל ? – אַף אֶחָד	Who called? – No one

To make an adjective negative, one can place לֹא directly in front of it:

הוּא הָיָה קְצָת לֹא נָעִים	He was a bit unpleasant
זֶה מְאֹד לֹא בָּרוּר	It's very unclear

With adjectives formed from verbs or nouns, Hebrew often uses the negative prefix בִּלְתִּי:

בִּלְתִּי־חוּקִי illegal	בִּלְתִּי־מְקוּבָּל unacceptable
בִּלְתִּי־קוֹנְבֶנְצִיוֹנָלִי unconventional	

With action nouns, use the negative prefix אִי־:

הָיְתָה אִי־הֲבָנָה	There was a misunderstanding
אִי־מְסִירַת חֲבִילוֹת	non-delivery of packages

but with nouns denoting a state, the negative prefix is usually חוֹסֶר and sometimes אִי:

חוֹסֶר־יְכוֹלֶת לְהָבִין	inability to understand
אִי־אַחֲרָיוּת or חוֹסֶר־אַחֲרָיוּת	irresponsibility

To express 'neither . . . nor', one may use a double לֹא:

אֶפְשָׁר שֶׁלֹּא יִבְחֲרוּ לֹא בְּזֶה וְלֹא בְּזֶה
It may be that they'll choose neither the one nor the other

101 Questions

a Questions using הַאִם

Questions expecting a 'yes' or 'no' can simply be signaled by tone of voice or question mark (see 39(a)). Alternatively, one can begin with the particle הַאִם, which is particularly common in formal or elegant usage:

הַאִם יֵשׁ לוֹרְדִים?	Are there any felt-tip pens?
הַאִם הֶרְצֶל יָדַע זֹאת?	Did Herzl know this?

Note also that negative questions of the type 'didn't he . . ., aren't you . . .' are simply rendered by adding לֹא (or אֵין) to the Hebrew question:

אֵין לוֹרְדִים? or הַאִם אֵין לוֹרְדִים?
Aren't there any felt-tips?

הֶרְצֶל לֹא יָדַע זֹאת? or הַאִם הֶרְצֶל לֹא יָדַע זֹאת?
Didn't Herzl know this?

But the equivalent of *tags*, such as 'didn't he?, aren't you?' is simply נָכוֹן?.

יֵשׁ שְׁאֵלוֹת, נָכוֹן?
There are questions, aren't there?

אֵין שְׁאֵלוֹת, נָכוֹן?
There aren't any questions, are there?

b Questions using אִם 'whether'

By contrast, *indirect* questions – that is, questions embedded in the overall sentence – start with an אִם, corresponding to 'whether':

אֲנִי לֹא בָּטוּחַ אִם יוֹרָם מְחַכֶּה
I'm not sure whether Yoram's waiting

Although אִם also means 'if' (i.e. 'in the event that . . .'), the two kinds of אִם will rarely be confused.

102 Wishes and requests

a 'I want (him) to . . .' . . . אֲנִי רוֹצֶה שֶׁ

While verbs of wishing such as רָצָה 'want', הֶעֱדִיף 'prefer', קִיוָּה 'hope' take . . . לְ 'to . . .' just as in English, this does not work when one wishes *someone else* to do something. In that case, שֶׁ is used + *future* tense, even if the action is in the past:

| אַתָּה רָצִיתָ שֶׁאַפְסִיק? | Did you want me to stop? |
| אֲנִי מַעֲדִיפָה שֶׁתִּשְׁכַּח מִזֶּה | I prefer you to forget about it |

b Commands with שֶׁ

Related to the preceding construction is the colloquial use of bare שֶׁ to express 'you must . . .' or 'he, she must' (a kind of forceful urging):

שֶׁלֹּא תִּשְׁכַּח	Don't you forget!
שֶׁיַּתְחִילוּ כְּבָר	Let them begin already!
שֶׁלֹּא נֵדַע מְצָרוֹת כָּאֵלֶּה	I hope we never know such troubles

103 'Either . . . or': אוֹ . . . אוֹ

'Either . . . or' with nouns is usually אוֹ . . . אוֹ, thus:

אֶפְשָׁר לְהִשְׁתַּמֵּשׁ אוֹ בְּאָפוֹר אוֹ בְּחוּם
You can use either gray or brown

When introducing a whole clause, Hebrew prefers אוֹ שֶׁ . . . אוֹ שֶׁ . . .:

אוֹ שֶׁתָּטוּס אִתָּנוּ אוֹ שֶׁתְּחַכֶּה עַד הַסְּתָיו
Either fly with us or wait till autumn

Level Two

In fact, a single שׁ או is common for 'or' when there is no 'either':

יֵשׁ עוֹד, אוֹ שֶׁאַתְּ עוֹד לֹא גָמַרְתְּ?
Is there more, or haven't you finished yet?

אֲנִי הוֹלֵךְ בָּרֶגֶל, אוֹ שֶׁאֲנִי לוֹקֵחַ מוֹנִית
I walk, or I take a cab

104 Clauses as subject: 'Painting is fun'

The Hebrew equivalent of the English verbal noun in '-ing' is either the *action noun*, e.g. צְבִיעָה 'painting', or else the *infinitive*, e.g. לִצְבּוֹעַ. For '-ing' as subject of a clause, particularly in speech, one usually finds an infinitive, something like:

לִצְבּוֹעַ זֶה כֵּיף	Painting is fun
לַעֲזוֹר קְצָת זֶה לֹא יַזִּיק לְךָ	Helping a bit isn't going to hurt you
הַבְעָרַת זֶבֶל גּוֹרֶמֶת זִיהוּם	Burning garbage causes pollution

Notice זֶה serving as the verb 'be' here – this often happens after an infinitive in constructions of this kind.

105 Relative clauses

a Relative clauses with a pronoun

The basic relative clause with שׁ for 'who, which' was introduced in 47. But to render 'with whom, with which, for whom, for which' and the like, one must insert an extra pronoun:

הַבָּחוּר שֶׁדִּיבַּרְתִּי אִתּוֹ	the guy I was speaking with
הַדּוּכָן שֶׁקָּנִיתִי בּוֹ פֵּרוֹת	the stall at which I bought fruit

160

This amounts to saying 'the man that I was speaking with him' and 'the
stall that I bought fruit at it': Hebrew's שֶׁ is in fact the equivalent of 'that'.
Formal Hebrew may also insert a pronoun אוֹתוֹ, אוֹתָה to do the work of
'whom, which':

הַמִּמְשָׁל בִּיטֵּל שְׁתֵּי יוֹזְמוֹת, שֶׁאוֹתָן הִנְהִיג הַמִּמְשָׁל הַקּוֹדֵם
The administration has canceled two initiatives which the previous
administration introduced

and this pronoun can even be used without a שֶׁ:

הַמִּמְשָׁל בִּיטֵּל שְׁתֵּי יוֹזְמוֹת, אוֹתָן הִנְהִיג הַמִּמְשָׁל הַקּוֹדֵם

Note in particular how to render 'whose':

סֵפֶר שֶׁהַמְחַבֵּר שֶׁלּוֹ הוּא תֵּימָנִי   a book whose author is a Yemenite
*(a book that the author of it is
a Yemenite)*

Similarly, 'where' is שֶׁ . . . שָׁם or simply שֶׁ . . . בּוֹ, thus:

הַתַּחֲנָה שֶׁחִיכִּינוּ שָׁם   the stop where we waited
(. . . that we waited there)

---

b   *מַה שֶׁ . . ., מִי שֶׁ . . ., אֵיפֹה שֶׁ . . .*

To express 'what I did, where I was, the person who rang', Hebrew
employs a special type of relative clause. It makes use of the question
words אֵיפֹה, מִי, מַה – but not, of course, as a question:

מָחַקְתִּי מַה שֶׁהִדְפַּסְתִּי   I erased what I typed

מִי שֶׁצִּלְצֵל לֹא הִזְדַּהָה   The person who called didn't
identify himself

תְּחַכֶּה אֵיפֹה שֶׁהַמּוֹנִיּוֹת עוֹמְדוֹת   Wait where the taxis are standing

To express 'whatever, whoever, wherever . . .', one often uses כָּל מַה,
כָּל מִי, בְּכָל מָקוֹם שֶׁ . . .:

הִיא מוֹחֶקֶת כָּל מַה שֶׁאֲנִי מַדְפִּיס   She erases whatever I type

כָּל מִי שֶׁיְנַחֵשׁ נָכוֹן יִזְכֶּה בְּפְּרָס   Whoever guesses right will win a prize

c Relative clauses with הַ

The relative clauses introduced thus far have the conjunction שֶׁ. Formal
Hebrew has an alternative, using הַ instead of שֶׁ in relative clauses like the
following:

מְכוֹנוֹת הַחוֹסְכוֹת בְּאֶנֶרְגִיָה   machines that save energy

הַ is permissible here because:

1   the subject of חוֹסְכוֹת is understood to be none other than the
    'antecedent noun', מְכוֹנוֹת, i.e. the *machines* are saving energy;

2   the verb חוֹסְכוֹת is in the present tense.

By contrast, the following relative clauses cannot have הַ, because the
subject of רָכַשְׁנוּ is understood to be אֲנַחְנוּ, not מְכוֹנוֹת (i.e. *we* did the
acquiring, not the machines):

מְכוֹנוֹת שֶׁרָכַשְׁנוּ עַתָּה   machines that we just acquired

or because the verb is not in the present tense:

מְכוֹנוֹת שֶׁחָסְכוּ בְּאֶנֶרְגִיָה   machines that saved energy

A final point: do not confuse this הַ with הַ meaning 'the'.

106 When the order is not subject–verb–object

The basic word order, subject–verb–object, is frequently overturned, with
confusing results.

a | Inverting subject and verb

1 Where the sentence begins not with the subject but with an adverb, an adverbial clause or the like, Hebrew often puts the verb ahead of the subject, making things 'lighter' and more 'balanced':

עַכְשָׁיו נֶעֶלְמוּ שְׁנֵיהֶם   Now both have vanished
(now have vanished both)

לְאַחַר שֶׁנוֹלַדְתִּי שָׁבוּ הוֹרַי אַרְצָה   After I was born my parents returned to Israel
(. . . returned my parents to Israel)

This also happens *inside* adverbial clauses and relative clauses. Observe what happens to subject + verb after אִם and לְאַחַר, for instance:

. . . לְאַחַר שֶׁגָּדְלוּ שְׁנֵי אַחַי   After my two brothers grew up, . . .

. . . אִם יִתְאַמְּתוּ דְּבָרָיו   If his words come true, . . .

and within the relative clause following שֶׁ:

כָּל מַה שֶׁרָאוּ עֵינַי הָיָה עָלוּב וּמוּזְנָח
All that my eyes saw was miserable and neglected

A similar situation arises when the sentence begins with an interrogative:

מָתַי חָזְרוּ הוֹרֶיךָ אַרְצָה?   When did your parents return to Israel?

כַּמָּה עוֹלִים הַחֲצִילִים?   How much do the eggplants cost?

However, where the subject is a pronoun, inversion of subject and verb is generally avoided:

מָתַי הֵם חָזְרוּ?   When did they return?

כַּמָּה זֶה עוֹלֶה?   How much does it cost?

2 As in English, a direct quotation is followed by an inversion:

"דַּי", אָמְרָה אֲחוֹתִי   'Stop it,' said my sister

b Starting with the object

Whereas English tends to use *tone of voice* for marking the focus and non-focus of a sentence, Hebrew tends to use *word order*. Thus, to indicate that a noun is already the topic of conversation or already in the hearer's mind, Hebrew likes to have it first in the sentence, even if it is the object:

אֶת הָרַדְיוֹ אַתָּה יָכוֹל לָקַחַת   You can take the radio
(implying: 'I know you're thinking about it already . . .' or 'by contrast with the other things . . .')

Similarly, to highlight a contrast or to stress a word, Hebrew likes to change the normal word order:

עוּגִיּוֹת אֲנִי קָנִיתִי, קְרָקֶרִים אֲנִי קָנִיתִי, אֲבָל וַפְלִים אֲנִי שָׁכַחְתִּי
I bought cookies, I bought crackers, but I forgot wafers

סוּבָּרוּ אַתָּה רוֹצֶה לִמְכּוֹר?   You want to sell a Subaru?

נְבֵלוֹת כָּל הָעִיתּוֹנָאִים הָאֵלֶה!   All these journalists are scum!

Such effects can be subtle in the extreme, and hard to define; but speakers of any language will know them when they hear them.

c Presentative verbs

When a subject noun is being presented or introduced, it is commonly held back for effect – with the 'presentative' verb coming first:

קַיָּם חֲשָׁשׁ שֶׁהַפְּרוֹיֶיקְט לֹא יְאוּשַׁר
A risk exists that the project will not be approved

הִגִּיעַ הַזְּמָן לִפְעוֹל   The time has come to act

פָּנוּ אֵלֵינוּ שְׁלוֹשָׁה מוּעֲמָדִים   Three candidates have applied to us

יוֹרֵד גֶּשֶׁם   It's raining (*lit.* descends rain)

107 Backtracking

Hebrew, both colloquial and formal, sometimes begins sentences with the *topic* under discussion and then backtracks to the subject. (This is known as ייחוד.)

הַמוֹנִית הַזֹּאת, מִי הִזְמִין אוֹתָהּ?
This cab, who ordered it?

אָז הַקַּבְּלָן הַזֶּה, אֲנִי רוֹאֶה שֶׁהוּא סִידֵּר אוֹתְךָ
So this builder, I see that he ripped you off

This is particularly common in sentences of 'having' and 'containing': besides:

לִמְרַכֵּז הַמֶּשֶׁק יֵשׁ הַרְבֵּה אוֹיְבִים
The farm manager has many enemies

it is equally common to say or write:

מְרַכֵּז הַמֶּשֶׁק יֵשׁ לוֹ הַרְבֵּה אוֹיְבִים
The farm manager has (lit. he has) many enemies

Similarly:

פֶּרֶק זֶה יֵשׁ בּוֹ עֲשָׂרָה סְעִיפִים
This chapter has (lit. there are in it) ten sections

108 Israeli spelling

For students writing Hebrew or using any kind of dictionary, the habits of Israeli spelling are a severe headache.

In a nutshell, Hebrew writers followed two separate spelling standards until the nineteenth century. Biblical Hebrew had been sparing in its use of vowel letters, hence it has הָלַךְ more commonly than הוֹלֵךְ, שֻׁלְחָן rather than שׁוּלְחָן and so on, though there were no hard and fast rules. This was the ongoing practice of Hebrew poets. By contrast, post-Biblical Hebrew made very full use of vowel letters, and this practice was followed by most prose writers and copyists through the ages.

Came the nineteenth century, and many Maskilim ('modern-minded' intellectuals) insisted on reverting to Biblical spelling, especially teachers. And when the quasi-official Vaad Halashon determined the spelling rules for schools in Eretz Yisrael early in the twentieth century, it actually insisted on Biblical spelling even where no nikkud was being used: ארך rather than ארוך, הכנס rather than הוכנס, דבר rather than דיבר.

This is still the practice of many dictionaries. But the adult public, and many publishers and newspapers, went on spelling with full vowel letters as they always had. There were thus two spelling systems in simultaneous use.

After the State was established, the Hebrew Language Academy in Jerusalem tried to simplify things, but no one paid much attention. Finally in 1970, its journal *Leshonenu La'am* published the Academy's full official rules for spelling native Hebrew words (without nikkud).

These rules have some official force, and some newer dictionaries have adopted them, but the public and press still cling to old habits.

These rules *are* worth knowing, as a firm basis. They are rather complex, and are best explained by an experienced teacher. Here they are in a nutshell:

1   All 'u' sounds are to be written as ו, thus:

טומאה, שולחן, הופל, כולם

2   The 'cholam' is to be written as ו, thus:

בוקר, קודש, יופי, לשמור, הכול

Exceptions:

לא, צאן, ראש, שמאל, כה, פה, איפה, יאבד, תאמר, (construct) כל

3   Most 'i' sounds in an open syllable are to be written with י, thus:

דיבור, יישוב, חמישה, עיור (+ עיורים), חיטה, מגילה, זימן (+זימנה), ניתן, תישמר, שנייה

Do not use י for 'i' in a closed syllable:

שמחה, מכתב, דמיון, תשמור, שמרו (שָׁמְרוּ), הלבשת

4   When י is 'y', it is best written as a *single* י at the beginning of the word: ילד, הילד, and as a *double* י elsewhere: סוסיי, צייר, התיישבות. Exceptions:

Use a single י next to another vowel letter (as in מסוים) and in nouns of the pattern קיץ, בית.

Exercises

The following exercise numbers correspond to the grammar section of the same number in Level 1 or Level 2.

2 'Me Tarzan, you Jane'

2a

Translate 2a through to 5:

1 Noam's clever, in fact all the family's clever.
2 The dog's filthy, absolutely filthy!
3 Ronit and Chagit are happy now.
4 The camera's wonderful.
5 The cat's so soft.
6 Now the dog's clean.
7 The dog and the cat are so clever.

2b

1 The radio is from Uncle Zvi.
2 The video is under the TV.
3 Dov's already in Israel.
4 This is probably for Grandpa or Grandma.
5 Chana's always with Shula and the kids.

2c

1 The neighbor is a lawyer.
2 The tape-recorder is a present for Mommy.
3 The computer is a bit of a problem.
4 Sometimes Jackie is really a pain-in-the-neck.
5 Daddy is a lawyer, too.
6 Rachel is a nurse.
7 Rachel is the nurse from Hadassa.
8 Chaim is the lawyer from New Jersey.

3 The personal pronouns

1 You're hungry, Moshe and Chaim?
2 And Yafa and Shoshana? They're also busy?
3 You're first, Tirtza.
4 She and I are still very busy.
5 Hey, Benny, is that you? It's me again.

4 The definite article

1 The blanket's in the drier.
2 I'm going back to the store.
3 Something's burning in the kitchen.
4 I put food from the micro-wave straight on the table.
5 What? You throw bottles right away into the garbage?
6 It's either in the oven or on the gas.
7 The sheet's in the closet.
8 So you're going to the mountains?
9 No, the opposite, I'm going to the sea.
10 Maybe the blanket's on the line on the balcony.

5 'a, some'

1 Some friends came from the Galilee.
2 I'm buying some postcards with views of Jerusalem and Hebron.
3 Dudu is visiting in Haifa with some relatives.
4 In Beer-Sheva there's usually some time for some Coca-Cola.
5 There are some yoghurts in the fridge, darling.

6 Masculine and feminine nouns

Depending on whether the noun is masculine or feminine, add יָפֶה or יָפָה 'beautiful':

חֶדֶר, גִּינָה, דִּירָה, קִיר, מִרְפֶּסֶת, חַלּוֹן, בַּיִת, הוֹל, דֶּלֶת, אַמְבַּטְיָה, סָלוֹן, וִילָה, מִטְבָּח, רִצְפָּה, מִקְלָט

And for these, add יָפִים or יָפוֹת:

סָלוֹן וּמִטְבָּח, רִצְפָּה וְתִקְרָה, הוֹל וּכְנִיסָה, אַמְבַּטְיָה וְכִיּוֹר, דֶּלֶת וְחַלּוֹן, מִרְפֶּסֶת וְגִינָה, דִּירוֹת וְוִילוֹת

7 The feminine and plural of nouns

7a וֹת and יִם

Give the plural of:

סְוֶדֶר, חוּלְצָה, חֲצָאִית, חֲגוֹרָה, שַׂרְווּל, גּוּפִיָּה, מְעִיל, דּוּבּוֹן, כִּיפָּה, כּוֹבַע, עֲנִיבָה, סַנְדָּל

1 The family spent five hard years in camps for immigrants.

2 The soldiers came in trucks, buses, cars, and even in cabs.

3 They haven't put handles on all the drawers.

4 In the apartment there are a few beds.

5 There are also some dirty tables.

6 Customers rarely keep till-receipts.

7 There are many cases of unemployment.

8 These structures are dangerous.

9 Tenured teachers will receive compensation.

7b | The type דָּבָר

Give the plural of:

בָּרָק, מָטוֹס, מָדוֹר, מַצְלֵמָה, מַחְשֵׁב, מָסוֹק, פַּרְפַּר, שָׁפָן, נָמֵל, סַפָּר, חַיָּיט,
כָּבֵד, חָבֵר, חָתָן, בַּלָּשׁ

and of:

יָעֵל, טַיָּיס, רָחֵל, מַרְבָד, עָקֵב, טַבָּח, נָחָשׁ, קַצָּב, אָבִיב, צָעִיף, שָׁעוֹן, כַּדּוּר,
עַכְבָּר

7c | The type סֶרֶט

Give the plural of:

בֶּרֶז, כֶּתֶר, בּוֹרֶג, מֶלֶךְ, צֶבַע, כֶּנֶס, זֶרַע, כּוֹתֶל, בֶּלֶם, סֶלַע, שַׁעַר, לַחַץ,
קֶבֶר, שֶׁלֶג, נַחַל, תּוֹאַר, שֶׁקֶר

and of:

עֵדֶר, חֵפֶץ, חֶסֶד, עֵמֶק, גֶּשֶׁם, שֶׁלֶט, אֶפֶס, אֶבֶן, קוֹמֶץ, קֹצֶר, עֶבֶד, קֶרֶשׁ,
חֶדֶר, עֵבֶר, יַעַד, בּוֹחַן, אֶלֶף

7d | Plural of ות

1 Take advantage of all the opportunities.

2 Embassies make lots of mistakes.

3 All his priorities are wrong.

4 Because of the heat they've cancelled some activities.

5 New developments in the Middle East?

6 Commitments about rights of immigrants? Nonsense.

7e *Feminine denoting people*

1 This is a photo of the Queen as a little girl.

2 Ofra Haza is even a star in the USA.

3 Our neighbor, Ofra, is a teacher in some high school.

4 He's marrying a French woman apparently.

5 Like the other Russian woman in the building, she's a doctor.

6 You're looking for a good typist?

7 Well, there's Natasha – she's a student from the USSR.

8 She's an artist, I think, or maybe an actress.

9 Naava is a lawyer in Ramle.

8 **The feminine and plural of adjectives**

8a *The simplest adjective type*

Give the plural of these adjectives:

קוֹמוּנִיסְטִית, דֶמוֹקְרָטִי, רַע, אַחֲרוֹנָה, נֶחְמָד, קַר, נִפְלָאָה, זְוַעֲתִי, אִיטִית,
אַנְגְלִי, אַמֶרִיקָאִית

8b *Adjectives ending in הָ*

Put anything singular into the plural:

1 הַפֶּרַח שָׁם כָּל־כָּךְ יָפֶה 2 יֵשׁ רַק צֶבַע כֵּהֶה 3 הִיא גָרָה בְּדִירָה נָאָה
4 אֲנִי רוֹצֶה תִּקְרָה עָבָה

8c *The type גָּדוֹל*

Give the masculine plural of these adjectives:

סָבִיר, אָדִיר, סָגוּר, כַּבִּיר, תָּמִים, צָמֵא, חָדָשׁ, רָעֵב, יַצִּיב, יָעִיל, נָבוֹן,
מַצְחִיק, עָשִׁיר, קָצָר, רָחָב

9 יֶלֶד קָטָן

1 I need a cheap lamp – which lamp is cheap?

2 We want good pillows – a good pillow is important.

3 Chests of drawers are so expensive. Is this a strong chest of drawers?

4 You like a warm duvet? Great, every duvet here is warm.

10 Quantity phrases

1 A lot of tax 2 All the bargains 3 A few sales 4 Most prices 5 A little discount 6 More bills 7 Several receipts 8 A hundred customers 9 In twenty installments 10 How much Value Added Tax? 11 Sixty percent 12 One supermarket 13 A few shops

11 'This . . ., the same . . ., which . . .'

1 Which pajamas? 2 Any suit 3 A coat like this (=such a coat) 4 The same bathrobe 5 What blouse, the blouse over there? 6 This coat 7 That jacket 8 Such a zipper 9 Any skirt is OK. 10 It's a sort of belt. 11 Which outfit is good for Rosh Hashanah? 12 She's wearing a sort of Arab dress. 13 I need the same button, of course. 14 What pants do you have? 15 Which hanger is good for that sweater?

12 Agreement of ה

12a Noun + adjective

1 The next festival 2 The great day 3 The special celebration 4 On the first day 5 Till the big fast 6 In the last heatwave 7 The long summer 8 For the coming spring 9 The beautiful autumns 10 The second winter 11 Silly Danny 12 Stupid Dr Frankenstein 13 Dr Frankenstein's brilliant. 14 Where's the new booklet from the Hebrew University? 15 Who wrote the long article on it for the religious newspaper? 16 The other book's on the small bookcase.

12b Noun + זֶה

1 Who is this author, anyway?
2 This form is compulsory.
3 This circular is the final warning.
4 I was coming back from this meeting . . .
5 . . . And this guy suddenly shouts.

13 Agreement for gender and number

13a Adjectives

1 The pictures are gorgeous.
2 The old mirror's worth a lot.
3 Yuk, the stairs are still dirty.
4 There are some colored rugs.
5 Where, in the big bathroom upstairs?

13c Particles of being

1 Rachel is a kindergarten teacher.
2 Dov and Ya'ir are engineers.
3 Dov is also a lecturer in Bar-Ilan.
4 Her friends are either secretaries or clerks.

13d Determiners

1 That suggestion 2 Such ideas 3 The same agreements 4 Which complaints? 5 That nonsense 6 Such pleasure 7 This baby girl 8 These brainwaves 9 Any problems 10 Such a blessing

13e Quantity words

1 How many combs? 2 More soap and water 3 Less dirt 4 Several Italian films 5 Lots of tables and chairs 6 How much furniture? 7 Too much furniture 8 Enough armchairs 9 Many perfumes 10 Fewer baths
11 Few Israelis take a bath. 12 Most Israelis take showers. 13 You didn't find a toilet? But there are loads of toilets here!

14 Numerals

14a

1 Three bottles 2 Six cups and six glasses 3 Two trays 4 Five knives
5 One kettle 6 We need two menus. 7 Three saucepans 8 Four teaspoons 9 There are only three restaurants. 10 Eight waiters and ten waitresses 11 Four wine-glasses 12 Nine napkins 13 Nine bowls for cereal 14 Two can-openers, one meaty and one dairy 15 Two forks and two spoons

14b

1 Twelve stamps 2 Sixteen air-letters 3 Eleven postcards 4 Nineteen letters to Israel and fourteen to overseas 5 Thirteen small packages
6 Eighteen telegrams 7 Twelve official letters 8 Fifteen forms
9 Nineteen calls today 10 There are seventeen mail-boxes at the entrance.

14c

1 Ninety kibbutzim 2 Thirty-three moshavs 3 Eighty-seven villages
4 Twenty-two vineyards 5 Sixty orchards along the highway 6 Forty-nine trees 7 Seventy-five fields 8 About fifty or sixty tracks 9 Over eighty farms

15 Partitives: 'many of the . . ., all of the . . .'

1 Most of the eggs are off!

2 The rest of the butter is on the plate.

3 On some of the sandwiches there's margarine and on some there's mayonnaise.

4 Three of the challahs are no good – they fell on the ground.

5 How much of the milk is left?

6 The kids have finished nearly all of the jelly!

7 How many of the guys want hummus and pitta?

8 Many of the products aren't kosher.

9 I've put juice in four of the glasses.

16 Pronouns etc.

16a Definite pronouns

1 Your passport, honey? It's in the small bag.

2 Here's a trolley, thank heavens. Oh no, it's broken.

3 Come over to this line, it's moving.

4 The plane's late again, it's a disgrace!

5 I have two suitcases – is that OK?

6 Four plastic bags and a shoulder bag! It's a cheek.

16b Indefinite pronouns

1 Someone's pushing. Hey, what's happening here?

2 Hang on, I'm asking something at the counter.

3 We're landing at an airport somewhere in Europe.

4 Come to visit some time.

5 Is someone checking the tickets?

6 Once they did a check in customs, do you remember?

7 Is something wrong?

8 There's a message for someone called Gila.

16c Adjectives without their noun

1 This plum's no good? Then here's another one.

2 I don't like those apples. Do you have a red one?

3 What, you're not eating this one? I don't have any more fruit!

4 Those grapes are the black ones – they're sour.

16d *Numerals without their noun*

1 How many mistakes did you find? I found five.

2 One moment, does this word have one meaning or two?

3 You only speak one language? In Israel many people speak six or seven.

17 **Possessives and constructs**

17a *Possessive 'of'*

1 Ben-Gurion's influence 2 Whose promise? 3 Britain's promise
4 Egypt's aims 5 Begin's concessions 6 Hussein's plans 7 Whose brother
are you? 8 Whose are those sandals on the floor? Menachem's or
Shimon's?

17b *'My, your'*

1 Her Fiat 2 Your Peugeot 3 My Volvo 4 Their stupidity 5 Your sense
6 Our experience 7 His sister 8 My girl-friend 9 I love your wig, Chava.
10 I like your shtreimel, Gershon.

17c *The construct: set phrases*

1 A pear tree 2 An olive tree 3 A tennis match 4 A soccer pitch 5 A
summer camp 6 A camp director 7 Apple juice 8 Orange juice 9 A juice
carton 10 An orange grove 11 Chicken meat 12 Life insurance

17d *Construct endings*

1 Mitzi the cat wants breakfast.

2 My sister-in-law is a beauty queen.

3 Natan has written to an insurance company.

4 There are at least three insurance companies on this street.

5 Good TV programs!

6 TV sets are expensive.

7 Video sets are just as expensive.

8 I got a video camera.

9 How much did you pay for wedding photos?

10 I hate receptions.

17e *ה in construct phrases*

1 The school 2 The hospital 3 The lunches 4 The synagogue 5 The circumcision 6 The swimsuit 7 The barmitzvah 8 The barmitzvah suit 9 The video set 10 The video camera 11 How much does the swimsuit cost? 12 The school costs a lot of money. 13 The treatment at this hospital is free. 14 When is the service at the synagogue on Friday night? 15 Is the circumcision at the synagogue or at home?

19 The past tense

19a *Form of the past tense*

Using the verb זָז 'move', give the appropriate past tense forms:

‎1 אַתָּה... ‏2 אֲנַחְנוּ... ‏3 אֲנִי... ‏4 הֵם... ‏5 אַתְּ... ‏6 הֵן...
‎7 אַתֶּם... ‏8 הוּא... ‏9 אַתֶּן... ‏10 הִיא... ‏11 דָנִי וְבֶנִי...
‎12 הַתּוֹר... ‏13 אֲנִי... ‏14 הַשַּׁבְּלוּל... ‏15 הִיא...

and now using the verb שָׁר 'sing':

‎1 אַתָּה... ‏2 אֲנַחְנוּ... ‏3 אֲנִי... ‏4 הֵם... ‏5 אַתְּ... ‏6 הֵן...
‎7 אַתֶּם... ‏8 הוּא... ‏9 אַתֶּן... ‏10 הִיא... ‏11 דָנִי וְבֶנִי...
‎12 הָעוֹרֵב... ‏13 אֲנִי... ‏14 הַחַזָּן... ‏15 הִיא...

19b *Syntax of the past tense*

1 I've moved. 2 The cow's moved. 3 The cockroach has moved. 4 The sheep have moved. 5 The baby's moved. 6 She's just moved. 7 You've moved, dope! 8 We moved slightly. 9 The lizard's moved. 10 Have the flies moved? 11 He moved. 12 Immediately, she moved.

19c *Meaning of the past tense*

1 When did he last rest? 2 She was resting a moment ago! 3 It's all right, I've already rested. 4 We rested all the evening. 5 Devorah was just resting. 6 Sorry, Esther, were you resting?

20 The present tense

1 OK, OK, we're moving soon.
2 The old man moves very slowly.
3 Why are Esther and Yehudit moving all the time?
4 It's moving. Well done!
5 You're moving slightly, Yael.
6 The car's moving! Quick, third gear!

Exercises

21 The future tense

21a Form of the future tense

Using the verb זָז 'move', give the appropriate future tense forms:

אַתָּה ... 1   אֲנַחְנוּ ... 2   אֲנִי ... 3   הֵם ... 4   אַתְּ ... 5   הֵן ... 6
אַתֶּם ... 7   הוּא ... 8   אַתֶּן ... 9   הִיא ... 10   דָּנִי וְבְנִי ... 11
הַתּוֹר ... 12   אֲנִי ... 13   הַשַּׁבְּלוּל ... 14   הִיא ... 15

and now using the verb שָׁר 'sing':

אַתָּה ... 1   אֲנַחְנוּ ... 2   אֲנִי ... 3   הֵם ... 4   אַתְּ ... 5   הֵן ... 6
אַתֶּם ... 7   הוּא ... 8   אַתֶּן ... 9   הִיא ... 10   דָּנִי וְבְנִי ... 11
הָעוֹרֵב ... 12   אֲנִי ... 13   הַחַזָּן ... 14   הִיא ... 15

21b Use of the future tense

1 Rest a few minutes, David.
2 Chana, rest a while, too.
3 I'll rest half an hour and that's enough.
4 Children, move right away!
5 If you'll move, buddy, I'll move.
6 But will they really rest?
7 Don't move, guys!
8 Chava, please don't rest now.
9 A scorpion, Yosef – don't move at all!
10 He'll rest afterwards.

22 Form and use of the imperative

1 Go to another till.
2 Come after the lunch-hour.
3 Put these checks into the account.
4 Get down from there, sweetheart.
5 Leave off, I'm busy.
6 Temporary fault. Please wait.
7 In event of fire, leave through the emergency exit.
8 Take the money and the receipt.
9 Give more to charity.
10 Sit and wait. Do not run.
11 The engine's running, so go!
12 Put the checkbook into the folder.

24 Root and base

Write separately (without *nikkud*) the root, base, and prefix or suffix of any of these verbs:

שִׁיפַּרְתִּי 1 הָלַכְתִּי 2 קִיבַּלְתִּי 3 דִּיבְּרוּ 4 אָקוּם 5 תָּקוּמוּ 6 יָשׁוּבוּ 7
טִיפֵּל 8

Identify the meanings of these groups of words, and debate whether they are semantically related by virtue of sharing the same root letters:

ס.פ.ר: סַפִּיר, סִפְרָה, סַפָּר, מִסְפָּר, הִסְתַּפֵּר, סֵפֶר, סִיפֵּר, סָפַר 1
ס.מ.ך: הִסְתַּמֵּךְ, סַמְכוּת, סָמַךְ עַל, סָמִיךְ, מוּסְמָךְ 2
ז.כ.ר: זָכַר, הִזְכִּיר, זָכָר, מַזְכֶּרֶת, מַזְכִּירוּת 3
ד.ב.ר: דִּיבֵּר, הִדְבִּיר, דְּבוֹרָה, דֶּבֶר, מִדְבָּר, דַּבְרָן, הַדַּבְרוּת, דָּבָר 4
ש.ל.ם: שָׁלוֹם, נִשְׁלַם, תַּשְׁלוּם, שָׁלֵם, מוּשְׁלָם, הִשְׁלִים עִם מַשֶּׁהוּ 5
ס.פ.ק: מַסְפִּיק, סָפֵק, הִסְפִּיק (לַעֲשׂוֹת), אַסְפָּקָה, סַפְקָנוּת, סִיפֵּק 6
ע.נ.ה: עָנָה, עִינָה, תַּעֲנִית, עָנִי, מַעַן 7

25 Word patterns: *binyanim* and *mishkalim*

25b *Functions of the verb patterns*

Which *binyanim* do these verbs belong to? (They are all in the past tense.)

נִשְׁבַּר 1 קָבַץ 2 טוּפַּל 3 הוּכְפַּל 4 הִתְמַצֵּא 5 דָּחַף 6 שׁוּתַּף 7
נִרְדַּף 8 הִתְלַבֵּט 9 מוּקַם 10 הִרְגִּישׁ 11 הוּזְהַר 12 נִלְמַד 13
חוּנַּךְ 14 פָּתַר 15 הוּרְגַּשׁ 16

Form the passives of:

הִכְנִיס 1 גָּזַל 2 לָקַח 3 נִיתֵּק 4 בָּחַר 5 הִטְרִיד 6 סִילֵּק 7 הִזְכִּיר 8
שָׁמַר 9 בִּיטֵל 10

On the basis of probability, and given the meaning of the first word, what might the second word mean?

1 רָטוֹב 'wet': שָׁכַב *הִרְטִיב* 2 'lie down': *הִשְׁכִּיב* 3 פָּחַד 'be afraid': *הִפְחִיד*
4 גָּבוֹהַּ 'high': *הִגְבִּיהַּ* 5 קִיצֵר 'shorten': *הִתְקַצֵּר* 6 פִּיתַּח 'develop': *הִתְפַּתַּח*
7 רוֹקֵן 'to empty': *הִתְרוֹקֵן* 8 פִּיזֵּר 'disperse': *הִתְפַּזֵּר* 9 שָׁמֵן 'fat': *הִשְׁמִין*
10 לָבָן 'white': *הִלְבִּין* 11 נִכְנַע 'surrender': *הִכְנִיעַ* 12 שָׁפֵל 'lowly': *הִשְׁפִּיל*
13 זָרַק 'throw': *נִזְרַק* 14 שִׁיפֵּץ 'renovate': *שׁוּפַּץ* 15 הִקְטִין 'reduce': *הוּקְטַן*
16 נִיתֵּק 'sever': *הִתְנַתֵּק* 17 עִבְרִית 'Hebrew': *עִבְרֵת* 18 טֶלֶפוֹן 'telephone': *טִילְפֵּן*
19 חִיבֵּק 'hug (someone)': *הִתְחַבֵּק* 20 תַּמְלִיל 'script': *תִּמְלֵל* 21 נִכְנַס 'enter': *הִכְנִיס*

26 Two-syllable and one-syllable PA'AL

Put שָׁטַף 'to rinse', זָרַק 'to throw', שָׁמַר 'to keep', טָס 'to fly', רָץ 'to run', שָׂם 'to put', בָּא 'to come' into the appropriate past tense forms:

1 אַתָּה ... 2 אֲנַחְנוּ ... 3 אֲנִי ... 4 הֵם ... 5 אַתְּ ... 6 הֵן ...

7 אַתֶּם ... 8 הוּא ... 9 אַתֶּן ... 10 הִיא ... 11 דָּנִי וּמַיָה ...

12 הַסַּמָּל ... 13 אֲנִי ... 14 הַסַּפָּר ... 15 הִיא ...

and into the appropriate future tense:

1 אַתֶּן ... 2 הִיא ... 3 דָּנִי וּבְנִי ... 4 הַסַּמָּל ... 5 אֲנִי ...

6 הַסַּפָּר ... 7 הִיא ... 8 אַתָּה ... 9 אֲנַחְנוּ ... 10 אֲנִי ...

11 הֵם ... 12 אַתְּ ... 13 הֵן ... 14 אַתֶּם ... 15 הוּא ...

Turn into the singular or into the plural:

1 חוֹרְשׁוֹת 2 קוֹצְרִים 3 טוֹחֶנֶת 4 גּוֹזֵז 5 אוֹרְגוֹת 6 קוֹשֵׁר 7 תּוֹפְרִים

8 סוֹתֶרֶת 9 בָּאִים 10 גָּרָה 11 בָּאוֹת 12 גָּר 13 צָפוֹת 14 צָפָה

15 גָּרִים

Give the infinitive and the action noun for:

1 שָׁטַף 2 זָרַק 3 שָׁמַר 4 קָצַר 5 טָחַן 6 גָּזַז 7 רָחַץ 8 מָשַׁךְ

9 נָשַׁךְ 10 דָּהַר 11 רָץ 12 שָׁב 13 לָן 14 שָׁר

27 Binyan HIF'IL

Put הִקְלִיט 'to record', הִרְבִּיץ 'to hit', הִגְדִּיר 'to define', הִזְנִיחַ 'to neglect', הִשְׁפִּיעַ 'to influence' into the appropriate past tense forms:

1 אֲנַחְנוּ ... 2 אַתָּה ... 3 הֵם ... 4 אֲנִי ... 5 אַתֶּם ... 6 אַתְּ ...

7 הֵן ... 8 אַתֶּן ... 9 הוּא ... 10 יוֹסִי וְצְבִי ... 11 מִי ...

12 הִיא ... 13 הָאָחוֹת ... 14 הַחֶבְרָ'ה ... 15 שָׂרָה וְלֵאָה וְאֲנִי ...

and into the appropriate future tense:

1 אֲנַחְנוּ ... 2 אַתָּה ... 3 הֵם ... 4 אֲנִי ... 5 אַתֶּם ... 6 אַתְּ ...

7 הֵן ... 8 אַתֶּן ... 9 הוּא ... 10 יוֹסִי וְצְבִי ... 11 מִי ...

12 הִיא ... 13 הָאָחוֹת ... 14 הַחֶבְרָ'ה ... 15 שָׂרָה וְלֵאָה וְאֲנִי ...

Translate:

1 We're recording soon.
2 Mommy, she's hitting.
3 Sara and Rivka promise to come.
4 I always explain.
5 The girls want to explain, but they don't explain.
6 It's hard to define commitment.
7 These sweaters won't fit you.
8 The forecast doesn't frighten me.
9 I got them out at the last moment.
10 When will you make up your mind, guys? Or have you already?
11 We ordered the other newspaper.
12 Sit him down here, Shoshana.

Give the infinitive and the action noun for:

הִדְבִּיר, הִסְבִּיר, הִגְדִּיר, הִרְבִּיץ, הִקְלִיט, הִנְמִיךְ, הִרְטִיב, הִבְלִיט, הִזְמִין

28 Binyan PI'EL

Put שִׁדֵּר 'to broadcast', קִילֵּל 'to curse', שִׁלֵּם 'to pay', הִימֵר 'to bet', סִידֵּר 'to tidy up', סִיוֵּוג 'to sort', זִיֵּיף 'to sing out of tune' into the appropriate past tense forms:

1 אֲנַחְנוּ . . . 2 אַתָּה . . . 3 הֵם . . . 4 אֲנִי . . . 5 אַתֶּם . . . 6 אַתְּ . . .
7 הֵן . . . 8 אַתֶּן . . . 9 הוּא . . . 10 יוֹסִי וְצְבִי . . . 11 מִי . . .
12 הִיא . . . 13 הָאֲחוֹת . . . 14 הַחֲבֵרְ'ה . . . 15 שָׂרָה וְלֵאָה וְאֲנִי . . .

and into the appropriate future tense:

1 אֲנַחְנוּ . . . 2 אַתָּה . . . 3 הֵם . . . 4 אֲנִי . . . 5 אַתֶּם . . . 6 אַתְּ . . .
7 הֵן . . . 8 אַתֶּן . . . 9 הוּא . . . 10 יוֹסִי וְצְבִי . . . 11 מִי . . .
12 הִיא . . . 13 הָאֲחוֹת . . . 14 הַחֲבֵרְ'ה . . . 15 שָׂרָה וְלֵאָה וְאֲנִי . . .

Translate:

1 We're late.
2 Mommy, she's lying.
3 Sara and Rivka are asking to come.
4 I always tidy up.
5 The girls also get payment.
6 She's canceled the class again!

7 Ariela, ask to hear the beginning.

8 We've distributed loads of matzot but we're distributing more.

9 Pay if you want, Yael, but I won't pay.

10 They're visiting their mother.

11 Have you spoken with the director yourselves?

12 She'll speak with the embassy and explain.

Give the infinitive and the action noun for:

חִפֵּשׂ, סִידֵּר, לִיטֵּף, נִיתֵּק, אִיחֵר, מִיזֵג, רִיפֵּד, שִׁפֵּר, עִיכֵּל, שִׁיהֵק

29 Binyan HITPA'EL

Put הִתְפַּטֵּר 'to resign', הִתְקַבֵּל 'to be accepted', הִתְלַבֵּט 'to be in two minds', הִתְגַּבֵּר 'to overcome', הִתְאַמֵּן 'to train', הִתְרַחֵץ 'to bathe', הִתְלַבֵּשׁ 'to get dressed' into the appropriate past tense forms:

1 אַתָּה . . . 2 אֲנַחְנוּ . . . 3 אֲנִי . . . 4 הֵם . . . 5 אַתְּ . . . 6 הֵן . . .
7 אַתֶּם . . . 8 הוּא . . . 9 אַתֶּן . . . 10 הִיא . . . 11 דָּנִי וּמַיָה . . .
12 הַסַּמָּל . . . 13 אֲנִי . . . 14 הַסַּפָּר . . . 15 הִיא . . .

and into the appropriate future tense:

1 אַתֶּן . . . 2 הִיא . . . 3 דָּנִי וְבֶּנִי . . . 4 הַסַּמָּל . . . 5 אֲנִי . . .
6 הַסַּפָּר . . . 7 הִיא . . . 8 אַתָּה . . . 9 אֲנַחְנוּ . . . 10 אֲנִי . . .
11 הֵם . . . 12 אַתְּ . . . 13 הֵן . . . 14 אַתֶּם . . . 15 הוּא . . .

Turn into the singular or into the plural:

1 מִתְפַּטְּרִים 2 מִתְקַבְּלוֹת 3 מִתְלַבֶּטֶת 4 מִתְגַּבֵּר 5 מִתְאַמְּנוֹת
6 מִתְרַחֵץ 7 מִתְלַבְּשִׁים 8 מִתְפַּטֶּרֶת 9 מִתְפַּשְּׁטִים 10 מִתְעָרֵב

1 I wasn't so impressed with it.

2 Were you impressed, Yehudit?

3 When are you marrying, Miriam?

4 They say they'll marry in the spring.

5 Has she used this cup?

6 She's not really sorry.

7 I'll shave and run to the store.

30 Binyan NIF'AL

1 Using the verb נִסְרַט 'was scratched', give the appropriate past tense forms:

1 אַתָּה ... 2 אֲנַחְנוּ ... 3 אֲנִי ... 4 הֵם ... 5 אַתְּ ... 6 הֵן ...
7 אַתֶּם ... 8 הוּא ... 9 אַתֶּן ... 10 הִיא ... 11 דָּנִי וְבֶנִי ...
12 הָרֶכֶב ... 13 אֲנִי ... 14 הַטַּבָּעוֹת ... 15 הִיא ...

and the appropriate future tense:

1 אַתֶּן ... 2 הִיא ... 3 דָּנִי וְבֶנִי ... 4 הַסַּמָל ... 5 אֲנִי ...
6 הַסַּפָּר ... 7 הִיא ... 8 אַתָּה ... 9 אֲנַחְנוּ ... 10 אֲנִי ...
11 הֵם ... 12 אַתְּ ... 13 הֵן ... 14 אַתֶּם ... 15 הוּא ...

2 Give the four present tense forms of:

לְהִמָּלֵט 'to flee', לְהִשָּׁעֵן 'to lean', לְהִיבָּדֵק 'to be inspected', לְהִקָּלֵט 'to be absorbed'

3 Give the infinitive of:

נִגְמַר 'to be finished', נִתְקַל 'to run into', נִמְסַר 'to be handed', נִקְנַס 'to be fined', נִרְדָּף 'to be persecuted'

Translate:

1 Messages were sent to various governments.
2 Different solutions were examined.
3 A peace conference was held.
4 The negotiations were ended.
5 A peace agreement was signed.
6 You'll be examined in the small room.
7 They've already calmed down.
8 There's such a tension that I can't calm down.
9 This shirt's been stretched.
10 The tickets are selling very quickly.
11 Run, the door's closing!
12 Why are they getting into his car?

31 Binyan HUF'AL

1 Using the verb הוּקְלַט 'be recorded', give the past tense forms:

1 אַתֶּן ... 2 הִיא ... 3 דָנִי וְבֶנִי ... 4 אֶשְׁתִּי ... 5 אֲנִי ...
6 הַסַּפָּר ... 7 הִיא ... 8 אַתָּה ... 9 אֲנַחְנוּ ... 10 אֲנִי ...
11 הֵם ... 12 אַתְּ ... 13 הֵן ... 14 אַתֶּם ... 15 הוּא ...

and the future tense:

1 אַתָּה ... 2 אֲנַחְנוּ ... 3 אֲנִי ... 4 הֵם ... 5 אַתְּ ... 6 הֵן ...
7 אַתֶּם ... 8 הוּא ... 9 אַתֶּן ... 10 הִיא ... 11 דָנִי וְבֶנִי ...
12 הָרַב ... 13 אֲנִי ... 14 הַזַּמְרוֹת ... 15 הִיא ...

2 Give the four present tense forms of:

הוּחְזַר 'was returned', הוּזְנַח 'was neglected', הוּמְלַץ 'was recommended', הוּפְקַד 'was deposited', הוּגְבַּל 'was restricted'

Translate:

1 The ports of the enemy have been bombed.
2 Many factories have been destroyed.
3 Missile launchpads have also been attacked.
4 Chemical weapons have not been employed.
5 Paratroopers have been parachuted behind the front.

32 Binyan PU'AL

Put these PI'EL forms into the corresponding PU'AL:

יָנַצְּלוּ, נִתֵּק, תְּנַצֵּל, אֲמַקֵּם, נִיצַּלְתִּי, נִיתַּקְתְּ, צִילְמָה, סִימַנְתֶּם, צִילְמוּ,
תְּסַמְּנוּ, יְסַלְקוּ, סִילַקְתָּ

Convert into the plural:

מְסוּמָן, מְקוּבֶּלֶת, מְשׁוּמָשׁ, מְפוּזָר, מְחוּנֶּכֶת

1 The situation was gradually improved.
2 The Negev was suddenly cut off.
3 Rifles were distributed to civilians.
4 Several villages in the Jezreel Valley were also cut off.
5 The Jordan Valley was cut off from the rest of the country.

34 Object markers

34a The object marker אֶת

1 I'm looking for the brush.

2 She's wiping the sink.

3 Take the rag.

4 Take the soap and a towel.

5 Who is he looking for?

6 I hate it!

7 Who are you inviting?

8 What were you cooking?

9 Go on, take it!

10 No, I'm reading it!

11 Rinse the toothbrush or take another toothbrush.

12 The cleaning-lady's wiping the toilet-bowl.

13 Chana, who do you want here? Benny or Kobi?

34b Indirect objects

Using a good dictionary, give the prepositions governed by:

1 טִיפֵּל   2 חִיכָּה   3 הִתְנַגֵּד   4 הִתְאַהֵב   5 הִמְלִיץ   6 הִתְחַשֵּׁב   7 כָּעַס
8 וִיתֵּר   9 יָרֵא   10 הִשְׁתַּמֵּשׁ

Translate:

1 This belongs to the woman downstairs.

2 We're very proud of the door actually.

3 I'm quite satisfied with the paint.

4 But I'm not so pleased with the whitewash.

5 They're aware of the dangers.

6 Why did you touch the window?

7 But meanwhile, who'll look after the wood outside in the yard?

8 Don't listen to the carpenter – the closet's fantastic.

9 I'm not an expert in kitchen cabinets.

10 I meant the dining corner, not the living room!

35 Preposition + suffix

35a Preposition + suffix: בְּ, לְ

Add the appropriate suffixes:

בְּ:   Us, him, them, you (masc. sing.), me, you (masc. pl.), them (fem.), her, us, me, him

לְ:   Him, me, us, him, them, you (masc. sing.), me, you (masc. pl.), them (fem.), her

And now translate:

1 Judaism? I'm very interested in it.
2 Everyone is jealous of them.
3 Her parents are proud of her.
4 Do you trust me?
5 What beautiful customs! I fell in love with them.
6 Hi, guys – is someone dealing with you?
7 Yes, sure, they're already dealing with us.
8 The secular parties scarcely trust them.
9 I don't suspect you, Chaim, heaven forbid!
10 I'm gradually falling in love with you, Golda.
11 He's helping us.
12 Everyone's listening to you, Devora.
13 I'm giving them a lot of advice and help.
14 But what do they give me?
15 You're always bothering her.

35b Preposition + suffix: ... אוֹתוֹ

Add the appropriate suffixes:

Us, him, them, you (masc. sing.), me, you (masc. pl.), them (fem.), her, us, me, him

And now translate:

1 You surprised me.
2 Sonny and Cher? I remember them.
3 The atmosphere here annoys us.
4 It kind of amuses me.
5 The threat still worries him.

6 Films like this frighten you?
7 I'm taking a photo of you next to the map.
8 The worry is killing us.
9 He's finally fired her.
10 She's finally divorced him.

35c *Preposition + suffix:* עִם, מִ

Add the appropriate suffixes:

מִ: Us, him, them, you (masc. sing.), me, you (masc. pl.), them (fem.), her, us, me, him

עִם: Him, me, us, him, them, you (masc. sing.), me, you (masc. pl.), them (fem.), her

And now translate:

1 My mother-in-law always quarrels with her.
2 My fiancee is cross with me at the moment.
3 Are you afraid of him?
4 My cousin Shlomo is very impressed with you, Zeev.
5 His mother and father are coming with us.
6 Why is he starting with her suddenly?
7 Yafa, do you really care about him?
8 I'm fed up with them already.
9 You recently received a reminder from us.
10 I have received a notification from you.

35d *Preposition + suffix:* בִּשְׁבִיל *etc.*

1 The mezuzah is for you, auntie.
2 The candies are for them, for the festival.
3 Because of me, he forgot the prayer-book.
4 We sat in the sukkah, with loads of bees and flies around us.
5 There are always so many friends around her.
6 What, the celebration's because of you?
7 It's quite obvious – there's a cemetery opposite us.
8 He's crazy – opposite them there's a cinema!
9 Near him there's a big yeshivah.
10 There's a bookcase near you, with a Bible, I think.
11 What's all the noise near me! I'm cooking something for you for Passover!
12 Another prayer-shawl for him? But now he has five!

35e *Preposition + suffix:* אחרי, לפני, אל, על

Add the appropriate suffixes:

אל: Us, him, them, you (masc. sing.), me, you (masc. pl.), them (fem.), her, us, me, him

על: Him, me, us, him, them, you (masc. sing.), me, you (masc. pl.), them (fem.), her

לפני: Us, him, them, you (masc. sing.), me, you (masc. pl.), them (fem.), her, us, me, him

אחרי: Him, me, us, him, them, you (masc. sing.), me, you (masc. pl.), them (fem.), her

37 יֵשׁ

1 There's a bus at the bus-stop.
2 Careful, there aren't traffic-lights at this intersection.
3 There'll be lanes just for buses!
4 Maybe there's a parking lot in a side-street.
5 There's no sidewalk on this side of the street!
6 So walk on the other side, there's a sidewalk there.
7 There were huge jams.
8 But there wasn't an Ayalon Highway then.

38 'I have'

1 Israel had large forces along the southern border.
2 The air force has mainly American planes.
3 So you'll have a lift to the base after Shabbat?
4 We have two sons in the Golani brigade.
5 Aharon has another year in the Israeli Army.
6 Perhaps they have the nuclear bomb.
7 I don't have a rifle here.
8 Miki doesn't have reserve duty till Chanukah.
9 In the War of Independence they barely had a navy.

39 Questions

1 Is there a post office here?
2 Does the butcher sell turkey, too, or just meat?
3 When does the bank close?
4 How did you find the bakery?
5 What do you pay with, cash or credit card? Or a check?
6 She's shopping? Who with?
7 He's gone to the food store. You know who for?
8 What time does the laundry open?

40 Negation

1 Yossi, don't order the soup, it's salty.
2 Kids, don't finish all the salad.
3 I'm not cutting more lettuce.
4 There isn't any coffee in the house?
5 Why didn't you boil some water, Rina?
6 You won't put in sugar, I hope.
7 Don't put in any Sucrazit, please.

41 'The cake in the fridge'

1 The bus to Jericho.
2 The season ticket in your wallet.
3 The stop at the corner.
4 The number on the front of the bus.
5 The cab from Nesher.

42 Degree words

1 Their new show's rather boring.
2 The second film was so dumb!
3 She's particularly interested in Israeli art.
4 There's a very good play at Habima.
5 I quite like that Naomi Shemer record.
6 A bit louder please. Ah, that's better.
7 Chaim Topol as director is extremely successful.
8 The late show doesn't end so late.
9 I'm so sorry, sir. This seat is taken.
10 I liked the acting a lot.

43 Adverbs of time and place

1 Sometimes I fix it myself.
2 We usually keep the brooms on the balcony.
3 First I'm turning off the washing machine.
4 I always leave the laundry here.
5 Put all the second-hand furniture in the storeroom.
6 Iddo often does the ironing downstairs in the basement.
7 We're sleeping in the shelter tonight.
8 Yesterday we ate in the courtyard – what fun!

44 'I want to sneeze'

1 The bus driver began shouting.
2 Then my mother started screaming.
3 All the passengers went on laughing a long time.
4 We're hoping to go to Switzerland or France.
5 Egged has stopped picking up by the gas station.
6 Your brother wants to learn to drive? He's only 17!
7 I expected to be back by midnight.
8 I hate catching a lift.
9 Try to smile instead.

45 'It's good to smile'

1 It's so easy to write with this pen.
2 It's good that the teacher's sick today.
3 It's hard to get into this course in the first semester.
4 Actually it's surprising that we don't have a paper – or at least an exercise.
5 What, the class has been cancelled again? It's weird that it happens.
6 It's better to talk to them in the cafeteria.
7 It's obvious that you passed.
8 You have to do three subjects for the Master's.

46 Reported thoughts

1 I told him I'm leaving.
2 I think it's too cold.
3 She said there was something about it on the news.
4 I'm afraid I threw away the Shabbat supplement.
5 I knew I was right!

47 Relative clauses with שֶׁ

1 Where's the whatchumacallit that locks the windows?
2 Oh darn, this is the key that doesn't work.
3 The policeman I asked didn't know.
4 They've found the things that the burglars took.
5 This parking ticket you got – is it a lot of money?
6 Is that the person who went to the police?

48 Adverbial clauses

1 When we left, it was already snowing.
2 If the weather's nice, can we go back to the pool?
3 In the end we didn't go to Eilat, because there was a hamsin.
4 What if the forecast says that it will be hot and dry?
5 There's always a strong wind before it rains.
6 Although it was wet, it was fun.
7 When the temperature's over forty, they tell the soldiers to drink and drink.
8 While we were on vacation on the Hermon, there was a huge storm.
9 Thunder's really great, especially when there's lots of lightning.
10 Dry your hands before turning on the light.
11 After packing, we grabbed some sleep.
12 While sleeping in the sun, the counselor got a bad headache.
13 Watch out instead of whispering all the time.
14 How can you buy without using a credit card?
15 They opened my bag without me seeing.
16 You're holding the steering wheel like you've never driven.
17 As I said, we have to keep the stairway clean.
18 Zelda makes chicken like her mother made it.
19 The police are talking as if I ran someone over.
20 I'm in charge, although I don't understand much.
21 Shoshana took a lot of things, though not everything.
22 I asked him, so I know already.
23 We left early so as to see the first movie.
24 I'm telling her so that she won't use it.

49 Sentences without a subject

1 How do they choose the prime minister?
2 You vote once in four years in Israel, it's fixed.
3 A pity the Foreign Minister didn't come to the shiva.

4 It is possible that they will put together a now coalition.
5 Lucky there were enough MKs for a debate.
6 Another political crisis? It's impossible.
7 Can I turn off the air conditioning? – It's not so hot.

50 ל׳ה roots

1 Using the verbs שָׂחָה 'swim', קָנָה 'buy', זָכָה 'win', give the past tense forms:

1 אַתֶּן ... 2 הִיא ... 3 דָּנִי וְבֶנִי ... 4 אִשְׁתִּי ... 5 אֲנִי ...
6 הַכֶּלֶב ... 7 הִיא ... 8 אַתָּה ... 9 אֲנַחְנוּ ... 10 אֲנִי ...
11 הֵם ... 12 אַתְּ ... 13 הֵן ... 14 אַתֶּם ... 15 הוּא ...

and the future tense:

1 אַתָּה ... 2 אֲנַחְנוּ ... 3 אֲנִי ... 4 הֵם ... 5 אַתְּ ... 6 הֵן ...
7 אַתֶּם ... 8 הוּא ... 9 אַתֶּן ... 10 הִיא ... 11 דָּנִי וְבֶנִי ...
12 הָרַב ... 13 אֲנִי ... 14 הַגְּמַלִים ... 15 הִיא ...

2 Using the verbs חִיכָּה 'wait', נִיקָה 'clean', נִיסָה 'try', give the past tense forms:

1 אַתָּה ... 2 אֲנַחְנוּ ... 3 אֲנִי ... 4 הֵם ... 5 אַתְּ ... 6 הֵן ...
7 אַתֶּם ... 8 הוּא ... 9 אַתֶּן ... 10 הִיא ... 11 עוֹפְרָה וְיָפָה ...
12 הָרַב ... 13 אֲנִי ... 14 הַחַיָּילוֹת ... 15 הִיא ...

and the future tense:

1 אַתֶּן ... 2 הִיא ... 3 דָּנִי וְבֶנִי ... 4 אִשְׁתִּי ... 5 אֲנִי ...
6 הַמָּשִׁיחַ ... 7 הִיא ... 8 אַתָּה ... 9 אֲנַחְנוּ ... 10 אֲנִי ...
11 הֵם ... 12 אַתְּ ... 13 הֵן ... 14 אַתֶּם ... 15 הוּא ...

3 Turn into the infinitive:

מִינָה 'appointed', קִיוְוָה 'hoped', טָעָה 'made a mistake', לִיוָוה 'accompanied', שָׁתָה 'drank', שָׂחָה 'swim', קָנָה 'bought', מִיצָה 'exhausted', שִׁינָה 'altered', תָּלָה 'hung'

4 Using the verbs הִשְׁקָה 'irrigate', הִשְׁוָוה 'compare', הִטְעָה 'mislead', supply the present tense for:

1 אַתָּה ... 2 אֲנַחְנוּ ... 3 אִמָּא ... 4 הֵם ... 5 אַתְּ ... 6 הֵן ...
7 אַתֶּם ... 8 הוּא ... 9 אַתֶּן ... 10 הִיא ... 11 דָּנִי וְבֶנִי ...
12 הַחַקְלָאי ... 13 אֲנִי ... 14 הַנַּעֲרָה ...

5 Using the verbs הִתְפַּנָּה 'become free', הִתְגַּלָה 'were discovered', הִתְאַדָּה 'evaporate', give the past tense forms:

1 אַתָּה . . . 2 אֲנַחְנוּ . . . 3 אֲנִי . . . 4 הֵם . . . 5 אַתְּ . . . 6 הֵן . . .
7 אַתֶּם . . . 8 הוּא . . . 9 אַתֶּן . . . 10 הִיא . . . 11 עוֹפְרָה וְיָפָה . . .
12 הָרַב . . . 13 אֲנִי . . . 14 הַמַּיִם . . . 15 הִיא . . .

and the future tense:

1 אַתֶּן . . . 2 הִיא . . . 3 דַּנִי וְבֶנִי . . . 4 אִשְׁתִּי . . . 5 אֲנִי . . .
6 הַבְּרֵכָה . . . 7 הִיא . . . 8 אַתָּה . . . 9 אֲנַחְנוּ . . . 10 אֲנִי . . .
11 הֵם . . . 12 אַתְּ . . . 13 הֵן . . . 14 אַתֶּם . . . 15 הוּא . . .

6 Give the full past and present tense of נִרְאָה 'seem' and the full present and future of נִמְנָה 'count'.

7 Use a NIF'AL verb:

1 She enjoyed the film.
2 You seem tired, Yafa.
3 Chagit seems happy.
4 I won't enjoy this book.
5 Where were the tomatoes bought?
6 Tomatoes are usually bought in the market.
7 We really enjoyed the meal on Shabbat.
8 Are cars made in Israel?
9 The situation was gradually being made more comfortable.
10 Our payments were made every month.

51 Roots with 'gutturals'

51b When the first letter is a 'guttural'

1 Pronounce the following:

תַחְקוֹר 'investigate', תַחְסוֹךְ 'save', תִכְתּוֹב 'write', יַחֲזוֹר 'he'll return', יִכְבּוֹשׁ 'he'll capture', נַחְשׁוֹב 'we'll think', אַחְקוֹר 'I'll investigate', תַחְזְרוּ 'return', יַהֲרוֹג 'he'll kill', יַעֲבוֹד 'he'll work', תַעֲזוֹב 'leave', נַעֲזוֹר 'we'll help', אֶעֱבוֹד 'I'll work', אֶעֱמוֹד 'I'll stand', יַעֲמוֹד 'he'll stand', תַעֲצוֹר 'stop', נֶאֱרוֹג 'we'll weave', תֶאֱרוֹז 'pack', תֶאֱסוֹף 'gather'

193

2 and:

העביר 'he decided', הכתיר 'he crowned', החמיץ 'he missed', החליט 'he transferred', העסיק 'he employed', הנמיך 'he lowered', החמיר 'he was stringent', העמיד 'he placed', תעביר 'transfer', האכיל 'he fed', תאכיל 'feed', תסביר 'explain', תחליף 'switch', החליף 'he switched'

3 and finally:

ייחקר 'will be investigated', ייהנה 'will enjoy', ייעשה 'will become', נעזב 'was abandoned', נעדר 'was missing', נשמר 'was kept', נחתם 'was signed', ייחתם 'will be signed', נעשה 'became', נעצר 'was arrested', ייעצר 'will be arrested', ייגמר 'will end'

4 Form the infinitive of:

החליט 'decided', העמיד 'placed', האזין 'listened', העסיק 'employed', חזר 'returned', עבד 'worked', הרג 'killed', אסף 'gathered', עצר 'arrested', אכל 'ate', נדד 'wandered', עקב 'followed', נעמד 'rose', נעדר 'was missing', חצב 'excavated', נעלב 'was offended'

51c When the middle letter is a 'guttural'

1 Pronounce the following:

בוערים 'burning', טוענים 'loading', תואמות 'matching', פעלו 'acted', יבחר 'chose', בערו 'burned', לטעון 'to load', לבחור 'to choose', בחרו 'he'll choose', יבחן 'he'll test', תדחוף 'push', יצחק 'he'll laugh', יצחקו 'they'll laugh', צוחקים 'laughing'

2 and:

ננעלו 'were locked', יינעלו 'will be locked', נזהרו 'were careful', נזכרו 'were mentioned', הופעלו 'were activated', הופצצו 'were bombed', הובהרה 'was clarified', הורעלה 'was poisoned', תבאר 'elucidate', תטהרי 'purify', תשחקי 'play', תתארו 'describe', תטפסו 'climb', יבארו 'they'll elucidate', ימהרו 'they'll rush', תואר 'was described', בירך 'congratulated', התנערה 'shook herself', התנקמה 'took revenge', יתפארו 'they'll boast', התפעלו 'they were impressed'

3 and:

תיאום 'event', שיעור 'lesson', מיעוט 'minority', שירות 'service', אירוע 'coordination', גיהוץ 'ironing', טירוף 'insanity', ריהוט 'furniture', צירוף 'phrase'

51d *When the final letter is a 'guttural'*

1   Form the infinitive and future 3rd masc. sing. of:

שמע 'heard', נשמע 'sounded', שח 'spoke', בטח 'trusted', קיפח 'deprived', בלע 'swallowed'

2   What is the future of:

ביצע 'carried out', קרע 'tore', הזניח 'neglected', נמנע 'refrained', נכנעה 'surrendered', התגלח 'shaved himself', גילחה 'shaved', טרח 'bothered', ניצח 'won', נפתח 'was opened'

3   What is the feminine of:

רוצח 'murdering', מתקלח 'taking a shower', מבצע 'carrying out', מפצח 'cracking', מורגש 'felt', מובלע 'swallowed', מצביע 'pointing', נוגע 'touching', משובח 'praised', מתנפח 'swelling'

52 Roots with ב, כ, פ

1   Pronounce the following:

פיטר 'sacked', תיעב 'detested', ביטל 'cancelled', כינה 'named', פצע 'injured', יפטר 'will sack', התפטר 'resigned', מפוטר 'is sacked', נבגד 'is betrayed', ייבגד 'will be betrayed', יבגוד 'will betray', נפצע 'was injured', תפצע 'she'll injure', תיפצע 'she'll be injured', בלט 'stood out', לבלוט 'to stand out', הבליט 'highlighted', הובלטו 'were highlighted', שובת 'striking', השבית 'brought to a standstill', יושבת 'will be brought to a standstill', מגביר 'increasing', נתגבר 'we shall overcome', גבר 'prevailed', גיבש 'crystallize', מגובש 'crystallized'

2   Form the infinitive from:

בחן 'tested', דפק 'knocked', טבל 'dipped', תפס 'caught', נפסל 'was disqualified', ביים 'staged', ביטל 'cancelled', נבנה 'was built', פיהק 'yawned', התבטל 'was cancelled', נבלע 'was swallowed', נכתב 'was written', ריפד 'upholstered', נפלט 'was emitted', נשפך 'was spilled', נתפס 'was caught', עיכל 'digested', נמכר 'was sold'

53 Four-consonant roots

Using the verbs צִילְצֵל 'ring', פִּירְסֵם 'publish', and הִתְמַרְמֵר 'become embittered', give the appropriate past tense forms:

1 אַתָּה ... 2 אֲנַחְנוּ ... 3 אֲנִי ... 4 הֵם ... 5 אַתְּ ... 6 הֵן ...
7 אַתֶּם ... 8 הוּא ... 9 אַתֶּן ... 10 הִיא ... 11 הַמַּרְצִים ...
12 הָרַב ... 13 אֲנִי ... 14 הַחַיָּילוֹת... 15 הִיא ...

and the future tense:

1 אַתֶּן ... 2 הִיא ... 3 דָּנִי וְבֶנִי ... 4 אֶשְׁתִּי ... 5 אֲנִי ...
6 הַבּוֹס שֶׁלְךָ ... 7 הִיא ... 8 אַתָּה ... 9 אֲנַחְנוּ ... 10 אֲנִי ...
11 הֵם ... 12 אַתְּ ... 13 הֵן ... 14 אַתֶּם ... 15 הוּא ...

54 פ"י verbs

54a פ"י roots

1 If he won't get down, get him down, Chaim.
2 You must sit down, kids.
3 Perhaps I'll initiate a pressure group.
4 For heaven's sake, you can't get 'em out and sit 'em down?
5 Pnina, come out of there and sit down immediately.
6 Let me know tomorrow or the day after, I need to know.
7 Call Magen David Adom, my wife's about to give birth!
8 When will the office know?
9 An international crisis is likely to be created.
10 How about going out together some time?

55 'Cross-over' roots

Create HITPA'EL verbs (in the past tense 3 masc. sing.) from these roots:

צ־ל־ם, ס־פ־ר, שׁ־נ־ה, ס־ע־ר, שׂ־ר־ע, ס־מ־ן, ז־ק־ק, ז־ה־ה, צ־ד־ק,
שׁ־פ־ר

and in the future 3 masc. sing. from these:

שׁ־ז־ף, שׁ־ח־ר־ר, ס־נ־ן, צ־ר־ף, שׂ־כ־ל־ל, שׁ־ר־ך, שׁ־מ־ע, ס־ב־ך,
ז־מ־ן

56 Maverick verbs

56a פ״נ roots

Using the verbs נָתַן 'give', נָגַשׁ 'walk up to', and נָסַע 'travel', give the appropriate past tense forms:

1 אַתָּה ... 2 אֲנַחְנוּ ... 3 אֲנִי ... 4 הֵם ... 5 אַתְּ ... 6 הֵן ...
7 אַתֶּם ... 8 הוּא ... 9 אַתֶּן ... 10 הִיא ... 11 הַמַּרְצִים ...
12 הָרַב ... 13 אֲנִי ... 14 הַחַיָּילוֹת... 15 הִיא ...

and the future tense:

1 אַתֶּן ... 2 הִיא ... 3 דָּנִי וְבֶנִי ... 4 אִשְׁתִּי ... 5 אֲנִי ...
6 הַבּוֹס שֶׁלְךָ ... 7 הִיא ... 8 אַתָּה ... 9 אֲנַחְנוּ ... 10 אֲנִי ...
11 הֵם ... 12 אַתְּ ... 13 הֵן ... 14 אַתֶּם ... 15 הוּא ...

Translate:

1 I'm afraid to go up to him.
2 I prefer to give bills, not coins.
3 Give me, Yafa.
4 Watch out, Nechama, you'll fall.
5 It's not allowed to touch the wire.
6 I said 'Don't touch'!
7 The institute will bear the names of Zionist leaders.

56b לָקַח

1 Don't take all the cookies, Uncle Efrayim.
2 I've decided to take my husband.
3 Take a flashlight, Naomi.
4 I'll take the old jeans.
5 It'll take a few seconds.
6 It takes three weeks to get an answer.
7 It's better to take an ID with you.

56c הָלַךְ

1 We're going to the zoo.
2 You can go too.
3 'Go to hell,' he said to me!
4 I'll go to the cash-dispenser first of all.
5 Then we'll go to the beach at Bat-Yam.

56d | יָכוֹל, צָרִיךְ

1 He had to go to an ulpan.
2 Poor thing, did he have to spend a long time there?
3 Miss Berkovitz, you'll have to do a preparatory course in Hebrew.
4 What, I won't be able to get an exemption?
5 You can try to pass the Hebrew test, OK?
6 These foreign students will have to do four hours of Social Science.
7 They got bad grades in Hebrew – they couldn't even read the questions.
8 I couldn't get a room in the dorms.
9 So I had to rent in the center of town.
10 Gee, it must have been a drag.

56e | Some verbs beginning with א

1 Don't worry, Naama, one day you'll love him.
2 I'd like to tell Mr Yehoshua something, please.
3 Say that Mr Oz is asking to see him.
4 I'll tell him you're here.
5 Those ants will eat all your vegetables.
6 They'll love the bread – and the matza.
7 I'll eat in the corridor – it's just a pitta.
8 Eat, eat, Irving, it's healthy.

56g | חַי, מֵת

1 I'm dying to meet her.
2 I'm terribly sorry, she died yesterday.
3 She lived for five years in Haifa Bay.
4 Jackals still live in the desert.
5 Bears and lions once lived in the mountains of Lebanon.
6 She can live in Ramot – that's close to Jerusalem.

57 | הִכִּיר, הֵכִיל etc.

Using the verbs הֵכִין 'prepare', הִגִּיעַ 'arrive', הֵבִין 'understand', and הִבִּיט 'gaze', give the appropriate past tense forms:

1 אַתָּה . . . 2 אֲנַחְנוּ . . . 3 אֲנִי . . . 4 הֵם . . . 5 אַתְּ . . . 6 הֵן . . .
7 אַתֶּם . . . 8 הוּא . . . 9 אַתֶּן . . . 10 הִיא . . . 11 הַמַּרְצִים . . .
12 הָרַב . . . 13 אֲנִי . . . 14 הַחַיָּילוֹת . . . 15 הִיא . . .

and the future tense:

1 אֶתֵּן . . . 2 הִיא . . . 3 דָּנִי וְבֶנִי . . . 4 אִשְׁתִּי . . . 5 אֲנִי . . .
6 הַבּוֹס שֶׁלְּךָ . . . 7 הִיא . . . 8 אַתָּה . . . 9 אֲנַחְנוּ . . . 10 אֲנִי . . .
11 הֵם . . . 12 אַתְּ . . . 13 הֵן . . . 14 אַתֶּם . . . 15 הוּא . . .

and the present tense, too:

1 אַתָּה . . . 2 אֲנַחְנוּ . . . 3 אֲנִי . . . 4 הֵם . . . 5 אַתְּ . . . 6 הֵן . . .
7 אַתֶּם . . . 8 הוּא . . .

What verb are these action nouns related to? Pay special attention to the
second letter. Does it have a dagesh? If it is not a ב, כ, פ, you'll have to
check its nikkud in a dictionary.

הקמה, הפצה, הפלה, הזזה, הצעה, הנחה, הצלה, הגדה, הבנה, הבעה

58 PA'AL verbs with -i-a- in the future

1 Binyamin wants to ride the bicycle on the road.
2 Our little son will grow up and be an Egged driver.
3 During the sermon half of them were asleep.
4 I'm glad you aren't absent again, Orit.
5 Why was she absent from the lesson?
6 Lie down on the couch, it's more comfortable.
7 She reads Psalms while she waits for a bus.
8 Patience, we'll find it.
9 Read as far as page four.
10 Wear a tie, Mottele, it looks better.
11 He refused to wear a tie.
12 Ask your father how to put on a tie.
13 I'll lie down and sleep for a few minutes.
14 Devorah always finds mistakes in the Torah Reading.
15 If you're fasting, perhaps you want to lie down.
16 No, I'd rather study a chapter of something.
17 I've brought a Hagada of my own.
18 Did you bring tefillin and a prayer-book, Itzi?

59 PO'EL and HITPO'EL

Using the verbs שׂוֹחֵחַ 'chat', הִתְלוֹנֵן 'complain', הִתְרוֹצֵץ 'run about', give
the appropriate past tense forms:

1 אַתָּה . . . 2 אֲנַחְנוּ . . . 3 אֲנִי . . . 4 הֵם . . . 5 אַתְּ . . . 6 הֵן . . .
7 אַתֶּם . . . 8 הוּא . . . 9 אַתֶּן . . . 10 הִיא . . . 11 הַשּׁוֹמְרִים . . .
12 הָרַב . . . 13 אֲנִי . . . 14 הַחַיָּילוֹת . . . 15 הִיא . . .

and the future tense:

1 אֶתֵּן . . . 2 הִיא . . . 3 דָנִי וְבְנִי . . . 4 אִשְׁתִּי . . . 5 אֲנִי . . .
6 הַבֵּן־דּוֹד שֶׁלְךָ . . . 7 הִיא . . . 8 אַתָּה . . . 9 אֲנַחְנוּ . . . 10 אֲנִי . . .
11 הֵם . . . 12 אַתְּ . . . 13 הֵן . . . 14 אַתֶּם . . . 15 הוּא . . .

and the present tense, too:

1 אַתָּה . . . 2 אֲנַחְנוּ . . . 3 אֲנִי . . . 4 הֵם . . . 5 אַתְּ . . . 6 הֵן . . .
7 אַתֶּם . . . 8 הוּא . . .

60 More plurals of nouns

60a Plurals ending in ־יִם

1 A sparkling bicycle 2 Dark glasses 3 Sharp scissors 4 Sun glasses
5 Two ears 6 Five teeth 7 Iron teeth 8 Two arms 9 Brown eyes
10 Sport shoes 11 Wool socks 12 Warm water 13 A bright sky 14 Salt
water 15 A wide margin

60b Duals ending in ־יִם

1 He's two years old.
2 It will take two days at a minimum.
3 The curfew lasted two weeks.
4 They lost 2000 tanks and 200 planes.
5 Two months of tension passed.

60c Plural of מָסוֹרֶת etc.

Give the plural of:

תִּסְמוֹנֶת 'syndrome', חַיֶּלֶת 'girl-soldier', מִשְׁמֶרֶת 'shift', צַלַּחַת 'plate',
מַעֲבּוֹרֶת 'ferry', מַחְבֶּרֶת 'exercise book', גַּנֶּנֶת 'kindergarten teacher',
רַכֶּבֶת 'train', מִרְפֶּסֶת 'balcony', מַגֶּבֶת 'towel'

60d Exceptions

1 Three days 2 Five nights 3 Many bulls 4 Ten heads 5 Two markets
6 A brother and two sisters 7 Some houses 8 Four towns 9 Six names
10 Two walls 11 A thousand swords 12 Heavy tables 13 Important
places 14 Ultraorthodox women 15 Tall hotels 16 Young rabbis
17 Empty pits 18 Cans of coke 19 Beautiful daughters 20 Certain
advantages

61   כָּל, אָדוֹם

1 Most of them 2 All of us 3 All of you 4 Green men 5 Green women
6 Sweet challahs 7 Red rugs 8 Round spoons 9 New laws 10 Yellow
submarines 11 Yellow pages 12 A pink face 13 A red eye 14 A dark-
blue dress 15 Smelly goats 16 Fierce bears 17 Wonderful views 18 Nice
monkeys

62   Generic plurals

1 Snails eat leaves. 2 Birds catch snails. 3 Snakes hunt birds.

63   Plural loss: עֶשְׂרִים אִישׁ

1 Fifty kilometers 2 Two centimeters 3 Four kilometers 4 Ten days 5 In
sixty days 6 It lasted 170 years 7 Five liters 8 Eight persons 9 Four
million 10 A hundred watts 11 Seventy pounds sterling 12 Seventy kilos
13 Twenty years 14 Twelve years 15 7% 16 Two and a half pounds
17 Twenty minutes 18 40% 19 Twelve days 20 100%

64   Action nouns

Form action nouns from these verbs:

ספר 'count', טיפל 'treat', התמצא 'be familiar with', הרגיש 'feel',
הצטנן 'catch cold', שיפר 'improve', אישר 'approve', התנוון 'decay',
הרג 'kill', הפנה 'refer', שיתף 'share', נתקל 'encounter', מינה
'appoint', קנה 'buy', קלט 'absorb', השתנה 'change', התקיף 'attack'

These action nouns do not follow the normal pattern. What verb do they
belong to and what do they mean?

לִימוּד, עֲבוֹדָה, הֲנָאָה, אַהֲבָה, מַתָּן, רְפוּאָה, כְּנִיסָה, פַּחַד, מִשְׁלוֹחַ

What are the action nouns for these verbs? You probably won't find them
listed as such with their verb in a dictionary, so you may have to ask a
Hebrew speaker:

צָחַק, הִתְגָּרֵשׁ, נָח, גָּר, הִשְׁוָוֹנָה, צָעַק, רִיחֵם, הוֹסִיף, חָזַר

65 Nouns from adjectives

Form abstract nouns from these adjectives – and give the appropriate English translation:

כָּפוּל 'double', אָטוּם 'transparent', עֲמָמִי 'popular', כָּבֵד 'heavy', צָנוּעַ 'modest', שָׁבִיר 'fragile', יַלְדוּתִי 'childish', גָּמִישׁ 'flexible', עָיֵף 'tired', עָדִין 'gentle', מַדָּעִי 'scientific', מָתוּחַ 'tense'

קָבוּעַ 'permanent', חָבִיב 'lovable', דָּתִי 'religious', בָּרִיא 'healthy',

66 פַּעְלָן and פַּעָל

1 From these words, form 'job words' in the PA'AL pattern and suggest what they mean:

סִיֵּר 'to scout', כִּיס 'pocket', צָבַע 'to paint', כִּינוֹר 'violin', צִיֵּר 'to draw', בָּלַשׁ 'to search', חֲמוֹר 'donkey', פֶּסֶל 'statue', נִיוֵּט 'to navigate', דִּיבֵּר 'to speak'

2 Form words in the PA'ALAN pattern. (Where a verb ends in ה change it to י.) What might they mean? Remember, it might be an activity, a personality, or an object of some kind:

צְלָב 'cross', רָקַד 'to dance', בָּטֵל 'idle', הֶחְלִיף 'to exchange', בִּידֵר 'to entertain', חָלָב 'milk', סָקַר 'to scan', סֵפֶר 'book', יִיצֵר 'to manufacture', חָשַׁד 'to suspect', יָקָר 'expensive', חִיקָה 'to imitate', יֶרֶק 'vegetables', שִׁידֵךְ 'to marry off'

67 Nouns with the suffix ן ָ and אִי ָ

1 Use these words to form activity words with the ן ָ suffix and suggest a translation:

כַּדּוּרְסַל 'basketball', כַּרְטִיס 'ticket', תַּעֲשִׂייָה 'industry', יְצוּא 'exports', יַהֲלוֹם 'diamond'

2 And the same with אִי ָ:

מָתֵימָטִיקָה 'physics', פִיסִיקָה, מְכוֹנָה 'machine', פוֹנֵטִיקָה 'phonetics', מָתֵימָטִיקָה 'mathematics', פִּרְסוּם 'publicity', שִׁירְיוֹן 'armored corps', חַשְׁמָל 'electricity'

68 Some other noun patterns

1 Use these words to form 'device words' in the MAF'EL pattern and guess at the meaning:

שִׁידֵר 'to transmit', זָלַף 'to spray', צָבַר 'to accumulate', הִגְבִּיר 'to strengthen', צָפוֹן 'North', שִׁינֵק 'to choke', סִירֵק 'to comb', קָלַט 'to pick up (broadcasts)'

2 Use these words to form 'device words' in the MAF'ELA pattern and again guess at the meaning:

בָּחַן 'to test', גָּרַף 'to rake', זָמַר 'to prune', אֵפֶר 'ash', גָּלַשׁ 'to ski'

3 Use these words to form location or action/product words in the MIF'AL pattern:

כָּתַב 'write', רָדַף 'chase', גָּדוֹל 'big', שָׁפַט 'to judge', שָׁמַר 'to guard', עָבַר 'to make a transition'

4 Use these words to form location or organization words in the MIF'ALA pattern:

כִּיבֵּס 'launder', זֶבֶל 'garbage', חֵלֶק 'part', עָבַר 'to make a transition', סְפִינָה 'a ship', רִיפֵּא 'heal'

5 Use these words to form 'illness words' in the PA'ELET pattern:

כֶּלֶב 'dog', שָׁפַע 'to flow', אָדוֹם 'red', נָזַל 'to drip', קָצָר 'short'

6 Use these words to form outcome or product words in the TAF'IL pattern:

אָגַד 'combine', מִילֵל 'to utter', קִיצֵר 'to shorten', הִרְגִּיל 'to accustom', הִכְתִּיב 'dictate', פָּנָה 'turn' (instead of ה, use ת), גִּילָה 'discover'

8 Use these words to form diminutive nouns in the PE'AL'AL pattern:

שָׁפָן 'rabbit', בָּצָל 'onion', חֲזִיר 'pig'

9 On what words are the following based:

דּוּבּוֹן 'teddy-bear', סוּסוֹן 'foal', יַרְחוֹן 'monthly', מִילוֹן 'dictionary', עִתּוֹן 'newspaper', בִּרְכּוֹן 'Grace After Meals booklet', חִידוֹן 'quiz', תַּקָנוֹן 'rule-book', חֲזִירוֹן 'piglet', מְקוֹמוֹן 'local newspaper', מַעֲרְכוֹן 'skit', גַּרְבּוֹנִים 'tights'

14 What words are the basis for these compounds?

חַיְדַּק 'microbe', אוֹפַנּוֹעַ 'motorbike', מַחֲזֶמֶר 'a musical', מִגְדָּלוֹר 'lighthouse', חַמְשִׁיר 'limerick', רַכֶּבֶל 'cable-car', זַרְקוֹר 'searchlight', דַּחְפּוֹר 'bulldozer', רַמְזוֹר 'traffic light', מַדְחוֹם 'thermometer'

Use a good dictionary to find the source of these acronyms:

אֶשֶׁ״ל 'board and lodging expenses', חוּ״ל 'overseas (from Israel)', רַבַּ״ט 'corporal', מַכַּ״ם 'Radar', מוֹ״ל 'publisher', צַלַ״שׁ 'military award', חַזַ״ל 'the Sages', נַתְבַּ״ג 'Ben-Gurion Airport', גַדְנַ״ע 'Israeli Military Cadet Force', שַׁבַּ״כּ 'Israel Security Service'

15 Form verbs and TEFULA-type nouns from these roots, and use a dictionary to determine their meaning:

1 ע.ף 2 מ.ת 3 כ.ן 4 ב.ן 5 ק.ם 6 ז.ן 7 ב.ס

What is the meaning and the root of these nouns:

מוֹתָר, תוֹצָר, מוֹעֵד, מוֹרָד, תּוֹעֶלֶת, תּוֹבָלָה, מוֹרֶשֶׁת, מוֹרָשָׁה, תּוֹצָאָה, מוֹלֶדֶת

What is the root and meaning of these nouns? And what verbs are closely related to them?

מַטָע, מַשָׁב, מַגָע, מַפָּח, מַגֵפָה, מַפּוּחִית, מַטוֹל עִילִי, מַטָרָה, מַשָׂא, מַתָּנָה

69–71 ADJECTIVE TYPES

69 Passive adjectives (כָּנוּס, מוּכְנָס, מְכוּנָס)

1 A broken leg 2 An injured thumb 3 A sun-tanned face 4 A shaved chin
5 A bent nose 6 A broken finger 7 A scratched arm 8 A burnt tongue
9 Two rows of polished teeth 10 Combed hair 11 Open eyes 12 Painted nails 13 A broken heart

70 Adjectives from nouns

Create adjectives from these nouns and suggest translations for them:

רְפוּאָה 'literature', סִפְרוּת 'type', טִיפּוּס 'religion', דָּת 'South', דָּרוֹם
'medicine', סְבִיבָה 'environment', מִקְצוֹעַ 'profession', נִיהוּל
'management', צָבָא 'army', מַלְכוּת 'monarchy', מַשְׁמָעוּת 'meaning',
מָקוֹם 'place', רֶוַח 'profit', יַחַס 'relation', הַתְחָלָה 'beginning'

71 Other meaningful adjective patterns

Use these words to form PA'ALAN adjectives and suggest translations:

פָּחַד 'to be afraid', נָבַח 'to bark', דִּיבֵּר 'to talk', שָׁמַר 'to conserve'

Use these words to create PA'IL adjectives and suggest meanings:

אָכַל 'eat', קִיבֵּל 'accept', שָׁבַר 'break', נִיגַשׁ 'to access'

Figure out the technical English equivalent of these phrasal adjectives.
(You may not find them all in a pocket dictionary.)

חוּץ־רַחֲמִי, תּוֹךְ־וְרִידִי, פְּנִים־יַבַּשְׁתִּי, תַּת־מוֹלְקוּלָרִי, בְּתַר־מִקְרָאִי,
חַד־צְדָדִי, דּוּ־פַּרְצוּפִי, רַב־לְשׁוֹנִי, עַל־אֱנוֹשִׁי, בֵּין־יַבַּשְׁתִּי, תַּת־הַכָּרָתִי,
בֵּין־כּוֹכָבִי, פְּרוֹ־מַעֲרָבִי, תְּלָת־עֶרְכִּי

72 Present tense 'verbs' as nouns and adjectives

From these verbs, make 'present tense nouns' and offer translations for
them:

סָחַר 'to trade', שָׁמַר 'to watch', תִּיוֵוךְ 'to mediate', רָעָה 'to graze',
הִתְקַדֵּם 'to advance', אָפָה 'to bake', רִיכֵּז 'to convene', שֵׁירֵת 'to serve',
הֶעֱסִיק 'to employ', פִּיקֵד 'to command', תִּכְנֵת 'to program', הִתְלַמֵּד
'to teach oneself', זָכָה 'to win', גָּלָה 'to go into exile' אִפְיֵין 'to
characterize', עָזַר 'to help', שָׁדַד 'to rob', הִתְפָּרֵעַ 'to run riot'

And from these make 'present tense adjectives':

הִדְהִים 'to astound', נָצַץ 'to sparkle', הִצְטַבֵּר 'to accumulate', שִׂימֵחַ 'to
delight', הִרְתִּיעַ 'to deter', דִּיכֵּא 'to depress', מִיצָה 'to exhaust', הִשְׁפִּיל
'to degrade', הִרְשִׁים 'to impress' עִנְיֵין 'to interest', הִטְרִיד 'to bother',
הִרְגִּיעַ 'to soothe', חָלַף 'to pass'

73 The construct as a possessive

(a) [Use possessive suffixes and constructs rather than שֶׁל.]

1 Their heavy breathing interrupted our delicious meal.
2 They were barely listening to my introduction.
3 His students are crazy about his lectures.
4 Her sons feared her cooking.
5 Our parents are paying for our trip to South America.
6 My husband has an elderly aunt in the north of Israel.
7 My wife's parents always forget her family name.
8 There's an exhibition of magazines from the time of the Mandate.
9 The great powers' reactions to the UN resolutions were disappointing.
10 I have a bit of pull, because my father knows the minister's secretary.
11 The copying of records is absolutely forbidden.
12 There's no reason to be ashamed of participation in a demo.
13 After closure of the Suez Canal came the intervention of the Western forces.

(b) Run through the suffixed forms (for both singular and plural) for:

חָבֵר 'friend', פְּנִייָה 'request', הִתְנַצְלוּת 'apology', תִּקְוָה 'hope'

(c) Translate:

1 *Hannah and her sisters* 2 *Me and my girl* 3 *All my sons* 4 *The sound of music* 5 *Dead poets' society*

(d) Translate:

1 A long-haired counselor
2 A green-eyed Frenchwoman
3 Two broad-shouldered butchers
4 A short-term opportunity
5 Snow-covered mountains
6 Her suitcase was full of books
7 A country of great beauty
8 Money-filled wallets
9 He's a person of influence
10 This book has an important message for everyone
11 She lacks friends
12 A country lacking in science

74 לְ of possession

1 Rub your eyes. 2 Shut your mouth. 3 Shake your head. 4 Shake my hand. 5 Hold my arm. 6 Pull her hair. 7 Raise your hand. 8 Stretch your legs. 9 Cut your nails. 10 Cut Meir's hair. 11 Wipe his chin. 12 Fold your arms. 13 Touch the baby's forehead.

75–6 CONSTRUCT NOUNS – VOWEL CHANGES

75 Construct segolates

1 The tribes of Israel 2 The tombs of kings 3 Store owners 4 Food colors 5 Army tents 6 The flag of Israel 7 Car parts 8 Men's clothes 9 Shabbat shoes 10 Shabbat Eves 11 Emergency teams 12 Art books 13 A science book

76 Some other vowel changes in constructs

Translate aloud:

1 The army of Jordan 2 Student dorms 3 Place of birth 4 Jet plane 5 The peace of the world 6 Evening newspaper 7 Passenger plane 8 Bus ticket 9 Place of work 10 Orange grove 11 Egged driver 12 Turkey meat 13 Chicken soup

and also:

1 The Likud party 2 Pine trees 3 The government of Syria 4 The Baath party 5 The Cohen family 6 The paratroop corps 7 Fig trees 8 A birthday greeting 9 The last names of the students 10 The Chief of Staff's statement

Form the construct of these words:

נְדָבָה 'donation', שְׁכָבוֹת 'layers', נְשָׁמוֹת 'souls', פְּצָצָה 'bomb', פְּצָצוֹת 'bombs', נְשָׁמָה 'soul', חֲבָרוֹת 'companies' (behaves like חֲרָדוֹת)

77 Double possessives: בֵּיתָהּ שֶׁל שָׂרָה

1 The doctors' strike 2 An engineer's salary 3 The dentist's bill 4 A nurse's work 5 A teacher's living 6 The manager's payslip 7 Avraham's expenses 8 The workers' demands 9 The management's offer 10 The president's vacation

78 Preposition + suffix: בְּלִי, בֵּין, כְּמוֹ

1 She's like me. 2 I'm like him. 3 You're like them. 4 I'm here without her. 5 She went without him. 6 What am I without you, Chaya? 7 Between me and you, she's a nobody. 8 What's happening between them? 9 Going without me? 10 They look like us.

79–80 NUMERALS

79 Definite numerals: 'The three idiots'

1 The two medicines 2 The ten pills 3 The two thermometers 4 The four doctors 5 The two of us 6 The three diseases 7 The sixty patients

80 Ordinals: 'first, second, third . . .'

1 The third man 2 The fiftieth step 3 The second latke 4 The sixth dreidel 5 The first candle 6 The eighth evening 7 The forty-ninth day 8 The fourth glass of wine 9 The second matza 10 The fifteenth word 11 His thirteenth birthday

81 Hundreds and thousands

Say aloud in Hebrew:

6000, 210, 390, 445, 14,220, 2000, 9083, 860, 10,100, 269, 104, 570, 613, 365, 248, 600,000, 11,504, 24,000, 967, 930, 175, 127, 120, 1756, 5751

82 Tense

1 My mother used to start cooking supper at 3 o'clock.
2 She used to iron each shirt.
3 Every Yom Kippur the community would cry and wail.
4 If I had a Chinese rug, I would put it here exactly.
5 What kind of cake would you make, wise guy?
6 If the vase were green, it would look nice on the shelf.
7 Oh Ruti, I thought you were going to clean.
8 He said he was tidying up but he wasn't.
9 I knew she was uptight.
10 Leave a light on when you leave.

11 A beggar sat on the bench, rattling a can.

12 If you give money, it'll be a good deed.

13 Sara rode her bicycle while holding a bag of pears in her hand.

14 Don't read while people are here, stupid!

15 I was just walking down the street thinking about the party.

83 The object suffix: לִבְנוֹתוֹ 'to build it'

1 To deny it   2 To see her   3 To approve them   4 To take it   5 To dismantle it   6 To criticize him   7 To praise them

84 Reflexives: 'myself, yourself . . .'

1 I'm teaching myself.

2 She always criticizes herself.

3 Shake yourself off now, silly boy.

4 The recruits undressed for a check-up.

5 Get dressed and comb your hair, you're both late!

6 I warn you, you won't forgive yourself.

7 Easy, I've done it myself.

8 Is there time to take a shower?

9 You have to know yourself.

10 He can't come to the phone, he's shaving.

11 It's the mayor – come on, introduce yourself!

12 I'm not introducing myself.

85 'One another'

1 The two officers hated one another.

2 From the day that we met, we've loved one another.

3 Look, the two ends join one another.

4 The companies have been competing with each other for years.

5 We told each other stories, jokes, gossip.

86 Experience adjectives: נוֹחַ לִי, קַר לִי

1 I'm so cold in bed.

2 Are you comfortable in those boots?

3 The children are hot there at the back.

4 They're OK in their two-storey house in Savyon.

5 I feel uncomfortable asking him.

87–90 COMPARATIVES

87 Comparative phrases

1 I'm warmer now, thank you.
2 Shoshi's nicer than the last baby-sitter.
3 This paper's much thicker.
4 Don't exaggerate – it's thinner, in fact.
5 This silverware is less expensive than the other.
6 There's been more rain in the Sharon than they expected.
7 It's better than yesterday.

88 'The most . . .'

1 He's just met the most beautiful girl in the world again.
2 Saudi Arabia is today the biggest oil exporter.
3 Is that the longest roll of paper towels?
4 Which city has the worst pollution?
5 That's the best way, I'm sure.

89 'as big as': . . . כְּמוֹ

1 It's as smooth as a baby's skin.
2 It's as cold as Chicago here!
3 He's not as smart as his brother, but that's not the main thing.
4 Did you find a place to park as quickly as last time?
5 There's no city as special as Jerusalem.

90 Measurement: מַה גּוֹדֶל . . . 'How big is . . .'

1 How long is the concert?
2 How wide is your station-wagon?
3 And how long is it?
4 We need a fridge one meter wide.
5 It's only for people aged fifteen and over.
6 How tall is that blond guy?
7 How high is the partition?
8 They've built a tower 90 meters high in the middle of the city.
9 This dress is 2 cm longer than the black dress.
10 Shabbat is two hours longer in summer.

91 Adverbs of manner: בִּמְהִירוּת 'quickly'

1 She's working hard with that guitar.
2 Yes, but she sings so badly.
3 Why does everyone drive so dangerously?
4 If you run over a pedestrian, you're automatically brought to court.
5 That shepherd plays the pipe well.
6 He stroked her hand gently.
7 He beat her savagely.
8 Can you write a bit more neatly?
9 I think he writes very nicely.
10 She's pregnant? She has to get to hospital urgently.
11 I want to clean my desk thoroughly.

92 Echo phrases, e.g. נִיצַּח נִצָּחוֹן מוּחְלָט 'won decisively'

Translate into English:

1 נֶהֱנֵיתִי הֲנָאָה מְרוּבָּה מִכַּתָּבַתְכֶם עַל הָעֲלִייָה הַשְּׁנִייָה.
2 הַחוֹלֶה עָלוּל לֶאֱכוֹל אֲכִילָה גַּסָה.
3 הַחֲטִיבָה נִלְחֲמָה בָּאוֹיֵב לְחִימָה עַזָּה.

93 בְּ of time, place and means

1 At the beginning of the school year we're leaving.
2 Next week I'm not coming.
3 There's a kiosk at the corner.
4 I'm calling at six.
5 Each time I put in a token there's no tone.
6 I was walking along the street when . . . .
7 Every Friday we have a free day now.
8 We waited nine years and then last year we got a phone.
9 Each time I dial I have problems.
10 Turn it with a screwdriver.

94 הַשָּׁנָה, הַיוֹם 'today, this year'

1 Where are you going for vacation this year?
2 This evening we're going for a walk to the Old City.
3 I'd rather take a cab this time.
4 This morning there was a serious incident.
5 This week there's a concert in the park.
6 The Dead Sea? That's the second time you've been this month!

95   הָ ֬ of destination, e.g. צָפוֹנָה 'northwards'

1 Turn left after the circle.

2 No, you're wrong, he has to turn right.

3 If you're traveling south, you're on the wrong road.

4 The steering-wheel pulls to the side.

5 It's OK, we can get home by dark.

6 Stuck in the mud? Try going forwards and then backwards.

7 At the next interchange, go east.

8 On Independence Day, everyone goes north to Lake Kinneret.

96   מִ of location, e.g. מִשְׂמֹאל 'on the left'

1 The ball's over the wall? Who's to blame?

2 The gas canisters are there on the right.

3 There's a fence, of course, all round the settlement.

4 Michael, can you change the light above the door?

5 On the left, there's a sign 'Ginossar'.

6 I keep the sticks under the steps.

97   The gerund: בְּהַגִּיעוֹ 'on his arrival'

Translate:

1   בִּהְיוֹתוֹ בִּסְפָרַד, הִכִּיר זַמָּר סְפָרַדִּי.

2   בְּצֵאתָם לְבַצֵּעַ פְּעוּלוֹת לַיְלָה, הֵם לוֹקְחִים צִיּוּד כָּבֵד.

3   אֶת אִשְׁתּוֹ פָּגַשׁ בִּהְיוֹתוֹ כְּבֶן תְּשַׁע־עֶשְׂרֵה.

4   עִם פְּרוֹץ מִלְחֶמֶת הָעוֹלָם . . . .

98   Where to position רַק and גַּם

1 I only have two potatoes, Sara.

2 Yossi's applying? Good, I'm also applying.

3 She plays tennis . . . and she also plays piano.

4 Only invalids can sit in these seats.

5 She even brought the baby-carriage into the plane!

6 You can buy diapers there, too.

7 I only knew two people at the party.

99–100 NEGATIVES

99 Inflexion of אֵין

1 The company does not accept responsibility.

2 If you do not agree, please write immediately.

3 Britain does not support this position.

4 I am incapable of influencing them.

5 If he is not a tourist, he need not register.

100 'No one, nothing, nowhere'

1 Who were you talking to? – Oh, no one . . . .

2 I have no questions. Do you?

3 No one saw the robbery.

4 The burglars didn't take anything.

5 We needed witnesses, but there was no one there.

6 They park on the sidewalks but they never get a ticket.

7 That's because you can't find a meter anywhere.

8 What did the policeman say to you? – Nothing special . . . .

9 I never drive without my license.

10 Calm down, Mrs Abu-Hatzeira, nothing happened.

What is the English equivalent of:

בִּלְתִּי־אֶפְשָׁרִי, בִּלְתִּי־יַצִּיב, בִּלְתִּי־פּוֹסֵק, בִּלְתִּי־נִמְנַע, חוֹסֶר־תֵּיאוּם, חוֹסֶר־סַבְלָנוּת, אִי־טִיפּוּל בְּחוֹלִים, בִּלְתִּי־כָּבִיס

101 Questions

1 Don't you have any envelopes?

2 You bought matches, didn't you?

3 Does he intend to marry her or not?

4 I'm not sure if the elevator's working.

5 The travel agent's on the fourth floor, isn't he?

6 You're not passing the university, are you?

7 I've no idea what he wants.

8 I wonder if there's a chance of a match between them.

102 Wishes and requests

1 I want her to join Gadna.
2 His parents prefer him to go to Hesder Yeshiva.
3 I was hoping she'd go to Nachal.
4 I wish they'd stop whispering.
5 Don't you dare, Yitzhak . . . .
6 Shoshi wanted the boys to go to university but they're in Kollel.
7 I want Ariela to play with me now – is it OK?

103 'Either . . . or': אוֹ . . . אוֹ

1 Get either vanilla flavor or chocolate flavor.
2 Should I buy the blue night-dress or do you prefer the pink?
3 Either you make your mind up now or we're going home.
4 Is the bank closing in a moment or do we still have time?
5 Either Monday or Tuesday will be all right.

104 Clauses as subject: 'Painting is fun'

1 Smelling every cottage cheese is disgusting.
2 Driving fast and honking is fun.
3 Earning big bucks is a problem.
4 Watching *Dallas* is a national sport.
5 I enjoy standing in line.
6 He enjoys pushing.

105 Relative clauses

105a Relative clauses with a pronoun

1 The neighborhood we live in is quite expensive.
2 Where's the contract you signed?
3 We're renting an apartment whose owner is abroad.
4 Is this the stairway where you lost it?
5 Look, that's the building we lived in last year.
6 In the first moshav we went to, there wasn't any electricity yet.
7 They're in that parking lot where they always play.
8 I only asked the tenants whose names I know.
9 Is this the housing project you were thinking about? It's a bit crowded.
10 What's the name of the girl whose parents live in Kfar Shemaryahu?

| 105b | מַה שֶׁ . . ., מִי שֶׁ . . ., אֵיפֹה שֶׁ . . .

1 The person who sells the flowers isn't there today.

2 I've put the typewriter where there's a bit of light.

3 At last – here's what I was looking for.

4 But that's not what I wanted to know!

5 I'm polite to whoever speaks to me.

6 What you said to him was very very rude.

7 Eat whatever there is in the freezer.

8 Come by whenever it's convenient to you, Miriam.

9 Give this note to the person who's in charge.

10 Allow him whatever you allow the others – it's obvious.

11 Anyone who calls information doesn't have to pay.

12 Take anything that fits.

| 105c | *Relative clauses with* הַ

Insert הַ as the relative conjunction in the blank space where possible:

1 הֲכִי "in" זֶה גֶּבֶר _מִתְלַבֵּשׁ יָפֶה וּמִתְקַשֵּׁט בִּצְבָעִים עֲלִיזִים . . . .

2 זוֹ לְמַעֲשֶׂה מַהֲפֵּכָה סוֹצְיַאלִית, _עֲשׂוּיָה לְהַחֲזִיר אֶת הַגְּבָרִים מֵאָתַיִם שָׁנָה לְאָחוֹר.

3 יֵשׁ אֲנָשִׁים _יִהְיֶה לָהֶם קָשֶׁה לְהִתְרַגֵּל לַמַּצָּב הֶחָדָשׁ הַזֶּה.

4 בָּחַרְתִּי מָקוֹם שׁוֹמֵם _עַל־פִּי הַמּוּמְחִים אֵינוֹ מַתְאִים לְחַקְלָאוּת.

5 פּוֹנִים יָמִינָה וְעוֹלִים עַל דֶּרֶךְ קְטַנָּה, _מִתְפַּתֶּלֶת בְּמַקְבִּיל לַנַּחַל.

6 מָצָאנוּ צָעִיר בְּלוֹנְדִינִי וְשָׁזוּף, _עָסַק בְּהַקָּמַת סֶכֶר קָטָן.

7 עוֹבְרִים כָּל שָׁנָה אַלְפֵי בְּנֵי נוֹעַר, _שׁוֹהִים בְּמַחֲנֶה גַּדְנַ"ע שֶׁבַּכְּפָר הַסָּמוּךְ.

106 When the order is not subject–verb–object

| 106a | *Inverting subject and verb*

1 After my relatives emigrated to Israel, I began to be interested in my roots.

2 Outside, three fat men with beards were waiting.

3 We had our own eggs until the hens all died.

4 In front of the house stood a hive.

5 When they heard about this, farmers stopped using chemical fertilizers.

6 If war breaks out, the result will be a catastrophe.

106b *Starting with the object*

1 I have silverware but I don't have napkins.
2 You want *30 shekels* for this?
3 I know Shoshana and Ariela – and I also know Yafa.
4 That newspaper's old, and I don't need this one either.

106c *Presentative verbs*

1 Five new people have come today.
2 It's snowing again.
3 A serious danger exists now.
4 Rachel, your friend's arrived.
5 Someone else is coming, I think.

Vocabulary for exercises

about (= concerning)	לְגַבֵּי
about (= approximately)	בְּעֵרֶךְ
to be about to	הָלַךְ לְ
abroad	בְּחוּץ לָאָרֶץ
to be absent	חָסֵר
absolutely	לְגַמְרֵי
account	חֶשְׁבּוֹן
acting	מִשְׂחָק
activity	פְּעִילוּת
actor	שַׂחְקָן
actually	בְּעֶצֶם
advantage of, to take	נִיצֵל
advice	עֵצָה
to be afraid	פָּחַד מ
after	אַחֲרֵי
afterwards	אַחַר-כָּךְ
again	עוֹד פַּעַם, שׁוּב
aged . . .	בְּגִיל . . .
(travel) agent	סוֹכֵן (נְסִיעוֹת)
ago	לִפְנֵי . . .
to agree	הִסְכִּים
agreement	הֶסְכֵּם
aim	מַטָּרָה
air conditioning	מִיזוּג אַוְוִיר
air force	חֵיל אַוְוִיר
air-letter	אִגֶּרֶת-אַוְוִיר
airport	נְמַל-תְּעוּפָה
all	כָּל
all right	בְּסֵדֶר
to allow	הִרְשָׁה
it is not allowed	אָסוּר
along	לְאוֹרֶךְ
already	כְּבָר
although	לַמְרוֹת שֶׁ
always	תָּמִיד
America	אַמֵרִיקָה
American	אַמֵרִיקָאִי

to amuse	הִצְחִיק
and	וְ
to annoy	הִרְגִיז
answer	תְּשׁוּבָה
ant	נְמָלָה (נְמָלִים)
any	כָּל
anyway	בִּכְלָל, עַל כָּל פָּנִים
apartment	דִירָה
apparently	כַּנִרְאֶה
apple	תַּפּוּחַ
to apply	הִגִישׁ בַּקָשָׁה
to approve	אִישֵׁר
Arab	עֲרָבִי
Ariela	אֲרִיאֵלָה
arm	יָד (יָדַיִים)
armchair	כּוּרְסָה
Army, the Israeli	צַהַ״ל
around	סָבִיב
art	אוֹמָנוּת
article (written)	מַאֲמָר
artist	צַיָיר
as	בְּתוֹר
to be ashamed	הִתְבַּיֵישׁ מִ
to ask (a question)	שָׁאַל
to ask (request)	בִּיקֵשׁ
to be asleep	יָשֵׁן
assignment	עֲבוֹדָה
at	בְּ
at all	בִּכְלָל
atmosphere	אַוְוִירָה
to attack	הִתְקִיף
Auntie	דוֹדָה
author	סוֹפֵר
autumn	סְתָיו
aware of	מוּדָע לְ
Ayalon Highway	נְתִיבֵי אַיָלוֹן

baby	תִּינוֹק
baby carriage	עֲגָלָה
baby girl	תִּינוֹקֶת
baby sitter	בֵּיבִּיסִיטֶר
to be back	חָזַר
bad	לֹא טוֹב
bad (pain etc.)	קָשֶׁה
bag	תִּיק
bakery	מַאֲפִייָה
balcony	מִרְפֶּסֶת
ball	כַּדוּר
bank	בַּנְק
barely	בְּקוֹשִׁי
bargain	מְצִיאָה
barmitzvah	בַּר־מִצְוָוה
base	בָּסִיס
basement	מַרְתֵּף
Bat Yam	בַּת־יָם
bath	אַמְבַּטְיָה
bath, to take a	עָשָׂה אַמְבַּטְיָה
bathrobe	חָלוּק
bathroom	אַמְבַּטְיָה
bay	מִפְרָץ
beach	חוֹף
bear	דוֹב (דוּבִּים)
to bear	נָשָׂא
beard	זָקָן
beautiful	יָפֶה
beauty	יוֹפִי
because	כִּי
because of	בִּגְלַל
bed	מִיטָה
bee	דְבוֹרָה (דְבוֹרִים)
Beer-Sheva	בְּאֵר־שֶׁבַע
before	לִפְנֵי
beggar	קַבְּצָן

to begin	הִתְחִיל
beginning	הַתְחָלָה
behind	מֵאֲחוֹרֵי
belt	חֲגוֹרָה
bench	סַפְסָל
to bend	עִיקֵם
Benny	בֶּנִי
better (preferable)	עָדִיף
Bible	תַּנַ"ךְ
bicycle	אוֹפַנַּיִים
big	גָּדוֹל
bill (money)	שְׁטָר (שְׁטָרוֹת)
bill	חֶשְׁבּוֹן
bird	צִיפּוֹר
to give birth	יָלַד
birth	לֵידָה
birthday	יוֹם הוּלֶדֶת
a bit	קְצָת
black	שָׁחוֹר
to be to blame	אָשֵׁם
blanket	שְׂמִיכָה
blessing	בְּרָכָה
blond	בְּלוֹנְדִינִי
blouse	חוּלְצָה
to boil	הִרְתִּיחַ
bomb	פְּצָצָה
to bomb	הִפְצִיץ
book	סֵפֶר
bookcase	כּוֹנָנִית
booklet	חוֹבֶרֶת
boot	מַגָּף (מַגָּפַיִים)
border	גְבוּל
boring	מְשַׁעֲמֵם
to bother	הִפְרִיעַ לְ
bottle	בַּקְבּוּק
bowl	צְלוֹחִית

brainwave	חוֹכְמָה
bread	לֶחֶם
to break	שָׁבַר
to break out (war)	פָּרַץ
breakfast	אֲרוּחַת־בּוֹקֶר
to breathe	נָשַׁם
brigade	חֲטִיבָה
bright	בָּהִיר
brilliant	מַבְרִיק
broken	שָׁבוּר
broom	מַטְאֲטֵא
brother	אָח
brown	חוּם
brush	מִבְרֶשֶׁת
buddy	חָבֵר
building	בִּנְיָן
burglar	פּוֹרֵץ
to burn (something)	שָׂרַף
to burn *intrans.*	נִשְׂרַף
bus	אוֹטוֹבּוּס
bus-stop	תַּחֲנָה
busy	עָסוּק
but	אֲבָל
butcher	קַצָּב
butter	חֶמְאָה
button	כַּפְתּוֹר
to buy	קָנָה
by (= at the latest)	עַד
by (= next to)	עַל־יַד
cab	מוֹנִית
cabinet	אָרוֹן
cafeteria	מֶנְסָה
cake	עוּגָה
a call (by phone)	שִׂיחָה
to call (by phone)	צִילְצֵל לְ

called (= by the name of)	בְּשֵׁם
to calm down	נִרְגַּע
camera	מַצְלֵמָה
camp	מַחֲנֶה
can	יָכוֹל
can I, can we?	אֶפְשָׁר
can-opener	פּוֹתְחָן
canal	תְּעָלָה
to cancel	בִּיטֵל
canister (gas)	בַּלוֹן
capable	מְסוּגָּל
car	מְכוֹנִית
careful!	זְהִירוּת !
(he) cares about	אִיכְפַּת לוֹ מְ . . .
carpenter	נַגָּר
carton	אֲרִיזָה
case (= instance)	מִקְרֶה
cash	מְזוּמָן
cash-dispenser	כַּסְפּוֹמָט
cat	חָתוּל
catastrophe	קָטַסְטְרוֹפָה
to catch	תָּפַס
celebration	שִׂמְחָה
cemetery	בֵּית־קְבָרוֹת
center	מֶרְכָּז
centimeter	סֶנְטִימֶטֶר
cereal	קוֹרְנְפְלֵיקְס
certain (= particular)	מְסוּיָּים
Chagit	חַגִּית
Chaim	חַיִּים
chair	כִּיסֵא (כִּיסְאוֹת)
challah	חַלָּה
Chana	חַנָּה
chance of . . .	סִיכּוּי לְ
Chanukkah	חֲנוּכָּה
chapter	פֶּרֶק

in charge	אַחֲרָאִי
charity	צְדָקָה
Chava	חַוָה
Chaya	חַיָה
cheap	זוֹל
check (money)	שֵׁק
check (= investigation)	בְּדִיקָה
check-up	בְּדִיקָה
to check	בָּדַק
checkbook	פִּנְקַס-שֵׁקִים
cheek!	חוּצְפָּה !
chemical	כִּימִי
chicken	עוֹף
Chief of Staff	רַמַטְכָּ"ל
chin	סַנְטֵר
Chinese	סִינִי
chocolate	שׁוֹקוֹ
to choose	בָּחַר בְּ
cinema	בֵּית-קוֹלְנוֹעַ
circle (traffic)	סִיבּוּב
circular noun	חוֹזֵר
circumcision	בְּרִית-מִילָה
civilian	אֶזְרָח
class	כִּיתָּה
clean	נָקִי
to clean	נִיקָה
cleaning lady	עוֹזֶרֶת
clerk	פָּקִיד
clever	חָכָם
close (= near)	קָרוֹב לְ
to close intrans.	נִסְגַּר
closet	אָרוֹן
coalition	קוֹאַלִיצְיָה
coat	מְעִיל
cockroach	ג'וּק
coffee	קָפֶה

coin	מַטְבֵּעַ (מַטְבְּעוֹת)
color	צֶבַע
colored	צִבְעוֹנִי
comb	מַסְרֵק
to comb	סֵרֵק
to come	בָּא
to come back	חָזַר
to come by	קָפַץ
to come out	יָצָא
comfortable	נוֹחַ
coming (= next)	בָּא
commitment	הִתְחַיְּיבוּת
community	קְהִילָה
company	חֶבְרָה
compensation	פִּיצוּיִים
to compete	הִתְחָרָה
complaint	תְּלוּנָה
compulsory	חוֹבָה
computer	מַחְשֵׁב
concert	קוֹנְצֶרְט
concession	וִיתּוּר
conference	וְעִידָה
contract	חוֹזֶה
convenient	נוֹחַ
to cook	בִּישֵּׁל
cookie	עוּגִיָּיה
to copy	הֶעֱתִיק
corner	פִּינָה
corridor	מִסְדְרוֹן
to cost	עָלָה
cottage cheese	קוֹטֶג'
couch	סַפָּה
counselor (camp)	מַדְרִיךְ
counter	דַלְפֵּק
country	מְדִינָה
course	קוּרְס

court (of law)	בֵּית־מִשְׁפָּט
courtyard	חָצֵר
cousin	בֶּן־דּוֹד
cow	פָּרָה
crazy	מְשׁוּגָּע
to create	יָצַר
credit card	כַּרְטִיס אַשְׁרַאי
crisis	מַשְׁבֵּר
to criticize	בִּיקֵּר
cross with	בְּרוֹגֶז עִם
crowded	צָפוּף
cup	סֵפֶל
curfew	עוֹצֶר
custom	מִנְהָג
customer	קוֹנֶה
customs	מֶכֶס
to cut	חָתַךְ
(nails)	גָּזַר
(hair)	סִיפֵּר
to cut off (= isolate)	נִיתֵּק
Daddy	אַבָּא
dairy *adj.*	חַלָבִי
danger	סַכָּנָה
dangerous	מְסוּכָּן
Danny	דָּנִי
to dare	הֵעֵיז
dark *noun*	חֲשֵׁכָה
dark	כֵּהֶה
dark blue	כָּחוֹל
darling	מוֹתֶק
David	דָּוִד
day	יוֹם
the day after tomorrow	מָחֳרָתַיִם
Dead Sea	יַם הַמֶּלַח
to deal with	טִיפֵּל בְּ

debate	דִּיּוּן
to decide	הֶחְלִיט
(good) deed	מִצְוָוה
delicious	טָעִים
a demand	תְּבִיעָה
demo	הַפְגָּנָה
dentist	רוֹפֵא שִׁינַיִים
to deny	הִכְחִישׁ
desert	מִדְבָּר
desk	שׁוּלְחָן
to destroy	הִשְׁמִיד
development	הִתְפַּתְּחוּת
Devora	דְּבוֹרָה
to dial	חִיֵּיג
diaper	חִיתּוּל
to die	מֵת
different	שׁוֹנֶה
dining corner	פִּינַת־אוֹכֶל
director	מְנַהֵל
director (theatrical)	בַּמַּאי
dirt	לִיכְלוּךְ
dirty	מְלוּכְלָךְ
disappointed	מְאוּכְזָב
discount	הֲנָחָה
disease	מַחֲלָה
disgrace	בּוּשָׁה
disgusting	מַגְעִיל
to dismantle	פֵּירֵק
to distribute	חִילֵּק
to divorce	גֵּירֵשׁ
to do	עָשָׂה
doctor	רוֹפֵא
dog	כֶּלֶב
door	דֶּלֶת
dope	טֶמְבֶּל
dorms	מָעוֹן

Dov	דֹב
downstairs	לְמַטָה
Dr	ד"ר
drag *noun*	טְרְחָה
dress	שִׂמְלָה
dresser	שִׁידָה
drier	דְרַייֶאר
to drink	שָׁתָה
to drive	נָהַג
driver	נֶהָג
dry	יָבֵשׁ
Dudu	דוּדוּ
dumb (= stupid)	מְטוּמְטָם
during	בִּשְׁעַת
duvet	כֶּסֶת
ear	אוֹזֶן
to earn	הִרְווִיחַ
East	מִזְרָח
easy	קַל
to eat	אָכַל
Efrayim	אֶפְרַיִם
egg	בֵּיצָה (בֵּיצִים)
Egypt	מִצְרַיִים
Eilat	אֵילַת
either . . . or	אוֹ . . . אוֹ
elderly	קָשִׁישׁ
electricity	חַשְׁמָל
elevator	מַעֲלִית
embassy	שַׁגְרִירוּת
emergency	חֵירוּם
to emigrate (to Israel)	עָלָה
to employ	הִפְעִיל
empty	רֵיק
end (physical)	קָצֶה (קְצָווֹת)
end	סוֹף

to end	נִגְמַר
enemy	אוֹיֵב
engine	מָנוֹעַ
engineer	מְהַנְדֵּס
to enjoy	נֶהֱנָה מִ
enough	מַסְפִּיק
entrance	כְּנִיסָה
envelope	מַעֲטָפָה
especially	בְּעִיקָר
Esther	אֶסְתֵּר
Europe	אֵירוֹפָּה
even	אֲפִילוּ
evening	עֶרֶב
(in the) event	בְּמִקְרֶה
every	כָּל
everyone	כָּל אֶחָד, כּוּלָם
exactly	בְּדִיּוּק
to examine	בָּדַק
exemption	פְּטוֹר
exercise	תַּרְגִּיל
exhibition	תַּעֲרוּכָה
exit	יְצִיאָה
to expect	צִיפָּה
expenses	הוֹצָאוֹת
expensive	יָקָר
experience	נִסָּיוֹן
expert in	מוּמְחֶה לְ
to explain	הִסְבִּיר
exporter	יְצוּאָן
extremely	בְּיוֹתֵר
eye	עַיִן (עֵינַיִם)
face	פָּנִים
(in) fact	בְּעֶצֶם
factory	מִפְעָל
to fall	נָפַל

to fall in love with	הִתְאָהֵב בְּ
family	מִשְׁפָּחָה
fantastic	פַנְטַסְטִי
(as) far as	עַד
farm	מֶשֶׁק
farmer	חַקְלַאי
fast (= quick)	מַהֵר
fast *noun*	צוֹם
to fast	צָם
fat	שָׁמֵן
father	אָב, אַבָּא
fault	תַּקָלָה
(he's) fed up with	. . . נִמְאַס לוֹ מִ
fence	גָּדֵר
fertilizer	דֶּשֶׁן
festival	חַג
few	מְעַט מְאֹד
a few	כַּמָּה, אֲחָדִים, מְעַטִים
fiancee	אֲרוּסָה
Fiat	פִיאַט
field	שָׂדֶה (שָׂדוֹת)
fierce	אַכְזָרִי
fig	תְּאֵנָה
film	סֶרֶט
filthy	מְטוּנָּף
final	סוֹפִי
finally	סוֹף סוֹף
to find	מָצָא
finger	אֶצְבַּע (אֶצְבָּעוֹת)
to finish	גָּמַר
fire (= a blaze)	דְּלֵיקָה
to fire	פִּיטֵר
first	רִאשׁוֹן
first (= firstly)	קוֹדֶם
first of all	קוֹדֶם-כָּל
to fit (clothes)	הִתְאִים

to fix	תִּיקֵן
fixed	קָבוּעַ
flashlight	פַּנָס
flavor	טַעַם
floor	רִצְפָּה
floor (= storey)	קוֹמָה
fly	זְבוּב
to fold (one's) hands	שִׁילֵב יָדַיִים
folder	תִּיק
food	אוֹכֶל
foodstore	מַכּוֹלֶת
for	בִּשְׁבִיל
for (= since)	זֶה, כְּבָר
forbidden	אָסוּר
force	כּוֹחַ (כּוֹחוֹת)
forecast	תַּחֲזִית
forehead	מֵצַח
foreign	זָר
Foreign Minister	שַׂר הַחוּץ
to forget	שָׁכַח
to forgive	סָלַח לְ
fork	מַזְלֵג (מַזְלֵגוֹת)
form	טוֹפֶס
France	צָרְפַת
free (= for free)	חִינָם
free (= empty)	פָּנוּי
freezer	פְרִיזֶר
Frenchman	צָרְפָתִי
Friday	יוֹם שִׁישִׁי
Friday night	לֵיל שַׁבָּת
fridge	מְקָרֵר
friend	חָבֵר
to frighten	הִפְחִיד
from	מְ
front	חָזִית
(in) front of	לְפָנֵי

a fruit	פְּרִי (פֵּרוֹת)
fun	כֵּיף
furniture	רִיהוּט
Gadna	גַדְנַ"ע
the Galilee	הַגָּלִיל
garbage	זֶבֶל
garden	גִּינָה
gas (for cooking etc.)	גַז
gas station	תַּחֲנַת דֶּלֶק
gear	הִילוּךְ
gentle	עָדִין
Gershon	גֵּרְשׁוֹן
to get (= receive)	קִיבֵּל
to get down	יָרַד
to get (someone) down	הוֹרִיד
to get into	נִכְנַס
to get (someone) out	הוֹצִיא
Gila	גִּילָה
girl	בַּחוּרָה
girl, little	יַלְדָּה
girl-friend	חֲבֵרָה
to give	נָתַן לְ
to be glad	שָׂמֵחַ
a glass	כּוֹס (כּוֹסוֹת)
glasses	מִשְׁקָפַיִם
to go	הָלַךְ
to go (travel)	נָסַע
to go back	חָזַר
to go on	הִמְשִׁיךְ
to go out	יָצָא
good	טוֹב
gorgeous	נֶהְדָּר
government	מֶמְשָׁלָה
to grab	חָטַף
grade	צִיּוּן

gradually	לְאַט לְאַט
Grandma	סַבְתָּא
Grandpa	סַבָּא
grape	עֵנָב (עֲנָבִים)
great!	מֵאָה אָחוּז !
great (= major)	גָּדוֹל
great (= fabulous)	מְשֻׁגָּע
green	יָרוֹק
ground	אֲדָמָה
group	קְבוּצָה
grove	פַּרְדֵּס
to grow (up)	גָּדַל
guitar	גִּיטָרָה
guy	בָּחוּר
guys	חֶבְרֶ'ה
Hagada	הַגָּדָה
Haifa	חֵיפָה
hair	שֵׂיעָר
half	חֵצִי
half an hour	חֲצִי שָׁעָה
hamsin	חַמְסִין
hand	יָד
hang on	חַכֵּה !
hanger	קוֹלָב
to happen	קָרָה
happy	מְאוּשָׁר
hard	קָשֶׁה
to hate	שָׂנֵא
to have	יֵשׁ . . . לְ
to have to (= must)	צָרִיךְ
head	ראשׁ
headache	כְּאֵב־ראשׁ
healthy	בָּרִיא
to hear (about)	שָׁמַע (עַל)
heart	לֵב

heat	חוֹם
heatwave	חַמְסִין
heaven forbid	חָלִילָה
(for) heaven's sake	בְּחַיֶּיךָ
heavy	כָּבֵד
Hebrew (language)	עִבְרִית
Hebrew *adj.*	עִבְרִי
Hebron	חֶבְרוֹן
(go to) hell	לֵךְ לַעֲזָאזֵל
help	עֶזְרָה
to help	עָזַר לְ
hen	תַּרְנְגוֹלֶת
here	פֹּה, כָּאן
here's . . .	הִנֵּה
the Hermon	הַחֶרְמוֹן
Hesder	הֶסְדֵר
hey!	הָלוֹ !
hi	שָׁלוֹם
high school	תִּיכוֹן
highway	כְּבִישׁ
to hit	הִרְבִּיץ
hive	כַּוֶּרֶת
to hold	הֶחֱזִיק
to hold (conference etc.)	עָרַךְ
home	הַבַּיִת
honey	מוֹתֶק
to honk	צִפְצֵף
to hope	קִיוָּה
hospital	בֵּית־חוֹלִים
hot	חַם
hour	שָׁעָה
house	בַּיִת
housing project	שִׁיכּוּן
how	אֵיךְ
how about . . .	מַה דַּעְתְּךָ שֶׁ . . .
how many	כַּמָּה

how much	כַּמָה
huge	עֲנָקִי
hummus	חוּמוּס
a hundred	מֵאָה
hungry	רָעֵב
to hunt	צָד
husband	בַּעַל
ID	תְּעוּדַת זֶהוּת
idea	מוּשָׂג
immediately	מִיָד
immigrant	עוֹלֶה
important	חָשׁוּב
(it's) impossible	אִי־אֶפְשָׁר
to be impressed with	הִתְרַשֵׁם מִ
to improve	שִׁיפֵּר
in	בְּ
incident	תַּקְרִית
Independence Day	יוֹם הָעַצְמָאוּת
India	הוֹדוּ
to influence	הִשְׁפִּיעַ
influence	הַשְׁפָּעָה
to initiate	יָזַם
to injure	פָּצַע
installment	תַּשְׁלוּם
instead	דַוְוקָא
institute	מָכוֹן
insurance	בִּיטוּחַ
to intend	הִתְכַּוֵון
interchange	מַחְלֵף
interested in	מְעוּנְיָין בְּ
international	בֵּינְלְאוּמִי
intersection	צוֹמֶת
to intervene	הִתְעָרֵב
into	לְתוֹךְ
to introduce	הִצִיג

invalid	נְכֶה
to invite	הִזְמִין
iron	בַּרְזֶל
to iron	גִּיהֵץ
ironing	גִּיהוּץ
Israel	יִשְׂרָאֵל
Israeli	יִשְׂרָאֵלִי
Italian	אִיטַלְקִי
jackal	תַּן
jacket	ז'קֶט
jam (traffic)	פְּקָק
to be jealous of	קִינֵּא בְּ
jeans	ג'ינְס
jelly	רִיבָּה
Jericho	יְרִיחוֹ
Jerusalem	יְרוּשָׁלַיִם
jet	סִילוֹן
Jezreel	יִזְרְעֶאל
to join intrans.	הִתְחַבֵּר
to join (a club)	הִצְטָרֵף לְ
joke	בְּדִיחָה
Jordan	יַרְדֵן
the Jordan Valley	הַבִּקְעָה
Judaism	יַהֲדוּת
juice	מִיץ
Junior High	חֲטִיבַת בֵּינַיִים
just (now)	עַכְשָׁיו
just (= only)	רַק
just as (= equally)	בְּאוֹתָהּ מִידָה
to keep	שָׁמַר
kettle	קוּמְקוּם
key	מַפְתֵּחַ
kibbutz	קִיבּוּץ
kid	יֶלֶד

to kill	הָרַג
kilo	קִילוֹ
kilometer	קִילוֹמֶטֶר
kind (= sort)	סוּג
kind of	כָּכָה
kindergarten teacher	גַּנֶּנֶת
king	מֶלֶךְ
kitchen	מִטְבָּח
knife	סַכִּין
to know (someone)	הִכִּיר
(something)	יָדַע
Kobi	קוֹבִּי
Kollel	כּוֹלֵל
kosher	כָּשֵׁר
Lake Kinneret	יַם כִּנֶּרֶת
lamp	מְנוֹרָה
to land	נָחַת
lane (on highway)	נָתִיב
language	שָׂפָה
large	גָּדוֹל
last adv.	בַּפַּעַם הָאַחֲרוֹנָה
last	אַחֲרוֹן
last (week, month . . .)	שֶׁעָבַר
to last	נִמְשַׁךְ
late	מְאוּחָר
late show	הַצָּגָה שְׁנִייָה
to be late	אִיחַר
to laugh	צָחַק
launchpad	כֵּן
laundry (place)	מַכְבֵּסָה
laundry (clothes)	כְּבִיסָה
lawyer	עוֹרֵךְ־דִּין
leader	מַנְהִיג
leaf	עָלֶה
to learn	לָמַד

(at) least	לְפָחוֹת
to leave (= quit)	עָזַב
to leave	הִשְׁאִיר
Lebanon	לְבָנוֹן
lecture	הַרְצָאָה
lecturer	מַרְצֶה
left	שְׂמֹאל
to be left	נִשְׁאַר
leg	רֶגֶל
less	פָּחוֹת
lesson	שִׁיעוּר
to let know	הוֹדִיעַ
letter	מִכְתָּב
lettuce	חַסָּה
library	סִפְרִייָה
license	רִשְׁיוֹן
to lie (= untruth)	שִׁיקֵר
to lie down	שָׁכַב
life	חַיִּים
lift (by car etc.)	טְרֶמְפּ
light	אוֹר
light blue	תְּכֵלֶת
lightning	בָּרָק
to like	אָהַב
likely to	עָלוּל לְ
line (for clothes)	חֶבֶל
line (of people)	תּוֹר
lion	אַרְיֵה (אֲרָיוֹת)
to listen	הִקְשִׁיב לְ
liter	לִיטֶר
a little	קְצָת
to live	חַי
a living	פַּרְנָסָה
living room	סָלוֹן
lizard	לְטָאָה
loads of	הָמוֹן

239

to lock	נָעַל
long	אָרוֹךְ
a long time	הַרְבֵּה זְמָן
to look (= appear)	נִרְאָה
to look after	שָׁמַר עַל
to look for	חִיפֵּשׂ
to lose	הִפְסִיד
to lose (= mislay, drop)	אִיבֵּד
lots of	הַרְבֵּה
loud	גָּבוֹהַּ
(it's) lucky	מַזָּל
lunch	אֲרוּחַת־צָהֳרַיִים

magazine	כְּתַב־עֵת
Magen David Adom	מָגֵן דָּוִד אָדוֹם
mailbox	תֵּיבַת־דוֹאַר
(the) main thing	הָעִיקָר
mainly	בְּעִיקָר
to make	עָשָׂה
man	גֶּבֶר
management	הַנְהָלָה
manager	מְנַהֵל
Mandate	מַנְדָּט
many	הַרְבֵּה, רַב
map	מַפָּה
margarine	מַרְגָּרִינָה
margin	שׁוּלַיִים
to marry	הִתְחַתֵּן עִם
Master's (MA degree)	מ.א., מַסְטֶר
match (fire)	גַּפְרוּר
match (matrimonial)	שִׁידּוּךְ
matza	מַצָּה
maybe	אוּלַי
mayonnaise	מַיוֹנֶז
mayor	רֹאשׁ הָעִיר
meal	אֲרוּחָה

to mean	הִתְכַּוֵּון לְ
meaning	מַשְׁמָעוּת
meanwhile	בֵּינְתַיִים
meat	בָּשָׂר
meaty	בְּשָׂרִי
medicine	תְּרוּפָה
to meet	פָּגַשׁ
meeting	יְשִׁיבָה
Meir	מֵאִיר
Menachem	מְנַחֵם
menu	תַּפְרִיט
message	מֶסֶר
mezuzah	מְזוּזָה
Michael	מִיכָאֵל
micro-wave	מִיקְרוֹ-גַל
middle	אֶמְצַע
the Middle East	הַמִּזְרָח הַתִּיכוֹן
midnight	חֲצוֹת
Miki	מִיקִי
milk	חָלָב
to make up one's mind	הֶחְלִיט
(at a) minimum	מִינִימוּם
minister	שַׂר
minute	דַּקָּה
Miriam	מִרְיָם
mirror	רְאִי (מַרְאוֹת)
missile	טִיל
mistake	טָעוּת
mister	מַר
MK (member of Knesset)	חֲבֵר כְּנֶסֶת
moment	רֶגַע
(at the) moment	כָּרֶגַע
(in a) moment	תֵּיכֶף
Mommy	אִמָּא
Monday	יוֹם שֵׁנִי
money	כֶּסֶף

monkey	קוֹף
month	חוֹדֶשׁ (חוֹדָשִׁים)
more (things)	עוֹד
more	יוֹתֵר
moshav	מוֹשָׁב
Moshe	מֹשֶׁה
most	רוֹב
mother	אֵם, אִמָּא
mother-in-law	חוֹתֶנֶת
mountain	הַר
mouth	פֶּה
to move	זָז
Mr	מַר
mud	בּוֹץ
music	מוּסִיקָה
must	צָרִיךְ
Naama	נַעֲמָה
Naava	נַאֲוָה
Nachal	נַחַ"ל
nail (of finger)	צִיפּוֹרֶן
name	שֵׁם (שֵׁמוֹת)
Naomi	נָעֳמִי
napkin	מַפִּית
national	לְאוּמִי
Navy	חֵיל הַיָּם
near	עַל־יַד
nearly	כִּמְעַט
neat	מְסוּדָּר
Nechama	נֶחָמָה
need	צָרִיךְ
(the) Negev	הַנֶּגֶב
negotiations	מַשָּׂא וּמַתָּן
neighbor	שָׁכֵן
neighborhood	שְׁכוּנָה
new	חָדָשׁ

news	חֲדָשׁוֹת
newspaper	עִתּוֹן
(the) next	הַבָּא
next to	עַל־יַד
nice	נֶחְמָד, נָאֶה
nice (person)	נֶחְמָד, סִימְפַּטִי
nightdress	כְּתוֹנֶת־לַיְלָה
no good	לֹא בְּסֵדֶר
Noam	נֹעַם
(a) nobody	אֶפֶס
noise	רַעַשׁ
nonsense	שְׁטוּיוֹת
nose	אַף
note (written)	פֶּתֶק
notification	הוֹדָעָה
now	עַכְשָׁיו
nuclear	גַּרְעִינִי
number	מִסְפָּר
nurse	אָחוֹת

objection	הִתְנַגְּדוּת
obvious	בָּרוּר
of course	כַּמּוּבָן
off (= bad)	מְקוּלְקָל
offer noun	הַצָּעָה
office	מִשְׂרָד
officer	קָצִין
official	רִשְׁמִי
Ofra	עָפְרָה
oh darn!	אוֹי וַאֲבוֹי !
oil (petroleum)	נֵפְט
O.K.	בְּסֵדֶר
old (of people)	זָקֵן
the Old City	הָעִיר הָעַתִּיקָה
old man	זָקֵן
old (of things)	יָשָׁן

olive	זַיִת
on	עַל
to be on (e.g. a light)	פָּתוּחַ
once	פַּעַם
one	אֶחָד
to open *intrans.*	נִפְתַּח
opportunity	הִזְדַּמְנוּת
opposite	מוּל
(the) opposite	הַהֵיפֶךְ
or	אוֹ
orange	תַּפּוּז
orchard	פַּרְדֵּס
to order (something)	הִזְמִין
Orit	אוֹרִית
other	אַחֵר
outfit	תִּלְבּוֹשֶׁת
outside	בַּחוּץ
oven	תַּנּוּר
over (= more than)	לְמַעֲלָה מִ
over there	שָׁמָּה
overseas	חוּץ־לָאָרֶץ
(of one's) own	מִשֶּׁל . . .
owner of . . .	בַּעַל . . .

to pack	אָרַז
package	חֲבִילָה
page	עַמּוּד
pain-in-the-neck	נוּדְנִיק
paint	צֶבַע
to paint (i.e. decorate)	צָבַע
pajamas	פִּיזַ׳מָה
pants	מִכְנָסַיִים
paper	נְיָיר
paper (school assignment)	חִיבּוּר
to parachute	הִצְנִיחַ
paratroop	צַנְחָן

parents	הוֹרִים
park *noun*	גַּן צִיבּוּרִי
to park *intrans.*	חָנָה
parking-lot	חֶנְיוֹן
parking meter	מַדְחָן
parking ticket	דוּ״ח
part	חֵלֶק
to participate	הִשְׁתַּתֵּף
particularly	בִּמְיוּחָד
partition	מְחִיצָה
party (political)	מִפְלָגָה
party (the other sort)	מְסִיבָּה
to pass (by)	עָבַר (עַל-יַד)
passenger	נוֹסֵעַ
Passover	פֶּסַח
passport	דַּרְכּוֹן
patience	סַבְלָנוּת
patient	חוֹלֶה
to pay	שִׁילֵם
payment	תַּשְׁלוּם
payslip	תְּלוּשׁ מַשְׂכּוֹרֶת
peace	שָׁלוֹם
pear	אַגָּס
pedestrian	הוֹלֵךְ-רֶגֶל
pen	עֵט
people	אֲנָשִׁים
percent	אָחוּז
perfume	בּוֹשֶׂם
perhaps	אוּלַי
person	אָדָם
Peugeot	פֶּז׳וֹ
photo	צִילוּם
(to take a) photo of	צִילֵם
piano	פְּסַנְתֵּר
to pick up (people)	אָסַף
picture	תְּמוּנָה

pill	כַּדּוּר
pillow	כַּר
pine	אוֹרֶן
pink	וָרֹד
pitch	מִגְרָשׁ
pitta	פִּיתָּה
(it's a) pity	חֲבָל
plan	תּוֹכְנִית
plane	מָטוֹס
plastic bag	שַׂקִּית נַיְילוֹן
plate	צַלַּחַת
play (theater)	מַחֲזֶה
to play (game)	שִׂיחֵק
to play (instruments)	נִיגֵּן
please	בְּבַקָּשָׁה
pleased	מְבֻסּוֹט
pleasure	תַּעֲנוּג
plum	שָׁזִיף
poet	מְשׁוֹרֵר
police	מִשְׁטָרָה
policeman	שׁוֹטֵר
to polish	צִחְצֵחַ
polite	אָדִיב
political	פּוֹלִיטִי
pollution	זִיהוּם
pool	בְּרֵכָה
poor thing!	מִסְכֵּן !
port	נָמֵל
position	עֶמְדָּה
(it is) possible that . . .	. . . יִתָּכֵן שֶׁ
post office	דּוֹאַר
postcard	גְּלוּיָה
potato	תַּפּוּחַ־אֲדָמָה
pound	לִירָה
a power (e.g. USA)	מַעֲצָמָה
to praise	שִׁיבֵּחַ

prayer-book	סִידוּר
prayer-shawl	טַלִית
to prefer	הֶעֱדִיף
pregnant	בְּהֵרָיוֹן
preparatory course	מְכִינָה
present (gift)	מַתָּנָה
pressure	לַחַץ
price	מְחִיר
Prime Minister	רֹאשׁ מֶמְשָׁלָה
priority	עֲדִיפוּת
probably	בֶּטַח
problem	בְּעָיָיה
product	מוּצָר
promise *noun*	הַבְטָחָה
to promise	הִבְטִיחַ
proud	גֵּאֶה
Psalms	תְּהִלִים
pull	פְּרוֹטֶקְצְיָה
to pull	מָשַׁךְ
to push	דָּחַף
to put	שָׂם
to put in	שָׂם
to put on (clothes)	לָבַשׁ
to put together (assemble)	הִרְכִּיב
to quarrel	רָב
queen	מַלְכָּה
question	שְׁאֵלָה
quickly	מַהֵר
quiet	שֶׁקֶט
quite	דַי
Rachel	רָחֵל
radio	רַדְיוֹ
rag	סְמַרְטוּט
to rain	יָרַד גֶּשֶׁם

to raise	הֵרִים
Ramle	רַמְלֶה
Ramot	רָמוֹת
rarely	לְעִתִּים רְחוֹקוֹת
rather	דַי
(would) rather	הֶעֱדִיף
to rattle	קִישְׁקֵשׁ
reaction	תְּגוּבָה
to read	קָרָא
really	מַמָּשׁ
reason *noun*	סִיבָּה
receipt	קַבָּלָה
to receive	קִיבֵּל
recently	בָּאַחֲרוֹנָה
reception	קַבָּלַת קָהָל
record (= disc)	תַּקְלִיט
to record	הִקְלִיט
recruit (army)	טִירוֹן
red	אָדוֹם
to refuse	סֵירֵב
to register (for)	נִרְשַׁם לְ
relative	קָרוֹב
religious	דָתִי
to remember	זָכַר
reminder	תַּזְכִּיר
to rent	שָׂכַר
reserve duty	מִילוּאִים
resolution	הַחְלָטָה
responsibility	אַחֲרָיוּת
(the) rest (= remainder)	שְׁאָר
to rest	נָח
restaurant	מִסְעָדָה
result	תּוֹצָאָה
to ride	רָכַב
rifle	רוֹבֶה
right (= entitlement)	זְכוּת

right (opp. of left)	יָמִין
to be right	צָדַק
right away	מִיָּד
Rina	רִינָה
to rinse	שָׁטַף
Rivka	רִבְקָה
road	כְּבִישׁ
robbery	שׁוֹד
Ronit	רוֹנִית
room	חֶדֶר
root	שׁוֹרֶשׁ
Rosh Hashanah	ראשׁ הַשָּׁנָה
round adj.	עָגוֹל
row (= line)	שׁוּרָה
to rub	שִׁפְשֵׁף
rude	גַּס
rug	מַרְבַד
to run	רָץ
to run over (someone)	דָּרַס
Russian	רוּסִי
Ruti	רוּתִי
salad	סָלָט
salary	מַשְׂכּוֹרֶת
sale	מִבְצָע
salt	מֶלַח
salty	מָלוּחַ
(the) same	אוֹתוֹ
sandal	סַנְדָּל
sandwich	סֶנְדְּוִויץ'
Sara	שָׂרָה
satisfied	מְרוּצֶּה
saucepan	סִיר
Saudi Arabia	עֲרָב הַסַּעוּדִית
savage	אַכְזָרִי
Savyon	סַבְיוֹן

to say	אָמַר
scarcely	בְּקוֹשִׁי
school	בֵּית־סֵפֶר
school year	שְׁנַת לִימוּדִים
science	מַדָּע
scissors	מִסְפָּרַיִם
scorpion	עַקְרָב
to scratch	שָׂרַט
scream	צָרַח
screwdriver	מַבְרֵג
season ticket	כַּרְטִיסִיָּיה
seat	מוֹשָׁב
(a) second (of time)	שְׁנִיָּיה
second	שֵׁנִי
second-hand	מְשׁוּמָּשׁ
secretary	מַזְכִּירָה
secular	חִילוֹנִי
to see	רָאָה
to sell	מָכַר
semester	סֶמֶסְטֶר
to send	שָׁלַח
sense	שֵׂכֶל
serious	רְצִינִי
sermon	דְּרָשָׁה
service (= prayers)	תְּפִילָה
set (TV etc.)	מַכְשִׁיר
settlement	יִישׁוּב
several	אֲחָדִים
Shabbat	שַׁבָּת
Shabbat Eve	עֶרֶב שַׁבָּת
to shake (head)	נִעֲנַע
(by the hand)	לָחַץ
(The) Sharon	הַשָּׁרוֹן
sharp	חַד
to shave	הִתְגַּלֵּחַ
sheep	כִּבְשָׂה

sheet	סָדִין
shelf	מַדָּף
shelter	מִקְלָט
Shimon	שִׁמְעוֹן
shirt	חוּלְצָה
shiva	שִׁבְעָה
Shlomo	שְׁלֹמֹה
shoe	נַעַל (נַעֲלַיִם)
shop	חֲנוּת
to shop	עָשָׂה קְנִיּוֹת
Shoshana	שׁוֹשַׁנָה
shoulder bag	תִּיק צַד
to shout	צָעַק
show	הַצָּגָה
shower, to take a	עָשָׂה מִקְלַחַת
shtreimel	שְׁטְרַיְימֶל
Shula	שׁוּלָה
to shut	סָגַר
sick	חוֹלֶה
side	צַד
sidestreet	סִימְטָה
sidewalk	מִדְרָכָה
sign	סִימָן
to sign	חָתַם
silly	מְטוּמְטָם
silverware	סַכּוּ"ם
simple	פָּשׁוּט
sink	כִּיּוֹר
sir	אֲדוֹנִי
sister	אָחוֹת
sister-in-law	גִּיסָה
to sit (down)	יָשַׁב
to sit (someone) down	הוֹשִׁיב
situation	מַצָּב
sixty	שִׁישִׁים
skin	עוֹר

skirt	חֲצָאִית
sky	שָׁמַיִם
sleep	שֵׁינָה
to sleep	יָשֵׁן
slightly	טִיפָּה
slowly	לְאַט
small	קָטָן
smart	חָכָם
to smell (something)	הֵרִיחַ
smelly	מַסְרִיחַ
to smile	חִיֵּיךְ
smooth	חָלָק
snail	שַׁבְּלוּל
snake	נָחָשׁ
to snow	יָרַד שֶׁלֶג
so	כָּל-כָּךְ
so (= therefore)	אָז
soap	סַבּוֹן
soccer	כַּדּוּרֶגֶל
social science	מַדְעֵי חֶבְרָה
society	חֶבְרָה
socks	גַּרְבַּיִם
soft	רַךְ
soldier	חַיָּיל
solution	פִּתָּרוֹן (פִּתְרוֹנוֹת)
some (= a certain)	אֵיזֶה
some (= a few)	כַּמָּה
something	מַשֶּׁהוּ
sometimes	לִפְעָמִים
son	בֵּן (בָּנִים)
soon	עוֹד מְעַט
sorry	סְלִיחָה
(to be) sorry	הִצְטַעֵר
(a) sort of	מִין
sound noun	קוֹל
soup	מָרָק

sour	חָמוּץ
South	דָּרוֹם
southern	דְּרוֹמִי
sparkling	מַבְרִיק
to speak	דִּיבֵּר
special	מְיוּחָד
to spend (time)	עָבַר
spoon	כַּף (כַּפּוֹת)
sport	סְפּוֹרְט
spring	אָבִיב
stair	מַדְרֵגָה
stairway	חֲדַר־מַדְרֵגוֹת
stamp	בּוּל
star	כּוֹכָב
to start	הִתְחִיל
to start with	הִתְחִיל עִם
statement	קְבִיעָה
station-wagon	סְטֵיישֶׁן
steering wheel	הֶגֶה
step	צַעַד
stick	מַקֵּל (מַקְלוֹת)
still	עוֹד
to stop (= halt)	עָצַר
to stop (doing something)	הִפְסִיק
storage room	מַחְסָן
store	חֲנוּת
two-storey	דּוּ־קוֹמָתִי
storm	סְעָרָה
story	סִיפּוּר
straight	יָשָׁר
street	רְחוֹב
to stretch	מָתַח
strike	שְׁבִיתָה
strong	חָזָק
structure	מִבְנֶה
stuck	תָּקוּעַ
student	סְטוּדֶנְט

to study	לָמַד
stupid	טִיפֵּשׁ
stupidity	טִפְּשׁוּת
subject (in school etc.)	מִקְצוֹעַ
submarine	צוֹלֶלֶת
successful	מַצְלִיחַ
such	כָּזֶה
sucrazit	סוּכְּרָזִית
suddenly	פִּתְאוֹם
Suez	סוּאֶץ
sugar	סוּכָּר
suggestion	הַצָעָה
suit	חֲלִיפָה
suitcase	מִזְוָודָה
sukkah	סוּכָּה
summer	קַיִץ
sun, sunshine	שֶׁמֶשׁ
to suntan	שִׁיזֵף
supermarket	סוּפֵּר
supper	אֲרוּחַת-עֶרֶב
supplement	מוּסָף
to support	תָּמַךְ בְּ
sure	בָּטוּחַ
sure!	בֶּטַח !
to surprise	הִפְתִּיעַ
surprising	מַפְתִּיעַ
to suspect	חָשַׁד בְּ
sweater	סְוֶודֶר
sweetheart	מוֹתֶק
swimsuit	בֶּגֶד-יָם
Switzerland	שְׁוֵויצָרְיָה
synagogue	בֵּית-כְּנֶסֶת
Syria	סוּרְיָה
table	שׁוּלְחָן
to take	לָקַח
taken (= occupied)	תָּפוּס

to talk to	דִּיבֵּר עִם
tall	גָּבוֹהַּ
tank (weapon)	טַנְק
tape-recorder	טֵייפּ
tax	מַס
teacher	מוֹרֶה
team	צֶוֶת
teaspoon	כַּפִּית
tefillin	תְּפִילִין
telegram	מִבְרָק
to tell	אָמַר, סִיפֵּר
temperature	טֶמְפֶּרָטוּרָה
temporary	זְמַנִּי
tenant	דַּייָר
tennis	טֶנִיס
tension	מֶתַח
tent	אוֹהֶל
tenured	קָבוּעַ
terribly	נוֹרָא
test	מִבְחָן
thank heavens	בָּרוּךְ הַשֵּׁם
thank you	תּוֹדָה
that *pron.*	זֶה
that (such-and-such)	זֶה, הַהוּא
then	אָז
there	שָׁם
there is / are	יֵשׁ
to be there	נִמְצָא
thermometer	מַדְחוֹם
thick	עָבֶה
thin (object)	דַּק
thing	דָּבָר
to think	חָשַׁב
third	שְׁלִישִׁי
this *pron.*	זֶה
this (such-and-such)	זֶה

thorough	יְסוֹדִי
through	דֶּרֶךְ
to throw (into)	זָרַק (לְ)
to throw away	זָרַק
thumb	בּוֹהֶן
thunder	רַעַם
Tiberias	טְבֶרְיָה
ticket	כַּרְטִיס
to tidy up	סִידֵּר
tie (necktie)	עֲנִיבָה
till *noun*	קוּפָּה
till-receipt	חֶשְׁבּוֹנִית
time	זְמָן
time (= period)	תְּקוּפָה
time (= instance)	פַּעַם
what time?	בְּאֵיזוֹ שָׁעָה
Tirtza	תִּרְצָה
today	הַיּוֹם
together	יַחַד
toilet	שֵׁירוּתִים
toilet-bowl	אַסְלָה
token (for telephone)	אַסִימוֹן
tomato	עַגְבָנִייָה
tomorrow	מָחָר
tongue	לָשׁוֹן
tonight	הַלַּיְלָה
too (= also)	גַּם־כֵּן
too much	יוֹתֵר מִדַּי
tooth	שֵׁן (שִׁינַיִים)
toothbrush	מִבְרֶשֶׁת־שִׁינַיִים
Torah	תּוֹרָה
to touch	נָגַע בְּ
tourist	תַּיָּיר
towel	מַגֶּבֶת
town	עִיר
track	שְׁבִיל

traffic-light	רַמְזוֹר
tray	מַגָּשׁ
treatment	טִיפּוּל
tree	עֵץ
tribe	שֵׁבֶט
trip	טִיוּל
trolley	עֲגָלָה
to trouble	הִטְרִיד
truck	מַשָּׂאִית
to try	נִסָּה
Tuesday	יוֹם שְׁלִישִׁי
turkey	הוֹדוּ
to turn	סוֹבֵב
to turn off	סָגַר
to turn on	פָּתַח, הִדְלִיק
TV	טֶלֶוִיזְיָה
twenty	עֶשְׂרִים
typewriter	מְכוֹנַת כְּתִיבָה
typist	כַּתְבָן
ulpan	אוּלְפָּן
ultraorthodox	חֲרֵדִי
UN	הָאוּ״ם
uncle	דּוֹד
under	תַּחַת
to undress	הִתְפַּשֵּׁט
unemployment	אַבְטָלָה
university	אוּנִיבֶרְסִיטָה
until	עַד
upstairs	לְמַעֲלָה
uptight	עַצְבָּנִי
urgent	דָּחוּף
USA	אַרְצוֹת הַבְּרִית
to use	הִשְׁתַּמֵּשׁ בְּ
USSR	בְּרִית הַמּוֹעֲצוֹת
usually	בְּדֶרֶךְ־כְּלָל

vacation	חוּפְשָׁה
valley	עֵמֶק
Value Added Tax	מַס עֵרֶךְ מוּסָף
vanilla	וַנִיל
various	שׁוֹנֶה
vase	צִנְצֶנֶת
vegetables	יְרָקוֹת
very	מְאֹד
video	וִידֵאוֹ
view	נוֹף
village	כְּפָר
vineyard	כֶּרֶם
to visit	בִּיקֵר
Volvo	ווֹלְווֹ
to vote	הִצְבִּיעַ
to wait for	חִיכָּה לְ
waiter	מֶלְצַר
to walk	הָלַךְ
wallet	אַרְנָק
to want	רָצָה
war	מִלְחָמָה
War of Independence	מִלְחֶמֶת הַשִׁיחְרוּר
warm	חַם
to warn	הִזְהִיר
warning	אַזְהָרָה
washing machine	מְכוֹנַת כְּבִיסָה
to watch	צָפָה בְּ
to watch out	שָׂם לֵב
water	מַיִם
way	דֶּרֶךְ
weapons	נֶשֶׁק
to wear	לָבַשׁ
weather	מֶזֶג אֲווִיר
wedding	חֲתוּנָה
week	שָׁבוּעַ (שָׁבוּעוֹת)

weird	מוּזָר
well	טוֹב
well done!	כָּל הַכָּבוֹד !
Western	מַעֲרָבִי
wet	רָטוֹב
what?	מַה
whatchamacallit	זֶה
when	כְּשֶׁ
which?	אֵיזֶה
while	בִּזְמַן שֶׁ
to whisper	לָחַשׁ
whitewash	סִיּוּד
who?	מִי ?
why?	לָמָה
wide	רָחָב
wife	אִישָׁה
wig	פֵּאָה
wind	רוּחַ
window	חַלּוֹן
wine-glass	כּוֹסִית
winter	חוֹרֶף
to wipe	נִיגֵּב
wire	חוּט
wise guy	חָכָם
with	עִם
witness	עֵד
woman	אִישָׁה
(I) wonder	מְעַנְיֵין לָדַעַת . . .
wonderful	נִפְלָא
wood	עֵץ
wool	צֶמֶר
word	מִלָּה
work	עֲבוֹדָה
to work	עָבַד
world	עוֹלָם

worry	דְּאָגָה
to worry	דָּאַג
to worry (someone)	הִדְאִיג
worth	שָׁוֶוה
to write	כָּתַב
wrong	לֹא נָכוֹן

Yael	יָעֵל
Yafa	יָפָה
Yair	יָאִיר
yard	חָצֵר
year	שָׁנָה
Yehudit	יְהוּדִית
yes	כֵּן
yeshivah	יְשִׁיבָה
yesterday	אֶתְמוֹל
(not . . .) yet	עוֹד לֹא
Yitzhak	יִצְחָק
yoghurt	יוֹגוּרְט
Yosef	יוֹסֵף
Yossi	יוֹסִי
young	צָעִיר
yuk	אִיכְס

Zeev	זְאֵב
Zionist	צִיוֹנִי
zipper	רוֹכְסָן
zoo	גַּן־חַיּוֹת
Zvi	צְבִי

Key to exercises

2

2a

1 נועם חכם, בעצם כל המשפחה חכמה.   2 הכלב מטונף, לגמרי מטונף.
3 רונית וחגית מאושרות עכשיו.   4 המצלמה נפלאה.   5 החתול כל כך רך.
6 עכשיו הכלב נקי.   7 הכלב והחתול כל כך חכמים.

2b

1 הרדיו מדוד צבי.   2 הווידאו תחת הטלוויזיה.   3 דב כבר בישראל.   4 זה
בטח בשביל סבא וסבתא.   5 חנה תמיד עם שולה והילדים.

2c

1 השכן הוא עורך דין.   2 הטייפ הוא מתנה בשביל אמא.   3 המחשב הוא
קצת בעיה.   4 לפעמים ג'קי הוא ממש נודניק.   5 אבא הוא עורך דין גם כן.
6 רחל היא אחות.   7 רחל זה האחות מהדסה.   8 חיים זה העורך דין מניו
ג'רזי.

3

1 אתם רעבים, משה וחיים?   2 יפה ושושנה? גם הן עסוקות?   3 את
ראשונה, תרצה.   4 היא ואני מאוד עסוקות.   5 הי בני, זה אתה? זה אני שוב.

4

1 השמיכה בדרייר.   2 אני חוזר לחנות.   3 משהו נשרף במטבח.   4 אני שם
אוכל מהמיקרוגל ישר על השולחן.   5 מה? אתה זורק בקבוקים ישר לפח?
6 או שזה בתנור או שזה על הגז.   7 השמיכה בארון.   8 אז אתה נוסע
להרים?   9 לא, להיפך, אני נוסע לים.   10 אולי השמיכה על החבל
במרפסת.

5

1 חברים באו מהגליל.   2 אני קונה גלויות עם מראות של ירושלים וחברון.
3 דודי מבקר בחיפה עם קרובים.   4 בבאר שבע יש בדרך כלל זמן לקוקה
קולה.   5 יש יוגורטים במקרר, מותק.

263

6

סלון ומטבח יפים, רצפה ותקרה יפות, הול וכניסה יפים, אמבטיה וכיור
יפים, דלת וחלון יפים, מרפסת וגינה יפות, דירות ווילות יפות

7

7a

סוודרים, חולצות, חצאיות, חגורות, שרוולים, גופיות, מעילים, דובונים,
כיפות, כובעים, עניבות, סנדלים

1 המשפחה עברה חמש שנים קשות במחנות לעולים.   2 החיילים באו
במשאיות, אוטובוסים, מכוניות ואפילו במוניות. 3 לא שמו ידיות על כל
המגירות.   4 בדירה יש כמה מיטות.   5 יש גם כמה שולחנות מלוכלכים.
6 קונים שומרים חשבוניות לעיתים רחוקות.   7 יש הרבה מקרים של
אבטלה. 8 המבנים האלה מסוכנים. 9 מורים קבועים יקבלו פיצויים.

7b

ברקים, מטוסים, מדורים, מצלמות, מחשבים, מסוקים, פרפרים, שפנים,
נמלים, ספרים, חייטים, כבדים, חברים, חתנים, בלשים

יעלים, טייסים, רחלים, מרבדים, עקבות, טבחים, נחשים, קצבים, אביבים,
צעיפים, שעונים, כדורים, עכברים

7c

ברזים, כתרים, ברגים, מלכים, צבעים, כנסים, זרעים, כתלים, בלמים,
סלעים, שערים, לחצים, קברים, שלגים, נחלים, תארים, שקרים

עדרים, חפצים, חסדים, עמקים, גשמים, שלטים, אפסים, אבנים, קמצים,
קצרים, עבדים, קרשים, חדרים, עברים, יעדים, בחנים, אלפים

7d

1 נצל את כל ההזדמניות.   2 שגרירויות עושות הרבה טעויות.   3 כל
העדיפויות שלו לא נכונות.   4 בגלל החום ביטלו כמה פעילויות.
5 התפתחויות חדשות במזרח התיכון?   6 התחייבויות לגבי זכויות של
עולים? שטויות.

7e

1 זאת תמונה של המלכה בתור ילדה. 2 עופרה חזה היא אפילו כוכבת
בארצות הברית. 3 השכנה שלנו עופרה היא מורה באיזה תיכון. 4 הוא
מתחתן עם צרפתיה, כנראה. 5 כמו הרוסיות האחרות בבניין, היא רופאה.
6 אתה מחפש כתבנית טובה? 7 נו יש נטשה – היא סטודנטית מברית
המועצות. 8 היא אומנית, אני חושב, או אולי שחקנית. 9 נאוה היא עורכת
דין ברמלה.

8

8a

קומוניסטיות, דמוקרטיים, רעים, אחרונות, נחמדים, קרים, נפלאות,
זוועתיים, אטיות, אנגליים, אמריקאיות

8b

1 הפרחים שם כל כך יפים. 2 יש רק צבעים כהים. 3 הם גרות בדירות
נאות. 4 אנחנו רוצים תקרות עבות.

8c

סבירים, אדירים, סגורים, כבירים, תמימים, צמאים, חדשים, רעבים,
יציבים, יעילים, נבונים, מצחיקים, עשירים, קצרים, רחבים

9

1 אני צריך מנורה זולה – איזה מנורה זולה? 2 שידות הן כל כך יקרות . . .
זו שידה חזקה? 3 אנחנו רוצים כרים טובים – כך טוב זה חשוב. 4 אתה
אוהב כסת חמה? מאה אחוז, כל כסת פה היא חמה.

10

1 הרבה מס 2 כל המציאות 3 כמה מבצעים 4 רוב המחירים 5 קצת הנחה
6 עוד חשבונות 7 כמה קבלות 8 מאה קונים 9 ב20 תשלומים 10 כמה מס
ערך מוסף ? 11 שישים אחוז 12 סופר אחד 13 כמה חנויות

11

1 איזה פיז׳מה? 2 כל חליפה 3 מעיל כזה 4 אותו חלוק 5 איזה חולצה?
החולצה שם? 6 המעיל הזה 7 הז׳קט הזה 8 רוכסן כזה 9 כל חצאית
בסדר 10 זה מין חגורה 11 איזה תלבושת טובה לראש השנה 12 היא
לובשת מין שמלה ערבית 13 אני צריך אותו כפתור כמובן 14 איזה
מכנסיים יש לך? 15 איזה קולב טוב לסוודר ההוא?

12

12a

1 החג הבא 2 היום הגדול 3 החגיגה המיוחדת 4 ביום הראשון 5 עד
הצום הגדול 6 בחמסין האחרון 7 הקיץ הארוך 8 בשביל האביב הבא
9 הסתווים היפים 10 החורף השני 11 דני המטומטם 12 ד״ר פרנקנשטיין
הטיפש 13 ד״ר פרנקנשטיין מבריק. 14 איפה החוברת החדשה
מהאוניברסיטה העברית? 15 מי כתב את המאמר הארוך על זה בשביל
העתון הדתי? 16 הספר האחר הוא על הכוונית הקטנה.

12b

1 מי הסופר הזה בכלל? 2 הטופס הזה הוא חובה. 3 חוזר זה הוא ההודעה
הסופית. 4 חזרתי מהישיבה הזאת .... 5 והבחור הזה צועק פתאום.

13

13a

1 התמונות נהדרות. 2 הראי הישן שווה הרבה. 3 איכס, המדרגות עדיין
מלוכלכות. 4 יש מרבדים צבעוניים. 5 איפה? באמבטיה הגדולה למעלה?

13c

1 רחל היא גננת. 2 דב ויאיר הם מהנדסים. 3 דב הוא גם מרצה בבר אילן.
4 החברות שלה הן או מזכירות או פקידות.

13d

1 ההצעה הזאת   2 רעיונות כאלה   3 אותם הסכמים   4 איזה תלונות
5 השטויות האלה   6 תענוג כזה   7 התינוקת הזאת   8 החוכמות האלה
9 בעיות כלשהן   10 ברכה כזאת

13e

1 כמה מסרקים?   2 עוד סבון ומים   3 פחות ליכלוך   4 סרטים איטלקיים
אחדים   5 המון שולחנות וכסאות   6 כמה ריהוט?   7 יותר מדי ריהוט
8 מספיק כורסות   9 הרבה בשמים   10 פחות אמבטיות   11 מעט מאוד
ישראלים עושים אמבטיה   12 רוב הישראלים עושים מקלחת   13 אתה לא
מצאת שירותים? אבל יש פה המון שירותים

14

14a

1 שלושה בקבוקים   2 שישה ספלים ושש כוסות   3 שני מגשים   4 חמישה
סכינים   5 קומקום אחד   6 אנחנו צריכים שני תפריטים   7 שלוש סירות
8 ארבע כפיות   9 יש רק שלוש מסעדות   10 שמונה מלצרים ועשר מלצריות
11 ארבע כוסיות   12 תשע מפיות   13 תשע צלוחיות בשביל קורנספלקס
14 שני פותחנים, אחד בשרי ואחד חלבי   15 שני מזלגות ושתי כפות

14b

1 שנים־עשר בולים   2 שש־עשרה אגרות אויר   3 אחת־עשרה גלויות
4 תשעה־עשר מכתבים לישראל וארבעה לחוץ לארץ   5 שלוש־עשרה
חבילות קטנות   6 שמונה־עשר מברקים   7 שנים־עשר מכתבים רשמיים
8 חמשה־עשר טפסים   9 תשע־עשרה שיחות היום   10 יש שבע־עשרה
תיבות דואר בכניסה

14c

1 תשעים קיבוצים   2 שלושים ושלושה מושבים   3 שמונים ושבעה כפרים
4 עשרים ושניים כרמים   5 שישים פרדסים לאורך הכביש   6 ארבעים
ותשעה עצים   7 שבעים וחמשה שדות   8 כחמשים או שישים שבילים
9 למעלה משמונים משקים

15

1 רוב הביצים מקולקלות.   2 שאר החמאה על הצלחת.   3 על כמה
מהסנדוויצ׳ים יש מרגרינה ועל כמה יש מיונז.   4 שלוש מהחלות לא טובות
– הן נפלו על האדמה.   5 כמה מהחלב נשאר?   6 הילדים גמרו כמעט את
כל הריבה.   7 כמה מהחבר׳ה רוצים חומוס ופיתה?   8 הרבה מהמוצרים הם
לא כשרים.   9 שמתי מיץ בארבע מהכוסות.

16

16a

1 הדרכון שלך, מותק? הוא בתיק הקטן.   2 הנה עגלה ברוך השם . . . אוי
ואבוי, היא שבורה.   3 בוא לתור הזה, הוא זז.   4 המטוס מאחר עוד פעם, זה
בושה.   5 יש לי שתי מזוודות – זה בסדר!   6 ארבע שקיות ניילון ותיק צד!
זה חוצפה.

16b

1 מישהו דוחף. הלו, מה קורה פה?   2 חכה, אני שואל משהו בדלפק.
3 אנחנו נוחתים בנמל תעופה באיזשהו מקום באירופה.   4 בוא לבקר פעם.
5 מישהו בודק את הכרטיסים?   6 פעם הם עשו בדיקה במכס, אתה זוכר?
7 משהו לא בסדר?   8 יש הודעה בשביל מישהי בשם גילה.

16c

1 השזיף הזה לא בסדר? אז הנה אחר.   2 אני לא אוהב את התפוחים האלה,
יש לך אדום?   3 מה? אתה לא אוכל את זה? אין לי עוד פירות.   4 הענבים
ההם הם השחורים – הם חמוצים.

16d

1 כמה טעויות אתה מצאת? אני מצאתי חמש.   2 רגע אחד, למלה הזאת יש
משמעות אחת או שתים?   3 אתה מדבר רק שפה אחת? בישראל הרבה
אנשים מדברים שש או שבע.

17

17a

1 ההשפעה של בן גוריון 2 ההבטחה של מי? 3 ההבטחה של בריטניה
4 המטרות של מצרים 5 הוויתורים של בגין 6 התוכניות של חוסיין 7 האח
של מי אתה? 8 של מי הסנדלים האלה על הרצפה? של מנחם או של
שמעון?

17b

1 הפיאט שלה 2 הפיג'ו שלך 3 הוולוו שלי 4 הטיפשות שלהם 5 השכל
שלך 6 הניסיון שלנו 7 האחות שלה 8 החברה שלי 9 אני אוהבת את
הפיאה שלך, חווה 10 אני אוהב את השטריימל שלך, גרשון

17c

1 עץ אגס 2 עץ זית 3 משחק טניס 4 מגרש כדורגל 5 מחנה קייץ 6 מנהל
מחנה 7 מיץ תפוחים 8 מיץ תפוזים 9 חבילת מיץ 10 פרדס תפוזים
11 בשר עוף 12 ביטוח חיים

17d

1 מיצי החתול רוצה ארוחת בוקר. 2 הגיסה שלי היא מלכת יופי. 3 נתן
כתב לחברת ביטוח. 4 יש לפחות שלוש חברות ביטוח ברחוב הזה.
5 תוכניות טלוויזיה טובות?! 6 מקלטי טלוויזיה הם יקרים. 7 מקלטי וידאו
הם יקרים באותה מידה. 8 קיבלתי מצלמת וידאו. 9 כמה שילמת בשביל
צילומי חתונה? 10 אני שונא קבלות פנים.

17e

1 בית הספר 2 בית החולים 3 ארוחות הצוהריים 4 בית הכנסת 5 הברית
מילה 6 הבגד־ים 7 הבר־מצווה 8 חליפת הבר־מצווה 9 מקלט הווידאו
10 מצלמת הווידאו 11 כמה עולה הבגד־ים? 12 בית הספר עולה הרבה
כסף. 13 הטיפול בבית החולים הזה הוא חינם. 14 מתי התפילה בבית
הכנסת בליל שבת? 15 האם הברית־מילה בבית הכנסת או בבית?

19

19a

1 זזת 2 זזנו 3 זזתי 4 זזו 5 זזת 6 זזו 7 זזתם 8 זז 9 זזתן 10 זזה 11 זזו
12 זז 13 זזתי 14 זז 15 זזה

1 שרת 2 שרנו 3 שרתי 4 שרו 5 שרת 6 שרו 7 שרתם 8 שר 9 שרתן
10 שרה 11 שרו 12 שר 13 שרתי 14 שר 15 שרה

19b

1 אני זזתי 2 הפרה זזה 3 הג׳וק זז 4 הכבשות זזו 5 התינוק זז 6 היא
עכשיו זזה 7 אתה זזת, טמבל 8 זזנו טיפה 9 הלטאה זזה 10 הזבובים זזו?
11 הוא זז 12 מיד היא זזה

19c

1 מתי הוא נח בפעם האחרונה? 2 היא נחה לפני רגע 3 זה בסדר, אני כבר
נחתי 4 נחנו כל הערב 5 דבורה רק נחה 6 סליחה אסתר, את נחת?

20

1 בסדר, בסדר, אנחנו זזים תיכף. 2 הזקן זז מאד לאט. 3 למה אסתר
ויהודית זזות כל הזמן? 4 זה זז . . . כל הכבוד. 5 את זזה טיפה, יעל.
6 המכונית זזה! מהר, הילוך שלישי!

21

21a

1 תזוז 2 נזוז 3 אזוז 4 יזוזו 5 תזוזי 6 יזוזי 7 תזוזו 8 יזוז 9 תזוזו
10 תזוז 11 יזוזו 12 יזוז 13 אזוז 14 יזוז 15 תזוז

1 תשיר 2 נשיר 3 אשיר 4 ישירו 5 תשירי 6 ישירי 7 תשירו 8 ישיר
9 תשירו 10 תשיר 11 ישירו 12 ישיר 13 אשיר 14 ישיר 15 תשיר

21b

1 תנוח כמה דקות, דוד.   2 חנה, תנוחי קצת גם כן.   3 אני אנוח חצי שעה ודי.   4 ילדים, תזוזו מיד!   5 אם אתה תזוז, חבר, אני אזוז.   6 אבל הם ממש ינוחו?   7 אל תזוזו חבר'ה.   8 חוה בבקשה אל תנוחי עכשיו.   9 עקרב, יוסף – אל תזוז בכלל!   10 הוא ינוח אחר כך.

22

1 לך לקופה אחרת.   2 בוא אחרי הצהריים.   3 שים את השיקים האלה בחשבון.   4 רד משם, מותק.   5 עזוב, אני עסוק.   6 תקלה זמנית. חכה בבקשה.   7 במקרה של אש צא דרך יציאת החרום.   8 קח את הכסף והקבלה.   9 תן יותר לצדקה.   10 שב וחכה. אל תרוץ.   11 המנוע רץ, אז סע.   12 שים את פנקס השיקים בתיק.

25

25b

1 נפעל   2 פעל   3 פועל   4 הופעל   5 התפעל   6 פעל   7 פועל   8 נפעל   9 התפעל   10 פועל   11 הפעיל   12 הופעל   13 נפעל   14 פועל   15 פעל   16 הופעל

1 הוכנס   2 נגזל   3 נלקח   4 נותק   5 נבחר   6 הוטרד   7 סולק   8 הוזכר   9 נשמר   10 בוטל

26

1 שטפת   2 שטפנו   3 שטפתי   4 שטפו   5 שטפת   6 שטפו   7 שטפתם   8 שטף   9 שטפתן   10 שטפה   11 שטפו   12 שטף   13 שטפתי   14 שטף   15 שטפה

1 תשטפו   2 תשטוף   3 ישטפו   4 ישטוף   5 אשטוף   6 ישטוף   7 תשטוף   8 תשטוף   9 נשטוף   10 אשטוף   11 ישטפו   12 תשטפי   13 ישטפו   14 תשטפו   15 ישטוף

1 חורשת 2 קוצר 3 טוחנות 4 גוזזים 5 אורגת 6 קושרים 7 תופר
8 סותרות 9 בא 10 גרות 11 באה 12 גרים 13 צפה 14 צפות 15 גר

1 לשטוף – שטיפה 2 לזרוק – זריקה 3 לשמור – שמירה 4 לקצור –
קצירה 5 לטחון – טחינה 6 לגזוז – גזיזה 7 לרחוץ – רחיצה 8 למשוך –
משיכה 9 לנשוך – נשיכה 10 לדהור – דהירה 11 לרוץ – ריצה 12 לשוב
– שיבה 13 ללון – לינה 14 לשיר – שירה

1 הקלטנו 2 הקלטה 3 הקליטו 4 הקלטתי 5 הקלטתם 6 הקלטת
7 הקליטו 8 הקלטתן 9 הקליט 10 הקליטו 11 הקליט 12 הקליטה
13 הקליטה 14 הקליטו 15 הקלטנו

1 נקליט 2 תקליט 3 יקליטו 4 אקליט 5 תקליטו 6 תקליטי 7 יקליטו
8 תקליטו 9 יקליט 10 יקליטו 11 יקליט 12 תקליט 13 תקליט
14 יקליטו 15 נקליט

1 אנחנו מקליטים עוד מעט. 2 אמא, היא מרביצה. 3 שרה ורבקה
מבטיחות לבוא. 4 אני תמיד מסביר. 5 הילדות רוצות להסביר אבל הן לא
מסבירות. 6 קשה להגדיר התחייבות. 7 הסוודרים האלה לא יתאימו לך.
8 התחזית לא מפחידה אותי. 9 הוצאתי אותם ברגע האחרון. 10 מתי
תחליטו, חבר׳ה? או שכבר החלטתם? 11 הזמננו את העיתון האחר.
12 תושיבי אותו פה, שושנה.

1 להדביר – הדברה 2 להסביר – הסברה 3 להגדיר – הגדרה 4 להרביץ –
הרבצה 5 להקליט – הקלטה 6 להנמיך – הנמכה 7 להרטיב – הרטבה
8 להבליט – הבלטה 9 להזמין – הזמנה

28

1 שידרנו 2 שידרת 3 שידרו 4 שידרתי 5 שידרתם 6 שידרת 7 שידרו
8 שידרתן 9 שידר 10 שידרו 11 שידר 12 שידרה 13 שידרה 14 שידרו
15 שידרנו

1 נשדר 2 תשדר 3 ישדרו 4 אשדר 5 תשדרו 6 תשדרי 7 ישדרו
8 תשדרו 9 ישדר 10 ישדרו 11 ישדר 12 תשדר 13 תשדר 14 ישדרו
15 נשדר

1 אנחנו מאחרים. 2 אמא, היא משקרת. 3 שרה ורבקה מבקשות לבוא.
4 אני תמיד מסדר. 5 הבנות גם מקבלות תשלום. 6 היא ביטלה את הכיתה
עוד פעם! 7 אריאלה, תבקשי לשמוע את ההתחלה. 8 חילקנו המון מצות
אבל אנחנו מחלקים עוד. 9 תשלמי אם את רוצה, יעל, אבל אני לא אשלם.
10 הם מבקרים את אמא שלהם. 11 אתם דיברתם עם המנהל בעצמכם?
12 היא תדבר עם השגרירות ותסביר.

1 לחפש – חיפוש 2 לסדר – סידור 3 ללטף – ליטוף 4 לנתק – ניתוק
5 לאחר – איחור 6 למזג – מיזוג 7 לרפד – ריפוד 8 לשפר – שיפור
9 לעקל – עיקול 10 לשהק – שיהוק

29

1 התפטרת 2 התפטרנו 3 התפטרתי 4 התפטרו 5 התפטרת 6 התפטרו
7 התפטרתם 8 התפטר 9 התפטרתן 10 התפטרה 11 התפטרו 12 התפטר
13 התפטרתי 14 התפטר 15 התפטרה

1 תתפטרו 2 תתפטר 3 יתפטרו 4 יתפטר 5 אתפטר 6 יתפטר 7 תתפטר
8 תתפטר 9 נתפטר 10 אתפטר 11 יתפטרו 12 תתפטרי 13 יתפטרו
14 תתפטרו 15 יתפטר

1 מתפטר 2 מתקבלת 3 מתלבטות 4 מתגברים 5 מתאמנת 6 מתרחצים
7 מתלבש 8 מתפטרות 9 מתפשט 10 מתערבים

1 לא התרשמתי כל-כך מזה. 2 את התרשמת, יהודית? 3 מתי את מתחתנת,
מרים? 4 הם אומרים שהם יתחתנו באביב. 5 היא השתמשה בכוס הזו?
6 היא לא ממש מצטערת. 7 אני אתגלח וארוץ לחנות.

273

30

1

1 נשרטת 2 נשרטנו 3 נשרטתי 4 נשרטו 5 נשרטת 6 נשרטו 7 נשרטתם
8 נשרט 9 נשרטתן 10 נשרטה 11 נשרטו 12 נשרט 13 נשרטתי
14 נשרטו 15 נשרטה

1 תישרטו 2 תישרט 3 יישרטו 4 יישרט 5 אשרט 6 יישרט 7 תישרט
8 תישרט 9 נישרט 10 אשרט 11 יישרטו 12 תישרטי 13 יישרטו
14 תישרטו 15 יישרט

2

1 נקלט, נקלטת, נקלטים, נקלטות   2 נבדק, נבדקת, נבדקים, נבדקות
3 נשען, נשענת, נשענים, נשענות 4 נמלט, נמלטת, נמלטים, נמלטות

3

1 להיגמר 2 להיתקל 3 להימסר 4 להיקנס 5 להירדף

1 מסרים נשלחו לממשלות שונות. 2 פתרונות שונים נבחנו. 3 ועידת שלום
נערכה. 4 המשא ומתן נגמר. 5 הסכם שלום נחתם. 6 אתה תיבדק בחדר
הקטן. 7 הם כבר נרגעו. 8 יש מתח כזה שאני לא יכול להירגע. 9 החולצה
הזאת נמתחה. 10 הכרטיסים נמכרים מהר מאד. 11 רוץ, הדלת נסגרת!
12 למה הם נכנסים למכונית שלו?

31

1

1 הוקלטתן 2 הוקלטה 3 הוקלטו 4 הוקלטה 5 הוקלטתי 6 הוקלט
7 הוקלטה 8 הוקלטת 9 הוקלטנו 10 הוקלטתי 11 הוקלטו 12 הוקלטת
13 הוקלטו 14 הוקלטתם 15 הוקלט

1 תוקלט 2 נוקלט 3 אוקלט 4 יוקלטי 5 תוקלטו 6 יוקלטו 7 תוקלטו
8 יוקלט 9 תוקלטו 10 תוקלט 11 יוקלטו 12 יוקלט 13 אוקלט
14 יוקלטו 15 תוקלט

2

1 מוחזר, מוחזרת, מוחזרים, מוחזרות 2 מוזנח, מוזנחת, מוזנחים, מוזנחות
3 מומלץ, מומלצת, מומלצים, מומלצות 4 מופקד, מופקדת, מופקדים,
מופקדות 5 מוגבל, מוגבלת, מוגבלים, מוגבלות

1 הנמלים של האויב הופצצו. 2 מפעלים רבים הושמדו. 3 גם כני טילים
הותקפו. 4 משק כימי לא הופעל. 5 צנחנים הוצנחו מאחורי החזית.

32

ינוצלו, נתוקן, תנוצל, אמוקם, נוצלתי, נותקת, צולמה, צולמת, סומנתם, צולמו,
תסומנו, יסולקו, סולקת

מסומנים, מקובלות, משומשים, מפוזרים, מחונכות

1 המצב לאט לאט שופר. 2 הנגב פתאום נותק. 3 רובים חולקו לאזרחים.
4 כפרים אחדים בעמק יזרעאל גם נותקו. 5 בקעת הירדן נותקה משאר
המדינה.

34

34a

1 אני מחפש את המברשת. 2 היא מנגבת את הכיור. 3 קח את הסמרטוט.
4 קח את הסבון ומגבת. 5 את מי הוא מחפש? 6 אני שונא את זה. 7 את
מי אתה מזמין? 8 מה את בישלת? 9 נו, קח את זה. 10 לא, אני קורא את
זה. 11 תשטוף את מברשת השיניים או קח מברשת אחרת. 12 העוזרת
מנגבת את האסלה. 13 חנה, את מי את רוצה פה? את בני או את קובי?

34b

1 טיפל ב 2 חיכה ל 3 התנגד ל 4 התאהב ב 5 המליץ על 6 התחשב ב
7 כעס על 8 ויתר על 9 ירא מ 10 השתמש ב

1 זה שייך לאשה למטה. 2 אנחנו מאוד גאים בדלת בעצם. 3 אני די מרוצה
מהצבע. 4 אבל אני לא כל כך מבסוט מהסיוד. 5 הם ערים לסכנות. 6 למה
נגעת בחלון? 7 אבל בינתיים מי ישמור על העץ בחוץ בחצר? 8 אל
תקשיב לנגר – הארון פנטסטי. 9 אני לא מומחה בארונות מטבח.
10 התכוונתי לפינת האוכל, לא לסלון!

35

35a

בנו, בו, בהם, בך, בי, בכם, בהן, בה, בנו, בי, בו

לו, לי, לנו, לו, להם, לך, לי, לכם, להן, לה

1 יהדות? אני מאוד מעוניין בה. 2 כולם מקנאים בהם. 3 ההורים שלה
גאים בה. 4 אתה בוטח בי? 5 איזה מנהגים יפים! אני התאהבתי בהם.
6 שלום, חברה – מישהו מטפל בכם? 7 כן בטח, הם כבר מטפלים בנו.
8 המפלגות החלוניות בקושי בוטחות בהם. 9 אני לא חושד בך, חיים,
חלילה. 10 אני לאט לאט מתאהב בך, גולדה. 11 הוא עוזר לנו. 12 כולם
מקשיבים לך, דבורה. 13 אני נותן להם הרבה עצות ועזרה. 14 אבל מה הם
נותנים לי? 15 אתה תמיד מפריע לה.

35b

אותנו, אותו, אותם, אותך, אותי, אתכם, אותן, אותה, אותנו, אותי, אותו

1 אתה הפתעת אותי. 2 סני ושר? אני זוכר אותם. 3 האווירה פה מרגיזה
אותנו. 4 זה ככה מצחיק אותי. 5 האיום עוד מדאיג אותו. 6 סרטים כאלה
מפחידים אותך? 7 אני מצלם אותך ליד המפה. 8 הדאגה הורגת אותנו.
9 הוא סוף סוף פיטר אותה. 10 היא סוף סוף גירשה אותו.

35c

ממנו, ממנו, מהם, ממך, ממני, מכם, מהן, ממנה, מאיתנו, ממני, ממנו

איתו, איתי, איתנו, איתו, איתם, איתך, איתי, אתכם, איתן, איתה

1 החותנת שלי תמיד רבה איתה. 2 הארוסה שלי כועסת עלי כרגע. 3 אתה מפחד ממנו? 4 הבן־דוד שלי שלמה מאוד מתרשם ממך, זאב. 5 אבא ואמא שלו באים איתנו. 6 למה הוא מתחיל איתה פתאום? 7 יפה, ממש איכפת לך ממנו? 8 נמאס לי מהם כבר. 9 באחרונה קיבלת תזכיר מאיתנו. 10 קיבלתי הודעה ממך.

35d

1 המזוזה בשבילך, דודה. 2 הסוכריות הן בשבילם, בשביל החג. 3 בגללי הוא שכח את הסידור. 4 ישבנו בסוכה עם המון דבורים וזבובים סביבנו. 5 יש תמיד כל כך הרבה חברות מסביב לה. 6 מה? השמחה בגללך? 7 זה די ברור, יש בית קברות מולנו. 8 הוא משוגע, מולם יש קולנוע. 9 לידו יש ישיבה גדולה. 10 יש כוונית לידך עם תנ״ך, אני חושב. 11 מה כל הרעש לידי! אני מבשל לכם משהו בשביל פסח. 12 עוד טלית בשבילו? אבל עכשיו יש לו חמש.

35e

אלינו, אליו, אליהם, אליך, אלי, אליכם, אליהן, אליה, אלינו, אלי, אליו

עליו, עלי, עלינו, עליו, עליהם, עליך, עלי, עליכם, עליהן, עליה

לפנינו, לפניו, לפניהם, לפניך, לפני, לפניכם, לפניהן, לפניה, לפנינו, לפני, לפניו

אחריו, אחרי, אחרינו, אחריו, אחריהם, אחריך, אחרי, אחריכם, אחריהן, אחריה

37

1 יש אוטובוס בתחנת האוטובוסים. 2 זהירות, אין רמזורים בצומת הזה. 3 יהיו נתיבים רק לאוטובוסים. 4 אולי יש חניון בסמטה. 5 אין מדרכה בצד הזה של הרחוב. 6 אז נלך מצד שני, יש שם מדרכה. 7 היו פקקים עצומים. 8 אבל לא היה אז נתיבי איילון.

38

1 לישראל היו כוחות גדולים לאורך הגבול הדרומי. 2 לחיל האויר יש
בעיקר מטוסים אמריקאיים. 3 אז יהיה לך טרמפ לבסיס אחרי שבת? 4 יש
לנו שני בנים בחטיבת גולני. 5 לאהרון יש עוד שנה בצה"ל. 6 אולי יש
להם את הפצצה הגרעינית. 7 אין לי פה רובה. 8 למיקי אין מילואים עד
לחנוכה. 9 במלחמת השחרור היה להם בקושי חיל ים.

39

1 יש כאן דואר? 2 האם הקצב מוכר גם הודו או רק בשר? 3 מתי הבנק
נסגר? 4 איך מוצאת את המאפייה? 5 במה אתה משלם, במזומן או בכרטיס
אשראי? או בשיק? 6 היא עושה קניות? עם מי? 7 הוא הלך למכולת. אתה
יודע בשביל מי? 8 באיזה שעה נפתחת המכבסה?

40

1 יוסי, אל תזמין את המרק, הוא מלוח. 2 ילדים, אל תגמרו את כל הסלט.
3 אני לא חותך עוד חסה. 4 אין עוד קפה בבית? 5 למה לא הרתחת מים,
רינה? 6 אתה לא תשים סוכר, אני מקווה. 7 אל תשים סוכרזית, בבקשה.

41

1 האוטובוס לירִיחוֹ. 2 הכרטיסיה בארנק שלך. 3 התחנה בפינה.
4 המספר בחזית האוטובוס. 5 המונית מנשר.

42

1 ההצגה החדשה שלהם די משעממת. 2 הסרט השני היה כל כך מטומטם.
3 היא מעניינת במיוחד באומנות ישראלית. 4 יש מחזה מאד טוב
בהבימה. 5 אני די אוהב את התקליט ההוא של נעמי שמר. 6 קצת יותר
גבוה בבקשה. אה, זה יותר טוב. 7 חיים טופול בתור במאי מצליח ביותר.
8 ההצגה השניה לא נגמרת כל כך מאוחר. 9 אני כל כך מצטער, אדוני.
המושב הזה תפוס. 10 אני מאוד אהבתי את המשחק.

43

1 לפעמים אני מתקן את זה בעצמי. 2 אנחנו בדרך כלל מחזיקים את
המטאטאים במרפסת. 3 קודם אני סוגר את מכונת הכביסה. 4 אני תמיד
משאירה את הכביסה פה. 5 שים את כל הריהוט המשומש במחסן. 6 עידו
הרבה פעמים עושה את הגיהוץ למטה במרתף. 7 אנחנו ישנים במקלט
הלילה. 8 אתמול אכלנו בחצר – איזה כיף !

44

1 נהג האוטובוס התחיל לצעוק. 2 אז אימי התחילה לצרוח. 3 כל הנוסעים
המשיכו לצחוק הרבה זמן. 4 אנחנו מקווים לנסוע לשוייצריה או צרפת.
5 אגד הפסיק לאסוף על יד תחנת הדלק. 6 אחיך רוצה ללמוד לנהוג ? הוא
רק בן 17. 7 אני ציפיתי לחזור עד חצות. 8 אני שונא לתפוס טרמפ.
9 תנסה לחייך דווקא.

45

1 כל כך קל לכתוב בעט הזה. 2 טוב שהמורה חולה היום. 3 קשה להכנס
לקורס הזה בסמסטר א׳. 4 זה מפתיע בעצם שאין לנו עבודה – או לפחות
תרגיל. 5 מה ? הכתה בוטלה עוד פעם ? מוזר שזה קורה. 6 יותר טוב לדבר
איתם במנוסה. 7 ברור שאתה עברת. 8 צריך לעשות שלושה מקצועות
למאסטר.

46

1 אמרתי לו שאני עוזב. 2 אני חושב שקר מדי. 3 היא אמרה שהיה על זה
משהו בחדשות. 4 אני חושש שזרקתי את המוסף של שבת. 5 ידעתי שאני
צודק !

47

1 איפה הזה שנועל את החלונות ? 2 אוי ואבוי, זה המפתח שלא עובד.
3 השוטר ששאלתי לא ידע. 4 מצאו את הדברים שהפורצים לקחו.
5 הדו״ח הזה שקיבלת, זה הרבה כסף ? 6 זה האדם שהלך למשטרה ?

48

1 כשעזבנו, כבר ירד שלג. 2 אם מזג האוויר יפה אפשר לחזור לבריכה? 3 בסוף לא נסענו לאילת, כי היה חמסין. 4 מה אם התחזית אומרת שיהיה חם ויבש? 5 יש תמיד רוח חזקה לפני שיורד גשם. 6 למרות שהיה רטוב זה היה כיף. 7 כשהטמפרטורה למעלה מ־40 אומרים לחיילים לשתות ולשתות. 8 כשהיינו בחופשה בחרמון היתה סערה ענקית. 9 רעם זה ממש משגע, במיוחד כשיש הרבה ברקים. 10 תייבש את הידיים לפני שאתה מדליק את האור. 11 אחרי שארזנו חטפנו שינה. 12 כשהוא ישן בשמש המדריך קיבל כאב ראש קשה. 13 תשים לב במקום ללחוש כל הזמן. 14 איך אתה יכול לקנות בלי להשתמש בכרטיס אשראי? 15 פתחו את התיק שלי בלי שראיתי. 16 אתה מחזיק בהגה כמו שאתה אף פעם לא נהגת. 17 כפי שאמרתי, אנחנו צריכים לשמור את חדר־המדרגות נקי. 18 זלדה עושה עוף כמו שאמא שלה עשתה אותו. 19 המשטרה מדברת כאילו דרסתי מישהו. 20 אני אחראי, אם כי אני לא מבין הרבה. 21 שושנה לקחה הרבה דברים, אם כי לא הכל. 22 אני שאלתי אותו, כך שאני יודע כבר. 23 אנחנו עזבנו מוקדם כדי לראות את הסרט הראשון. 24 אני אומר לה כדי שהיא לא תשתמש בזה.

49

1 איך בוחרים בראש הממשלה? 2 מצביעים אחת לארבע שנים בישראל, זה קבוע. 3 חבל ששר החוץ לא בא לשבעה. 4 ייתכן שהם ירכיבו קואליציה חדשה. 5 מזל שהיו מספיק חברי כנסת לדיון. 6 עוד משבר פוליטי? אי אפשר. 7 אפשר לסגור את מיזוג האוויר? ־ לא כל כך חם.

50

1

1 שחיתן 2 שחתה 3 שחו 4 שחתה 5 שחיתי 6 שחה 7 שחתה 8 שחית 9 שחינו 10 שחיתי 11 שחו 12 שחית 13 שחו 14 שחיתם 15 שחה

1 תשחה 2 נשחה 3 אשחה 4 ישחו 5 תשחי 6 ישחו 7 תשחו 8 ישחה 9 תשחו 10 תשחה 11 ישחו 12 ישחה 13 ישחה 14 אשחה 15 ישחו 15 תשחה

2

1 חיכית 2 חיכינו 3 חיכיתי 4 חיכו 5 חיכית 6 חיכו 7 חיכיתם 8 חיכה
9 חיכיתן 10 חיכתה 11 חיכו 12 חיכה 13 חיכיתי 14 חיכו 15 חיכתה

1 תחכו 2 תחכה 3 יחכו 4 תחכה 5 אחכה 6 יחכה 7 תחכה 8 תחכה
9 נחכה 10 אחכה 11 יחכו 12 תחכי 13 יחכו 14 תחכו 15 יחכה

3

1 למנות 2 לקוות 3 לטעות 4 ללוות 5 לשתות 6 לשחות 7 לקנות
8 למצות 9 לשנות 10 לתלות

4

1 משקה 2 משקים 3 משקה 4 משקים 5 משקה 6 משקות 7 משקים
8 משקה 9 משקות 10 משקה 11 משקים 12 משקה 13 משקה
14 משקה

5

1 הפתנית 2 התפנינו 3 התפניתי 4 התפנו 5 התפנית 6 התפנו
7 התפניתם 8 התפנה 9 התפניתן 10 התפניתה 11 התפנו 12 התפניה
13 התפניתי 14 התפנו 15 התפנתה

1 תתפנו 2 תתפנה 3 יתפנו 4 תתפנה 5 אתפנה 6 תתפנה 7 תתפנה
8 תתפנה 9 נתפנה 10 אתפנה 11 יתפנו 12 תתפני 13 יתפנו 14 תתפנו
15 יתפנה

6

1 נראיתי נראית נראית נראתה נראינו נראיתם נראיתן נראו 2 נראה
נראית נראים נראות 3 נמנה נמנית נמנים נמנות 4 אמנה תימנה תימני
יימנה תימנה נימנה תימנו יימנו

7

1 היא נהנתה מהסרט. 2 את נראית עייפה, יפה. 3 חגית נראית מאושרת.
4 אני לא אהנה מהספר הזה. 5 איפה העגבניות נקנו? 6 עגבניות נקנות
בדרך-כלל בשוק. 7 אנחנו ממש נהנינו מהארוחה בשבת. 8 האם מכוניות
נעשות בארץ? 9 המצב נעשה לאט לאט יותר נוח. 10 התשלומים שלנו
נעשו כל חודש.

281

51

51b

להחליט, להעמיד, להאזין, להעסיק, לחזור, לעבוד, להרוג, לאסוף, לעצור,
לאכול, לנדוד, לעקוב, להעמד, להעדר, לחצוב, להעלב

51d

1 לשמוע – ישמע, להישמע – יישמע, לשוח – ישוח, לבטוח – יבטח,
לקפח – יקפח, לבלוע – יבלע

2 יבצע, יקרע, יזניח, יימנע, תיכנע, יתגלח, תגלח, יטרח, ינצח, ייפתח

3 רוצחת, מתקלחת, מבצעת, מפצחת, מורגשת, מובלעת, מצביעה, נוגעת,
משובחת, מתנפחת

52

2 לבחון, לדפוק, לטבול, לתפוס, להיפסל, לביים, לבטל, להיבנות, לפהק,
להתבטל, להיבלע, להיכתב, לרפד, להיפלט, להישפך, להיתפס, לעכל,
להימכר

53

1 צלצלת 2 צלצלנו 3 צלצלתי 4 צלצלו 5 צלצלת 6 צלצלו 7 צלצלתם
8 צלצל 9 צלצלתן 10 צלצלה 11 צלצלו 12 צלצל 13 צלצלתי
14 צלצלו 15 צלצלה

1 תצלצלו 2 תצלצל 3 יצלצלו 4 תצלצל 5 אצלצל 6 יצלצל 7 תצלצל
8 תצלצל 9 נצלצל 10 אצלצל 11 יצלצלו 12 תצלצלי 13 יצלצלו
14 תצלצלו 15 יצלצל

54

54a

1 אם הוא לא ירד, תוריד אותו, חיים. 2 אתם צריכים לשבת, ילדים. 3 אולי
אני איזום קבוצת לחץ. 4 בחייך, אתה לא יכול להוציא אותם ולהושיב
אותם? 5 פנינה, צאי משם ושבי מיד. 6 תודיע לי מחר או מחרתיים, אני
צריך לדעת. 7 תקרא למגן דוד אדום, אשתי הולכת ללדת. 8 מתי המשרד
יידע? 9 משבר בין־לאומי עלול להיווצר. 10 מה דעתך שנצא יחד פעם?

55

הצטלם, הסתפר, השתנה, הסתער, השתרע, הסתמן, הזדקק, הזדהה,
הצטדק, השתפר

ישתזף, ישתחרר, יסתנן, יצטרף, ישתכלל, ישתרך, ישתמע, יסתבך, יזדמן

56

56a

1 נתת, נגשת, נסעת 2 נתנו, נגשנו, נסענו 3 נתתי, נגשתי, נסעתי 4 נתנו,
נגשו, נסעו 5 נתת, נגשת, נסעת 6 נתנו, נגשו, נסעו 7 נתתם, נגשתם,
נסעתם 8 נתן, נגש, נסע 9 נתתן, נגשתן, נסעתן 10 נתנה, נגשה, נסעה
11 נתנו, נגשו, נסעו 12 נתן, נגש, נסע 13 נתתי, נגשתי, נסעתי 14 נתנו,
נגשו, נסעו 15 נתנה, נגשה, נסעה

1 תתנו, תגשו, תסעו 2 תתן, תגש, תסע 3 יתנו, יגשו, יסעו 4 תתן, תגש,
תסע 5 אתן, אגש, אסע 6 יתן, יגש, יסע 7 תתן, תגש, תסע 8 תתן, תגש,
תסע 9 נתן, נגש, נסע 10 אתן, אגש, אסע 11 יתנו, יגשו, יסעו 12 תתני,
תגשי, תסעי 13 יתנו, יגשו, יסעו 14 תתנו, תגשו, תסעו 15 יתן, יגש, יסע

1 אני פוחד לגשת אליו. 2 אני מעדיף לתת שטרות, לא מטבעות. 3 תני לי,
יפה. 4 שימי לב, נחמה, את תיפלי. 5 אסור לנגוע בחוט. 6 אמרתי לא
לנגוע. 7 המוסד ישא את השמות של מנהיגים ציוניים.

283

56b

1 אל תקח את כל העוגיות, דוד אפריים. 2 החלטתי לקחת את בעלי. 3 קחי פנס, נעמי. 4 אני אקח את הג׳ינס הישן. 5 זה יקח כמה שניות. 6 זה לוקח שלושה שבועות לקבל תשובה. 7 יותר טוב לקחת אתך תעודת זהות.

56c

1 אנחנו הולכים לגן החיות. 2 אתה יכול ללכת גם כן. 3 לך לעזאזל, הוא אמר לי. 4 אני אלך לכספומט קודם כל. 5 אז נלך לחוף בבת-ים.

56d

1 הוא היה צריך ללכת לאולפן. 2 מסכן, הוא היה צריך לעבור שם הרבה זמן? 3 גברת בורקוביץ? את תצטרכי לעשות מכינה בעברית. 4 מה, אני לא אוכל לקבל פטור? 5 אתה יכול לנסות לעבור את המבחן העברי, בסדר? 6 הסטודנטים הזרים האלה יצטרכו לעשות ארבע שעות של מדעי חברה. 7 הם קיבלו ציונים לא טובים בעברית – הם אפילו לא יכלו לקרוא את השאלות. 8 לא יכולתי לקבל חדר במעונות. 9 אז הייתי צריך לשכור במרכז העיר. 10 או-אה, זה היה צריך להיות טרחה.

56e

1 אל תדאגי, נעמה, יום אחד את תאהבי אותו. 2 הייתי רוצה לומר משהו למר יהושוע, בבקשה. 3 תאמר שמר עוז מבקש לראות אותו. 4 אני אומר לו שאתה פה. 5 הנמלים האלה יאכלו את כל היקרות שלך. 6 הם יאהבו את הלחם ואת המצה. 7 אני אוכל במסדרון, זה רק פיתה. 8 תאכל תאכל, ארווינג, זה בריא.

56g

1 אני מת לפגוש אותה. 2 אני נורא מצטער, היא מתה אתמול. 3 היא חיה חמש שנים במפרץ חיפה. 4 תנים עוד חיים במדבר. 5 דובים ואריות חיו פעם בהרי לבנון. 6 היא יכולה לחיות ברמות – זה קרוב לירושלים.

57

1 הכנת 2 הכנו 3 הכנתי 4 הכינו 5 הכנת 6 הכינו 7 הכנתם 8 הכין 9 הכנתן 10 הכינה 11 הכינו 12 הכין 13 הכנתי 14 הכינו 15 הכינה

1 תכינו 2 תכין 3 יכינו 4 תכין 5 אכין 6 יכין 7 יכין 8 תכין 9 נכין
10 אכין 11 יכינו 12 תכיני 13 יכינו 14 תכינו 15 יכין

1 מכין 2 מכינים 3 מכין(ה) 4 מכינים 5 מכינה 6 מכינות 7 מכינים
8 מכין

הֵקִים, הֵפִיק, הִפִּיל, הֵזִיז, הִצִּיעַ, הֵנִיחַ/הִנִּיחַ, הִצִּיל, הִגִּיד, הֵבִין, הִבִּיעַ

58

1 בנימין רוצה לרכב על אופניים בכביש. 2 הילד שלנו יגדל ויהיה נהג
אגד. 3 בשעת הדרשה חצים ישנו. 4 אני שמח שאת לא חסרה שוב, אורית.
5 למה היא חסרה מהשיעור? 6 תשכב על הספה, זה יותר נוח. 7 היא
קוראת תהילים בזמן שהיא מחכה לאוטובוס. 8 סבלנות, נמצא את זה.
9 תקרא עד עמוד 4. 10 תלבש עניבה, מוטלה, זה נראה יותר טוב. 11 הוא
סרב ללבוש עניבה. 12 תשאל את אבא שלך איך ללבוש עניבה. 13 אני
אשכב ואישן כמה דקות. 14 דבורה תמיד מוצאת טעויות בקריאת התורה.
15 אם אתה צם, אולי אתה רוצה לשכב. 16 לא, אני מעדיף ללמוד פרק של
משהו. 17 הבאתי הגדה משלי. 18 הבאת תפילין וסידור, איצי?

59

1 שוחחת 2 שוחחנו 3 שוחחתי 4 שוחחו 5 שוחחת 6 שוחחו
7 שוחחתם 8 שוחח 9 שוחחתן 10 שוחחה 11 שוחחו 12 שוחח
13 שוחחתי 14 שוחחו 15 שוחחה

1 תשוחחו 2 תשוחח 3 ישוחחו 4 תשוחח 5 אשוחח 6 ישוחח 7 תשוחח
8 תשוחח 9 נשוחח 10 אשוחח 11 ישוחחו 12 תשוחחי 13 ישוחחו
14 תשוחחו 15 ישוחח

1 משוחח 2 משוחחים 3 משוחח(ת) 4 משוחחים 5 משוחחת
6 משוחחות 7 משוחחים 8 משוחח

60

60a

1 אופניים מבריקים 2 משקפיים כהים 3 מספריים חדים 4 משקפי שמש 5 שתי אוזניים 6 חמש שיניים 7 שיני ברזל 8 שתי ידיים 9 עיניים חומות 10 נעלי ספורט 11 גרבי צמר 12 מים חמים 13 שמיים בהירים 14 מי מלח 15 שוליים רחבים

60b

1 הוא בן שנתיים. 2 זה יקח יומיים מינימום. 3 העוצר נמשך שבועיים. 4 הם הפסידו אלפיים טנקים ומאתיים מטוסים. 5 חודשיים של מתח עברו.

60c

תסמונות, חיילות, משמרות, צלחות, מעבורות, מחברות, גננות, רכבות, מרפסות, מגבות

60d

1 שלושה ימים 2 חמישה לילות 3 הרבה שוורים 4 עשרה ראשים 5 שני שווקים 6 אח ושתי אחיות 7 כמה בתים 8 ארבע ערים 9 שישה שמות 10 שני קירות 11 אלף חרבות 12 שולחנות כבדים 13 מקומות חשובים 14 נשים חרדיות 15 מלונות גבוהים 16 רבנים צעירים 17 בורות ריקים 18 קופסאות של קולה 19 בנות יפות 20 יתרונות מסויימים

61

1 רובם 2 כולנו 3 כולכם 4 אנשים ירוקים 5 נשים ירוקות 6 חלות מתוקות 7 מרבדים אדומים 8 כפות עגולות 9 חוקים חדשים 10 צוללות צהובות 11 דפים צהובים 12 פנים ורודים 13 עיין אדומה 14 שמלה כחולה 15 עזים מסריחות 16 דובים אכזריים 17 נופים נפלאים 18 קופים נחמדים

62

1 שבלולים אוכלים עלים   2 ציפורים תופסות שבלולים   3 נחשים צדים
ציפורים

63

1 חמישים קילומטר   2 שני סנטימטר   3 ארבעה קילומטר   4 עשרה ימים
5 בעוד שישים יום   6 זה נמשך מאה שבעים שנה   7 חמישה ליטר   8 שמונה
איש   9 ארבעה מליון   10 מאה ואט   11 שבעים לירות סטרלינג   12 שבעים
קילו   13 עשרים שנה   14 שתים-עשרה שנה   15 שבעה אחוז   16 שתים
וחצי לירות   17 עשרים דקות   18 ארבעים אחוז   19 שנים-עשר יום
20 מאה אחוז

64

ספירה, טיפול, התמצאות, הרגשה, הצטננות, שיפור, אישור, התנוונות,
הריגה, הפניה, שיתוף, היתקלות, מיניו, קניה, קליטה, השתנות, התקפה

ריפא 'study', עבד 'work', נהנה 'enjoyment', אהב 'love', נתן 'giving', לימד
'healing, medicine', נכנס 'entrance, entry', פחד 'fear', שלח 'sending,
dispatch'

צחוק, גירושין, מנוחה, מגורים, השוואה, צעקה, רחמים, תוספת, חזרה

65

כפילות, אטימות, עממיות, כבדות, צניעות, שבירות, ילדותיות, גמישות,
עייפות, קביעות, חביבות, דתיות, בריאות, עדינות, מדעיות, מתיחות

66

1 סייר, כייס, צבע, כנר, צייר, בלש, חמר, פסל, נווט, דבר

2 צלבן, רקדן, בטלן, חלפן, בדרן, חלבן, סקרן, ספרן, יצרן, חשדן, יקרן,
חקיין, ירקן, שדכן

1 כדורסלן, כרטיסן, תעשיין, יצואן, יהלומן

2 פיסקאי, מכונאי, פונטיקאי, מתמטיקאי, פרסומאי, שריונאי, חשמלאי

1 משרד, מזלף, מצבר, מגבר, מצפן, משנק, מסרק, מקלט   2 מבחנה, מגרפה, מזמרה, מאפרה, מגלשה 3 מכתב, מרדף, מגדל, משפט, משמר, מעבר 4 מכבסה, מזבלה, מחלקה, מעברה, מספנה, מרפאה 5 כלבת, שפעת, אדמת, נזלת, קצרת 6 תאגיד, תמליל, תקציר, תרגיל, תכתיב, תפנית, תגלית 8 שפנפן, בצלצל, חזרזיר 9 דוב, סוס, ירח, מלה, עת, ברכה, חידה, תקנה, חזיר, מקום, מערכה, גרב

14 חי + דק, אופן + נוע, מחזה + זמר, מגדל + אור, חמש + שיר, רכבת + כבל, זרק + אור, דחף + חפר, רמז + אור, מדד + חום

אכילה שתייה לינה, חוץ לארץ, רב-טוראי, מכשירי כיוון ומרחק, מוציא לאור, ציון לשבח, חכמינו זכרונם לברכה, נמל תעופה בן-גוריון, גדודי נוער, שירות בטחון כללי

1 תעופה – עף 'flying', 2 תמותה – מת 'mortality', 3 תכונה – הכין 'property', 4 תבונה – הבין 'sense', 5 תקומה – קם 'resurgence', 6 – זן 'nutrition', 7 תבוסה – הביס 'defeat' תזונה

יתר 'luxury', יצר 'product', יעד 'time', ירד 'slope', יעל 'usefulness', יבל 'haulage', ירש 'heritage', ירש 'heredity', יצא 'result', ילד 'motherland'

נטע 'plantation', נשב 'draft', נגע 'contact', נפח 'frustration', נגף 'plague', נפח 'mouth-organ', נטל 'overhead projector', נטר 'guard', נשא 'burden', נתן 'gift'

69

1 רגל שבורה 2 בוהן פצועה 3 פנים שזופים 4 סנטר מגולח 5 אף מעוקם
6 אצבע שבורה 7 יד שרוטה 8 לשון שרופה 9 שתי שורות של שיניים
מצוחצחות 10 שיער מסורק 11 עיניים פתוחות 12 ציפורניים צבועות
13 לב שבור

70

ספורתי, טיפוסי, דתי, דרומי, רפואי, סביבתי, מקצועי, ניהולי, צבאי,
מלכותי, משמעותי, מקומי, רווחי, יחסי, התחלתי

71

פחדן, נבחן, דברן, שמרן

אכיל 'edible', קביל 'acceptable', שביר 'fragile', נגיש 'accessible'

extra-uterine, intravenous, inner-continental, submolecular, post-Biblical,
unilateral, two-faced, multilingual, superhuman, intercontinental,
subconscious, interstellar, pro-Western, trivalent

72

סוחר, שומר, מתווך, רועה, מתקדם, אופה, מרכז, משרת, מעסיק, מפקד,
מתכנת, מתלמד, זוכה, גולה, מאפיין, עוזר, שודד, מתפרע

מדהים, נוצץ, מצטבר, משמח, מרתיע, מדכא, ממצה, משפיל, מרשים,
מעניין, מטריד, מרגיע, חולף

1 נשימתם הכבדה הפסיקה את ארוחתנו הטעימה. 2 הם בקושי הקשיבו
להקדמתי. 3 תלמידיו משוגעים להרצאותיו. 4 בניה פחדו מבישולה.
5 הורינו משלמים בשביל טיולנו לדרום אמריקה. 6 לבעלי יש דודה
קשישה בצפון הארץ. 7 הורי אשתי תמיד שוכחים את שם משפחתה. 8 יש
תערוכה של כתבי עת מתקופת המנדט. 9 תגובות המעצמות הגדולות
להצעות האו"ם היו מאכזבות. 10 יש לי קצת פרוטקציה כי אבי מכיר את
מזכירת השר. 11 העתקת תקליטים אסורה בהחלט. 12 אין סיבה להתבייש
מהשתתפות בהפגנה. 13 לאחר סגירת תעלת סואץ באה התערבות כוחות
המערב.

1 חנה ואחיותיה 2 אני ונערתי 3 כל בני 4 קול המוסיקה 5 חברת
משוררים מתים

1 מדריך ארוך־שיער 2 צרפתייה ירוקת־עיניים 3 שני קצבים רחבי־כתפיים
4 הזדמנות קצרת־טווח 5 הרים מכוסי שלג 6 המזוודה שלה היתה מלאה
ספרים 7 ארץ בעלת יופי רב 8 ארנקים מלאי כסף 9 הוא אדם בעל
השפעה 10 הספר הזה בעל מסר חשוב לכל אחד 11 היא חסרה חברות
12 ארץ חסרת מדע

1 תשפשף בעיניים 2 תסתום את הפה 3 תנענע בראש 4 תלחץ לי את היד
5 תחזיק לי את היד 6 תמשוך לה בשיער 7 תרים את היד 8 תמתח את
הרגליים 9 תגזור את הציפורניים 10 תגזור למאיר את השיער 11 תנגב לו
את הסנטר 12 תשלב את הידיים 13 תגע לתינוק במצח

1 שבטי ישראל 2 קברות המלכים 3 בעלי חנויות 4 צבעי מאכל 5 אוהלי
צבא 6 דגל ישראל 7 חלקי מכונית 8 בגדי גברים 9 נעלי שבת 10 ערבי
שבתות 11 צוותי חרום 12 ספרי אומנות 13 ספר מדע

76

1 צבא ירדן 2 מעונות סטודנטים 3 מקום לידה 4 מטוס סילון 5 שלום העולם 6 עתון ערב 7 מטוס נוסעים 8 כרטיס אוטובוס 9 מקום עבודה 10 פרדס תפוזים 11 נהג אגד 12 בשר הודו 13 מרק עוף

1 מפלגת הליכוד 2 עצי אורן 3 ממשלת סוריה 4 מפלגת הבעת 5 משפחת כהן 6 חיל הצנחנים 7 ענפי תאינה 8 ברכת יום הולדת 9 שמות המשפחה של הסטודנטים 10 קביעת הרמטכ״ל

נִדְבַת, שְׁכְבוֹת, נִשְׁמוֹת, פִּצְצַת, פִּצְצוֹת, נִשְׁמַת, חֶבְרוֹת

77

1 שביתתם של הרופאים 2 משכורתו של מהנדס 3 חשבונו של רופא השיניים 4 עבודתה של אחות 5 פרנסתה של מורה 6 תלוש משכורתו של המנהל 7 הוצאותיו של אברהם 8 תביעותיהם של העובדים 9 הצעתה של ההנהלה 10 חופשתו של הנשיא

78

1 היא כמוני 2 אני כמוהו 3 אתה כמוהם 4 אני כאן בלעדיה 5 היא הלכה בלעדיו 6 מה אני בלעדיך, חיה? 7 ביני לבינך, היא אפס 8 מה קורה ביניהם 9 הולכים בלעדיי? 10 הם נראים כמונו

79

1 שתי התרופות 2 עשרת הכדורים 3 שני המדחומים 4 ארבעת הרופאים 5 שנינו 6 שלוש המחלות 7 שישים החולים

80

1 האיש השלישי 2 הצעד החמישים 3 הלביבה השניה 4 הסביבון השישי 5 הנר הראשון 6 הערב השמיני 7 היום הארבעים ותשעה 8 הכוס הרביעית של יין 9 המצה השניה 10 המלה החמש־עשרה 11 יום ההולדת השלושה־עשר שלו

82

1 אימי היתה מתחילה לבשל ארוחת ערב בשעה שלוש.   2 היא היתה
מגהצת כל חולצה.   3 כל יום כיפור הקהילה היתה בוכה ומיללת.   4 אם
היה לי מרבד סיני, הייתי שם אותו פה בדיוק.   5 איזה מין עוגה היית עושה,
חוכם?   6 אם הצנצנת היתה ירוקה, היא היתה נראית נחמד על המדף.
7 אוי רותי, חשבתי שאת תנקי.   8 הוא אמר שהוא מסדר אבל הוא לא סידר.
9 ידעתי שהיא עצבנית.   10 תשאיר אור פתוח כשתעזוב.   11 קבצן ישב על
הספסל, מקשקש בקופסא.   12 אם תתן כסף, זה יהיה מצווה.   13 שרה
רכבה על האופניים שלה, כשהיא מחזיקה שקית אגסים ביד.   14 אל תקרא
כשאנשים פה, טיפש!   15 אני עכשיו הלכתי ברחוב וחשבתי על המסיבה.

83

1 להכחישו 2 לראותה 3 לאשרם 4 לקחתו 5 לפרקו 6 לבקרו 7 לשבחם

84

1 אני מלמד את עצמי.   2 היא תמיד מבקרת את עצמה.   3 תתנער עכשיו,
ילד מטומטם.   4 הטירונים התפשטו לבדיקה.   5 תתלבש ותסתרק, שניכם
באיחור.   6 אני מזהיר אותך, אתה לא תסלח לעצמך.   7 זה קל, עשיתי את
זה בעצמי.   8 יש זמן להתקלח?   9 אתה צריך להכיר את עצמך.   10 הוא לא
יכול לבוא לטלפון, הוא מתגלח.   11 זה ראש העיר, נו, תציג את עצמך.
12 אני לא מציג את עצמי.

85

1 שני הקצינים שנאו אחד את השני.   2 מהיום שנפגשנו אהבנו זה את זה.
3 תראה, שני הקצוות מתחברים אחד עם השני.   4 החברות מתחרות אחת
עם השניה כבר שנים.   5 סיפרנו אחד לשני סיפורים, בדיחות, רכילות . . .

86

1 כל כך קר לי במיטה. 2 נוח לך במגפיים האלה? 3 כל כך חם לילדים שם
מאחורה. 4 טוב להם בבית הדו-קומתי שלהם בסביון. 5 לא נעים לי
לשאול אותו.

87

1 יותר חם לי עכשיו, תודה. 2 שושי יותר נחמדה מהבייביסיטרית
האחרונה. 3 הנייר הזה הרבה יותר עבה. 4 אל תגזים – זה דווקא יותר דק.
5 הסכו"ם הזה פחות יקר מהאחר. 6 ירד יותר גשם בשרון מאשר ציפו.
7 זה יותר טוב מאתמול.

88

1 הוא עכשיו פגש את הבחורה הכי יפה בעולם עוד פעם. 2 סעודיה היא
היום יצואנית הנפט הגדולה ביותר. 3 האם זה הגליל הכי ארוך של מגבות
נייר? 4 לאיזה עיר יש הזיהום הכי גבוה? 5 זאת הדרך הכי טובה, אני
בטוח.

89

1 זה חלק כמו העור של תינוק. 2 קר כמו שיקגו כאן. 3 הוא לא חכם כמו
אחיו אבל זה לא העיקר. 4 אתה מצאת מקום לחנות באותה מהירות כמו
בפעם הקודמת? 5 אין עיר מיוחדת כמו ירושלים.

90

1 מה אורך הקונצרט? 2 מה רוחב הסטיישן שלך? 3 ומה אורכו? 4 אנחנו
צריכים מקרר ברוחב של מטר אחד. 5 זה רק בשביל אנשים בני חמש-
עשרה ומעלה. 6 מה גובה הבחור הבלונדיני הזה? 7 מה גובה המחיצה?
8 בנו מגדל בגובה של 90 מטר באמצע העיר. 9 השמלה הזאת בשני
סנטימטר יותר ארוכה מהשמלה השחורה. 10 שבת יותר ארוכה בשעתיים
בקיץ.

91

1 היא עובדת קשה עם הגיטרה ההיא. 2 כן, אבל היא שרה כל כך לא טוב.
3 למה כולם נוהגים בצורה כל כך מסוכנת? 4 אם אתה דורס הולך־רגל,
מביאים אותך באופן אוטמטי לבית המשפט. 5 הרועה ההוא מנגן טוב
בחליל. 6 הוא ליטף את ידה בעדינות. 7 הוא היכה בה באכזריות. 8 אתה
יכול לכתוב קצת יותר מסודר? 9 אני חושב שהיא כותבת מאוד יפה.
10 היא בהריון? היא צריכה להגיע לבית חולים באופן דחוף. 11 אני רוצה
לנקות את השולחן שלי באופן יסודי.

92

1. I greatly enjoyed your report about the Second Aliyah.

2. The patient is likely to eat excessively.

3. The brigade fought fiercely with the enemy.

93

1 בתחילת שנת הלימודים אנחנו עוזבים. 2 בשבוע הבא אני לא בא. 3 יש
קיוסק בפינה. 4 אני מצלצל בשש. 5 כל פעם שאני מכניס אסימון אין
צליל. 6 אני הלכתי ברחוב כש . . . . 7 כל יום שישי יש לנו עכשיו יום
פנוי. 8 חיכינו תשע שנים ואז בשנה שעברה קיבלנו טלפון. 9 כל פעם
שאני מחייג יש לי בעיות. 10 תסובב את זה במברג.

94

1 לאן אתם נוסעים לחופשה השנה? 2 הערב אנחנו מטיילים לעיר
העתיקה. 3 אני מעדיף לקחת מונית הפעם. 4 הבוקר היתה תקרית רצינית.
5 השבוע יש קונצרט בגן? 6 ים המלח? 7 זאת הפעם השנייה שהייתם שם
החודש!

95

1 תפנה שמאלה אחרי הסיבוב. 2 לא, אתה טועה, הוא צריך לפנות ימינה. 3 אם אתה נוסע דרומה אתה בכביש הלא נכון. 4 ההגה מושך הצידה. 5 זה בסדר, אנחנו יכולים להגיע הביתה בחושך. 6 תקוע בבוץ? תנסה לנסוע קדימה ואז אחורה. 7 בצומת הבא תסע מזרחה. 8 ביום העצמאות כולם נוסעים צפונה לים כינרת.

96

1 הכדור מעבר לחומה לחומה? מי אשם? 2 בלוני הגאז שמה מימין. 3 יש גדר כמובן מסביב לישוב. 4 מיכאל, אתה יכול להחליף את האור מעל לדלת? 5 משמאל יש שלט "גינוסר". 6 אני מחזיק את המקלות מתחת למדרגות.

97

1. When in Spain, he got to know a Spanish singer.

2. When setting out to perform night actions, they take heavy equipment.

3. He met his wife when he was about 19.

4. When the world war broke out . . . .

98

1 יש לי רק שני תפוחי אדמה, שרה. 2 יוסי מגיש בקשה? טוב, גם אני מגיש בקשה. 3 היא משחקת טניס והיא גם מנגנת בפסנתר. 4 רק נכים יכולים לשבת במושבים האלה. 5 היא אפילו הביאה את העגלה לתוך המטוס. 6 אתה יכול לקנות שם גם חיתולים. 7 הכרתי רק שני אנשים במסיבה.

99

1 החברה אינה מקבלת אחריות. 2 אם אינך מסכים נא לכתוב מיד. 3 בריטניה אינה תומכת בעמדה זו. 4 אינני מסוגל להשפיע עליהם. 5 אם הוא אינו תייר אינו צריך להרשם.

100

‫1 עם מי דיברת? – עם אף אחד. 2 אין לי שאלות. לך יש? 3 אף אחד לא‬
‫ראה את השוד. 4 הפורצים לא לקחו כלום. 5 היינו צריכים עדים, אבל לא‬
‫היה שם אף אחד. 6 הם חונים על המדרכות, אבל אף פעם הם לא מקבלים‬
‫דו"ח. 7 זה משום שאתה לא יכול למצוא מדחן בשום מקום. 8 מה אמר‬
‫לך השוטר ההוא? – שום דבר מיוחד. 9 אני אף פעם לא נוהג בלי הרשיון‬
‫שלי. 10 תרגעי, גב׳ אבו־חצירה, שום דבר לא קרה.‬

Impossible, unstable, unending, unavoidable, lack of coordination,
impatience, non-treatment of patients, non-washable

101

‫1 אין לך מעטפות? 2 קנית גפרורים, נכון? 3 האם הוא מתכוון להתחתן‬
‫איתה או לא? 4 אני לא בטוח אם המעלית עובדת. 5 סוכן הנסיעות הוא‬
‫בקומה הרביעית, נכון? 6 אתה לא עובר על יד האוניברסיטה, נכון? 7 אין‬
‫לי מושג מה הוא רוצה. 8 מעניין לדעת אם יש סיכוי לשידוך ביניהם.‬

102

‫1 אני רוצה שהיא תצטרף לגדנ"ע. 2 הוריו מעדיפים שהוא ילך לישיבת‬
‫הסדר. 3 קיויתי שהיא תלך לנח"ל. 4 שהם יפסיקו ללחוש. 5 שלא תעיז,‬
‫יצחק. 6 שושי רצתה שהבנים ילכו לאוניברסיטה אבל הם בכולל. 7 אני‬
‫רוצה שאריאלה תשחק איתי. עכשיו זה בסדר?‬

103

‫1 תקנה או טעם וניל או טעם שוקו. 2 כדאי לי לקנות את כותנת הלילה‬
‫הכחולה, או שאת מעדיפה את הוורודה? 3 או שאתה מחליט עכשיו או‬
‫שאנחנו חוזרים הביתה. 4 האם הבנק נסגר בעוד רגע, או שיש לנו עוד‬
‫זמן? 5 או יום שני או יום שלישי יהיה בסדר.‬

104

1 להריח כל גבינת קוטג׳ זה מגעיל.   2 לנסוע מהר ולצפצף זה כיף.
3 להרוויח המון כסף זו בעיה.   4 לצפות בדאלאס זה ספורט לאומי.   5 אני
נהנה לעמוד בתור.   6 הוא נהנה לדחוף.

105

105a

1 השכונה שבה אנחנו גרים היא די יקרה.   2 איפה החוזה שחתמת עליו?
3 אנחנו שוכרים דירה שבעליה בחוץ לארץ.   4 זה חדר המדרגות שבו
איבדת את זה?   5 תראה, זה הבניין שגרנו בו בשנה שעברה.   6 במושב
הראשון שהלכנו אליו עוד לא היה חשמל.   7 הם בחניון הזה שהם תמיד
משחקים בו.   8 אני שאלתי רק את הדיירים שאני מכיר את השמות שלהם.
9 זה השיכון שחשבת עליו? הוא קצת צפוף.   10 מה השם של הבחורה
שהוריה גרים בכפר שמריהו?

105b

1 מי שמוכר את הפרחים לא נמצא היום.   2 שמתי את מכונת הכתיבה איפה
שיש קצת אור.   3 סוף סוף, הנה מה שחיפשתי.   4 אבל זה לא מה שרציתי
לדעת.   5 אני אדיב עם כל מי שמדבר אלי.   6 מה שאמרת לו היה מאוד
מאוד גס.   7 תאכל כל מה שיש בפריזר.   8 תקפצי מתי שנוח לך, מרים.
9 תן את הפתק הזה למי שאחראי.   10 תרשה לו כל מה שאתה מרשה
לאחרים, זה ברור.   11 מי שמחייג למודיעין, לא צריך לשלם.   12 קח כל
מה שמתאים.

106

106a

1 אחרי שעלו הקרובים שלי לישראל, התחלתי להתעניין בשורשים שלי.
2 בחוץ חיכו שלושה אנשים שמנים עם זקנים. 3 היו לנו ביצים משלנו, עד
שמתו כל התרנגולות. 4 לפני הבית עמדה כוורת. 5 כששמעו על זה
הפסיקו חקלאים להשתמש בדשנים כימיים. 6 אם תפרוץ מלחמה, תהיה
התוצאה קטסטרופה.

106b

1 יש לי סכו"ם אבל מפיות אין לי. 2 30 שקל את רוצה בשביל זה? 3 אני
מכירה את שושנה ואת אריאלה – וגם את יפה אני מכירה. 4 העיתון ההוא
ישן, וגם את זה אני לא צריך.

106c

1 באו חמישה אנשים חדשים היום. 2 יורד עוד פעם שלג. 3 קיימת עכשיו
סכנה רצינית. 4 רחל, הגיעה החברה שלך. 5 בא עוד מישהו, אני חושב.

Index

Numbers refer to sections

299